THE SHORT STORIES OF EDGAR ALLAN POE

OTHER TITLES IN THE GREENHAVEN PRESS LITERARY COMPANION SERIES:

THE GREENHAVEN PRESS
Literary Companion
TO AMERICAN LITERATURE

THE SHORT STORIES OF EDGAR ALLAN POE

Hayley Mitchell Haugen, *Book Editor*

Bonnie Szumski, *Series Editor*

Greenhaven Press, Inc., San Diego, CA

Every effort has been made to trace the owners of copy-righted material. The articles in this volume may have been edited for content, length, and/or reading level. The titles have been changed to enhance the editorial purpose. Those interested in locating the original source will find the complete citation on the first page of each article.

Library of Congress Cataloging-in-Publication Data

Readings on the short stories of Edgar Allan Poe / Hayley
  Mitchell Haugen, book editor.
      p.   cm. — (The Greenhaven Press literary
  companion to American literature)
    Includes bibliographical references and index.
    ISBN 0-7377-0692-9 (pbk. : alk. paper) —
  ISBN 0-7377-0693-7 (lib. bdg. : alk. paper)
    1. Poe, Edgar Allan, 1809–1849—Fictional works.
  2. Detective and mystery stories, American—History and
  criticism. 3. Fantasy fiction, American—History and
  criticism. 4. Horror tales, American—History and
  criticism. 5. Short story. I. Title: Short stories of Edgar
  Allan Poe. II. Haugen, Hayley Mitchell, 1968–   III. Series.

PS2642.F43 R4   2001
813'.3—dc21
                                                  00-069156
                                                      CIP

Cover photo: Harry Clarke/The Scriptorium
Harvard University Library, 23

Copyright © 2001 by Greenhaven Press, Inc.
PO Box 289009
San Diego, CA 92198-9009
Printed in the U.S.A.

66 *What the world calls genius is the state of mental disease arising from the undue predominance of some one of the faculties. The works of such genius are never sound in themselves and, in especial, always betray the general mental insanity.* 99

—Edgar Allan Poe

CONTENTS

Chapter 1: The Detective Stories

Chapter 2: Revenge, Murder, and Madness

FOREWORD

*"'Tis the good reader that
makes the good book."*

Ralph Waldo Emerson

The story's bare facts are simple: The captain, an old and scarred seafarer, walks with a peg leg made of whale ivory. He relentlessly drives his crew to hunt the world's oceans for the great white whale that crippled him. After a long search, the ship encounters the whale and a fierce battle ensues. Finally the captain drives his harpoon into the whale, but the harpoon line catches the captain about the neck and drags him to his death.

A simple story, a straightforward plot—yet, since the 1851 publication of Herman Melville's *Moby-Dick*, readers and critics have found many meanings in the struggle between Captain Ahab and the whale. To some, the novel is a cautionary tale that depicts how Ahab's obsession with revenge leads to his insanity and death. Others believe that the whale represents the unknowable secrets of the universe and that Ahab is a tragic hero who dares to challenge fate by attempting to discover this knowledge. Perhaps Melville intended Ahab as a criticism of Americans' tendency to become involved in well-intentioned but irrational causes. Or did Melville model Ahab after himself, letting his fictional character express his anger at what he perceived as a cruel and distant god?

Although literary critics disagree over the meaning of *Moby-Dick*, readers do not need to choose one particular interpretation in order to gain an understanding of Melville's novel. Instead, by examining various analyses, they can gain numerous insights into the issues that lie under the surface of the basic plot. Studying the writings of literary critics can also aid readers in making their own assessments of *Moby-Dick* and other literary works and in developing analytical thinking skills.

The Greenhaven Literary Companion Series was created with these goals in mind. Designed for young adults, this unique anthology series provides an engaging and comprehensive introduction to literary analysis and criticism. The essays included in the Literary Companion Series are chosen for their accessibility to a young adult audience and are expertly edited in consideration of both the reading and comprehension levels of this audience. In addition, each essay is introduced by a concise summation that presents the contributing writer's main themes and insights. Every anthology in the Literary Companion Series contains a varied selection of critical essays that cover a wide time span and express diverse views. Wherever possible, primary sources are represented through excerpts from authors' notebooks, letters, and journals and through contemporary criticism.

Each title in the Literary Companion Series pays careful consideration to the historical context of the particular author or literary work. In-depth biographies and detailed chronologies reveal important aspects of authors' lives and emphasize the historical events and social milieu that influenced their writings. To facilitate further research, every anthology includes primary and secondary source bibliographies of articles and/or books selected for their suitability for young adults. These engaging features make the Greenhaven Literary Companion Series ideal for introducing students to literary analysis in the classroom or as a library resource for young adults researching the world's great authors and literature.

Exceptional in its focus on young adults, the Greenhaven Literary Companion Series strives to present literary criticism in a compelling and accessible format. Every title in the series is intended to spark readers' interest in leading American and world authors, to help them broaden their understanding of literature, and to encourage them to formulate their own analyses of the literary works that they read. It is the editors' hope that young adult readers will find these anthologies to be true companions in their study of literature.

INTRODUCTION: PEERING INTO THE DARKNESS: PSYCHOLOGICAL REALITY IN POE

Few people will open this book without some knowledge of Edgar Allan Poe. His short stories continue to be well read at a time when many other classic authors have fallen into obscurity. He is the author of perhaps the most well remembered poem ever written, "The Raven," which lives on both in the original and in parody (even a Halloween episode of the cartoon show *The Simpsons* parodied the poem). His continued popularity among young adult readers, however, does not extend to adults, many of whom view Poe as one-dimensional. Indeed, Poe's themes and ideas do seem single-minded, as critic Lewis E. Gates notes:

> Whether the effect that Poe aims at is a shiver of surprise at the sudden ingenious resolution of a riddle, or a shudder of horror at the collapse of a haunted house, his methods of work are substantially the same, and the stuff from which he weaves his tale is equally unreal and remote from what ordinary life has to offer; it is all the product of an infinitely inventive intellect that devises and plans and adroitly arranges with an unflinching purpose to attain an effect.

Gates's analysis points out a primary truth about the majority of Poe's work, his tendency to deal with the "unreal and remote" leading to a sameness in much of his work. In story after story, poem after poem, Poe writes to achieve a single effect, a mood, drawing the reader into an intimate world of horror, death, and gruesome resurrection. His landscapes are crumbling houses, dank cellars, dark rooms, hearts pumping under floorboards—all challenging the reader to peer into the darkness to see the deeper, psychological reality that his characters and settings suggest.

Critic and scholar N. Bryllion Fagin, author of *The Histrionic Mr. Poe*, argues that Poe's true genius lies in his attempt to create this imaginative reality:

Poe did not write stories of character, of plot, or of place: all the usual designations break down in his case. He wrote stories which attempted to transcribe the totality of a mood or impression or feeling and to create within the reader the same totality of mood, impression, or feeling. Poe's great achievement was the creation and mastery of a method for capturing and evoking in others his special type of imaginative experience.

It is this achievement, perhaps, that keeps Poe's work in the public eye. Poe is not interested in presenting realistic characters or settings, but in achieving a reality that, for the span of the work, grips readers and holds them spellbound. Whatever the deeper meanings of much of his work, Poe is first and foremost a storyteller of the first magnitude. Whether readers enjoy his work on this level or appreciate the deeper themes addressed in many of the essays in this volume, Poe remains an essentially accessible, modern author.

Readings on Edgar Allan Poe attempts to illuminate Poe's themes and ideas in readable, intriguing essays. The book contains several helpful features for those new to literary criticism. Each essay's introduction summarizes the article's main ideas and gives a bit of background on the author. Notes explain difficult or unfamiliar words and concepts throughout the book. A chronology lists important dates in the life of the author and presents him in a broader historical context. A bibliography includes works for further research as well as historical works of interest. Finally, an annotated table of contents and thorough index make each volume in the *Literary Companion Series* a complete research tool in itself as well as a launching point for further exploration.

EDGAR ALLAN POE: A BIOGRAPHY

Edgar Allan Poe has been heralded as the founder of several literary disciplines: the short story, the detective story, even literary criticism as it is practiced today. Not only did Poe break new ground in these areas, but his critical works—on both other writers and his own writing—remain well-read pieces of good advice implemented by many writers. It is somewhat ironic, however, that Poe rarely followed his own advice, often ignoring his own precepts. He also rarely ventured outside his characteristic subject matter, plumbing the nature of death, resurrection, and the psychological horror of those obsessed with these subjects. Today, most readers of Poe outside of an appreciative critical circle think of him as a rather one-dimensional horror writer. Nevertheless, the timelessness of and attraction to Poe's work is evident in the fact that many people can still recite portions of Poe's famous poem "The Raven" and vividly remember such tales as "The Fall of the House of Usher," "The Tell-Tale Heart," and "The Cask of Amontillado."

A writer approaches the task of a biography of Poe, especially a short biography of Poe, with a great deal of caution, as both Poe and his biographers are responsible for a great deal of misinformation and exaggeration about his life. For example, immediately after Poe's death, the biographer Rufus Griswold roasted the author as a limited writer given to alcoholism, debauchery, drug addiction, and a variety of other sins. Griswold's biography remained mostly unchallenged for decades. Though later writers took issue with some of Griswold's conclusions, his life of Poe remained the accepted version. Then, in the second half of the twentieth century, a new appreciation for the works of Poe emerged. Scholars delved into Poe's correspondence, sought out and scrutinized the correspondence of others who knew Poe, and tried to ferret out the truth in the fiction about his life and works. Though much of Griswold's biography has been disproved, the basic facts of Poe's life are mired in half-truths. What continues to emerge today is Poe's role in the controversy. During his lifetime, Poe, ever eager to portray himself in the best, most aristocratic light, reinvented whole portions of his life, telling elaborate fictions about his origins and his career. N. Bryllion Fagin, author of *The Histrionic Mr. Poe*, has written that accepting Poe's tendency to reinvent his life is essential to understanding it. "For Poe, like the myth-making world, was a lusty romancer, and it is only by accepting his romancing about himself as part of the truth that we can form any picture of him at all. . . . Perhaps Poe really believed, at times, that he was the grandson of Benedict Arnold, or that he had been arrested in far-off St. Petersburg." While no doubt this biography too will contain elements that fall in the realm of the challenged facts, the editor aims to record the most agreed upon elements of Poe's life and present them fairly.

Poe was born in Boston on January 19, 1809, the second son of actors Elizabeth (Eliza) and David Poe. At the time of Poe's birth, few cities could afford to sponsor a permanent theater company, and actors such as Poe's parents toured from city to city. Thus Edgar's infancy was spent traveling from town to town on the East Coast. Elizabeth Poe was a talented actress capable of many demanding roles, but David Poe had only limited talent and was frequently skewered in theater reviews—sometimes the same reviews that praised Elizabeth. Despite Elizabeth's near constant employment, the Poes earned little as actors and constantly veered from one financial crisis to another. Edgar's father, disowned by his own father for taking up acting, tried to borrow money from other relatives when the family required it, but with little success. The birth of Poe's sister, Rosalie, in 1810, further strained the family's finances. While the facts surrounding the event remain obscure, most scholars believe that economic pressures coupled with his unsuccessful choice of profession led David Poe to abandon his young family sometime in 1811, virtually condemning Eliza to death.

Elizabeth attempted to continue acting to support her three children, but constant moves and grinding poverty either aggravated or contributed to her contracting tuberculosis, which worsened under the strain of her new responsibilities. Her last appearance on the stage was October 11, 1811. Shortly after, she fell desperately ill. The theater community rallied around her, giving a benefit performance to earn money for her care and posting public notices for contributions for her and the children, but Eliza died on December 8. Although Edgar Poe later claimed to not remember his mother, many scholars believe that her premature death, following the fevers, coughing of blood, hemorrhages, and pallid wasting away from tuberculosis, imprinted itself into Edgar's budding consciousness. Some scholars attribute his later fascination with the theme of young women dying tragically with this first example.

Henry Poe, Edgar's brother, went to live with David Poe's father, but because Edgar and Rosalie's maternal grandfather was himself deep in poverty, the younger orphans were not placed with relatives. Rosalie was taken into the care of William Mackenzie, a Richmond merchant, while Edgar was taken into the childless home of John and Frances Allan, also of Richmond.

After Edgar joined the Allan household, John Allan took his family to England and Scotland, where they remained for five years. The Allans were excessively proud of Edgar, who even at an early age had a talent for memorization, which the Allans encouraged by having Poe recite poems in company. While in England the Allans enrolled Poe at the age of nine in a boarding school in Stoke Newington, a small village four miles north of London. There Poe studied Latin, French, and mathematics. In an article written in 1878, scholar William Hunter describes Poe's success at the school and headmaster John Bransby's opinion of the youth:

> When he left it he was able to speak the French language, construe any easy Latin author, and was far better acquainted with history and literature than many boys of a more advanced age who had had greater advantages than he had had. I spoke to Dr. Bransby about him two or three times during my school days, having then, as now, a deep admiration for his poems. . . . In answer to my questions on one occasion, he said "Edgar Allan was a quick and clever boy and would have been a very good boy if he had not been spoilt by his parents, but they spoilt him, and allowed him an extravagant amount of pocket-money, which enabled him to get into all manner of mischief—still I liked the boy—poor fellow, his parents spoilt him!"

The Allans left England in 1820; John Allan's business

was failing and Frances Allan, after having contracted tuberculosis, was becoming seriously ill. Back in Richmond, the Allans enrolled Edgar in a school run by Joseph Clarke, a classical scholar, and, later, a school run by William Burke. In Clarke's school Poe studied mathematics and read Cicero, Caesar, Virgil, Horace, and Ovid in Latin as well as Homer and Xenophon in Greek. Clarke wrote of Poe:

> He was remarkable for self-respect, without haughtiness, strictly just and correct in his demeanor with his fellow playmates, which rendered him a favorite even with those above his years. . . . As a scholar he was ambitious to excel, and tho' not conspicuously studious always acquitted himself well in his classes. His imaginative powers seemed to take precedence of all his other faculties, he gave proof of this in some of his juvenile compositions addressed to his young female friends. He had a sensitive and tender heart, and would strain every nerve to oblige a friend.

In contrast to Poe's later, more melancholic bent, at Clarke's school he excelled at athletics. One of Poe's classmates, James Preston, said that Poe "was a swift runner, a wonderful leaper, and what was more rare, a boxer with some slight training." Indeed Poe set a broad-jump record of twenty-one feet six inches.

In 1825 or 1826 Poe fell in love with and became secretly engaged to Elmira Royster, the fifteen-year-old daughter of his neighbor. Around this time Poe became estranged from John Allan. Poe's continued interest in poetry and romantic pursuits severely clashed with Allan's practical nature. And Poe's melancholy seems to have irritated Allan. In a letter written to Edgar's older brother, Henry, on November 1, 1824, Allan expresses some of the same sort of dismay that parents of teenagers today might voice.

> [Edgar] has had little else to do for me, he does nothing & seems quite miserable, sulky & ill-tempered to all the Family. How we have acted to produce this is beyond my conception—why I have put up so long with his conduct is a little less wonderful. The boy possesses not a Spark of affection for us, not a particle of gratitude for all my care and kindness towards him. I have given him a much superior Education than ever I received myself.

In 1826 Poe enrolled at the University of Virginia in Charlottesville. (It is interesting to note that Poe attended the university while its founder, Thomas Jefferson, was still involved with the institution. Every week, Jefferson invited a few students to Monticello to dine with him.) Poe's years at the university have been scrutinized by scholars, since it is during these years that Poe and Allan became estranged. Though Poe excelled academically at the university, financially he got into disastrous trouble. Most scholars seem to agree that Allan did not give Poe sufficient funds to support himself at the university. Poe resorted to gambling to pay his debts, and whether the product of unscrupulous cheating or of his own bad luck, Poe was soon so deeply in debt that he had no hope of repaying without Allan's help. Allan, however, was not inclined to pay the debts and was infuriated by Poe's attempt to blame Allan for his insufficient funds. No longer able to pay for his education, his funds cut off by his foster father, Poe was forced to leave the university in December 1826.

Back in Richmond, Allan put Poe to work at his counting-house without pay. While engaged in this profession for which he had neither talent nor enthusiasm, Poe learned that Elmira Royster had become engaged to another man. Elmira's father had been intercepting Poe's correspondence to her, and Elmira, thinking herself abandoned by Poe, accepted the proposal of Alexander Shelton.

Suffering from the combined disappointments of leaving the university, working at the countinghouse, and losing his fiancée, Poe decided to leave Richmond for Boston in 1827. An aggrieved Poe wrote to Allan:

> My determination is at length taken—to leave your house and endeavor to find some place in this wide world, where I will be treated—not as *you* have treated me. . . .
>
> Since I have been able to think on any subject, my thoughts have aspired and have been taught by *you* to aspire, to eminence in public life—this cannot be attained without a good Education. . . .
>
> [I hope] to place myself in some situation where I may not only obtain a livelihood, but lay by a sum which one day or another will support me at the University.

Then, after berating Allan, Poe had the nerve to ask him for funds to leave. The shameless request would become a pattern with Poe, who never seemed to learn that this combination of scolding and pleading for money did nothing to endear him to Allan, who became increasingly frustrated and angry with Poe for his ingratitude.

From this moment on, Poe would never recover a stable life. Critic Edward Davidson sums up Poe's tragic existence this way:

Part of Poe's personal tragedy was that he was carefully reared through the first eighteen years of his life to conform to the manners and code of the aristocratic, landed gentry in the fashionable circles of sophisticated Richmond; then he was suddenly thrust into the business world where the only money he ever made came from that otherwise discredited instrument in the world of finance—a writer's pen.

Unable to find work for six weeks after arriving in Boston, Poe enlisted as a common soldier in the U.S. Army under the name of Edgar A. Perry. During this period, Poe paid to have his first book published. Entitled *Tamerlane and Other Poems*, it appeared without his name, the only attribution being "By a Bostonian."

Because of his superior education, in the army Poe was given a post as clerk, taking dictation from officers, preparing the payroll, and acting as a messenger. Although quickly disenchanted with the army and soon desperate to leave, Poe was a success there. In nineteen months he attained the highest enlisted rank. Nevertheless, unhappy because his lack of social standing prevented him from rising to the rank of officer, Poe decided to seek officer's rank by applying to West Point. He paid a man twenty-five dollars of a promised seventy-five dollars to take his place in the army (a necessity at the time if one wished to leave the military earlier than the promised five-year stint) and was discharged in April 1829.

A couple of months before his discharge, Poe had been able to forge a tentative reconciliation with his foster father after the death of his foster mother, Frances, in February 1829. On temporary leave in March, Poe and Allan found common ground in their grief. The reconciliation would not last, however, as Poe continued to dun Allan for money, and Allan resolutely continued to refuse, trying to force Poe to become more self-supporting.

Meanwhile, Poe solicited letters of recommendation to West Point from friends and finally entered the academy in 1830. He continued to pursue his literary ambitions as well, having obtained a publisher for his second book of poetry, *Al Aaraaf, Tamerlane and Minor Poems*, in 1829. Although this second volume, published in an edition of 250, gained slightly more critical notice than his first, it, too, failed to make the impact Poe desired.

Poe quickly found that West Point was not for him either. He balked at the rigors of the academy and almost immediately began pleading with Allan for permission to resign. Increasingly despondent, Poe turned once again to gambling and drinking for solace. When Allan refused to give permission for a resignation, Poe decided on a less honorable way to escape West Point by getting himself court-martialed. In January 1831 Poe disobeyed orders, failed to show up for roll call and guard duty, and generally violated enough rules to be tried for and convicted of gross neglect of duty and disobedience of orders. On March 6 Poe was dismissed.

As usual, Poe wrote Allan, blaming him for his fate at West Point and renewing his plea for money. Allan, who had remarried, and who would eventually have three children with his second wife as well as illegitimate twins with his mistress, was even less inclined to listen to Poe's pleas. With any hope of inheritance almost completely obliterated, Poe's continued self-pitying pleas further wearied Allan, who severed their relationship.

Now entirely on his own, Poe left for New York and then Baltimore, eventually settling with his biological father's widowed sister, Maria Clemm, and his nine-year-old cousin, Virginia, in May 1831. The Clemms lived on the edge of poverty, Maria supporting herself and her daughter by sewing and keeping boarders, aided by a pension to her bedridden mother, Elizabeth. While living with Maria, Poe renewed his relationship with his elder brother, Henry, who had been reared by Elizabeth and her husband. When Henry died of tuberculosis in 1831 at twenty-four, Poe took on his role as the man of the Clemm household.

During his years with the Clemms in Baltimore, Poe published five stories in the *Philadelphia Saturday Courier:* "Metzengerstein," "The Duc de l'Omelette," "A Tale of Jerusalem," "Bon Bon," and "Loss of Breath." Poe also won a literary contest sponsored by the Baltimore *Saturday Visiter* with "MS. Found in a Bottle." The small amount of money that Poe brought in from writing could not lift his newfound family out of poverty, and Poe again attempted a reconciliation with his foster father. Hearing that Allan was ill, Poe returned to Richmond on February 14, 1834. Instead of welcoming the prodigal son, however, Allan is said to have raised his cane, threatened him, and ordered him out. His father died six weeks later.

Ever in need of employment, especially after the death of Elizabeth Poe and the loss of her pension, Poe was able to attain with the help of friends the editorship of the *Southern*

Literary Messenger in Richmond. Though extremely adept at his task, Poe missed Maria and Virginia, still in Baltimore. He began to drink heavily and experience violent mood swings; his exasperated publisher Thomas Willis White sacked him.

The unemployed Poe returned to Baltimore and convinced the Clemms to join him in Richmond. Writing to White with promises to reform, Poe convinced White to reinstate him in December 1835. While at the *Messenger*, Poe became known for his scathing reviews of books, which provoked criticism from writers at other journals but were popular with Poe's readers. Poe also used the *Messenger* as a venue for his own work, including his seven *Tales of the Folio Club*, as well as "Berenice," "Morella," and "The Unparalleled Adventure of One Hans Pfaall."

While continuing to publish stories, Poe became tremendously productive at the *Messenger*, the stability of his home life contributing to his ability to work. He also devoted much of his time to educating Virginia Clemm, for whom at some point he began to feel more than brotherly love. On May 16, 1836, the twenty-seven-year-old Poe publicly married the fourteen-year-old Virginia. (He had actually married her at thirteen in a private ceremony a year earlier.) The marriage did little to improve Poe's spirits, however, as he continued to suffer from bouts of depression brought on by his drinking. Many scholars, including biographer Jeffrey Meyer, are convinced that Poe suffered from either an allergy or an extreme sensitivity to alcohol that made him irascible even after a single drink. Meyers, who believes Poe inherited his alcoholism from his father, describes Poe's alcoholism this way:

> The origins of Poe's alcoholism go back to his infancy, when his nurse tranquilized him with bread soaked in gin, and to his childhood, when he toasted the dinner guests. . . . At the university he compulsively gulped down alcohol during his drinking bouts at West Point. . . . Though Poe needed no excuse to start drinking, he sought relief in alcoholic binges during times of emotional stress. He drank when he was in danger of losing Virginia, after her first hemorrhage and after her death. He drank when overwhelmed by work and by poverty. . . . He drank to calm his nerves. . . . He drank before and after his public lectures in New York and Boston, incapacitating himself for the former and disgracing himself after the latter.

Poe's continued drinking frustrated White, publisher of the *Messenger*. Though Poe had made significant contributions to the journal, perhaps single-handedly increasing its circulation from five hundred to thirty-five hundred, White again reached the point of firing him:

> Highly as I really think of Mr. Poe's talents, I shall be forced to give him notice . . . that I can no longer recognize him as editor of my *Messenger*. Three months ago I felt it my duty to give him a similar notice—and was afterwards overpersuaded to restore him to his situation on certain conditions—which conditions he has again forfeited. Added to all this, I am cramped by him in the exercise of my own judgment, as to what articles I shall or shall not admit into my work. . . . I mean to dispense with Mr. Poe as my editor.

Thus, in January 1837 Poe left the *Messenger*.

After losing his job, Poe, Virginia, and Maria moved to New York, where they continued to live in poverty, but Poe cut back on his drinking. New York's high cost of living prompted a move to Philadelphia in the summer of 1838, where they acquired a black cat called Catterina who might have been the inspiration for Poe's story "The Black Cat." Poe continued to publish and work on *The Narrative of Arthur Gordon Pym*, two installments of which he had published while editor of the *Messenger*. *Pym* is a full-length novel depicting a supposed true-to-life adventure. Poe also published "Ligeia" in 1838.

In May 1839 Poe obtained an editorial position with *Burton's Gentleman's Magazine*. William Burton, owner of the magazine, and Poe began to clash almost immediately, mostly over Poe's caustic literary critiques. Burton wanted Poe to tone down the pieces. Poe replied, "You see I speak plainly, I cannot do otherwise upon such a subject." Despite such disagreements, Poe continued as assistant editor and, as was his custom, used the magazine as a venue for publishing his stories. He published "The Man That Was Used Up," and his most well known work, "The Fall of the House of Usher," in September 1839. The popularity of "Usher" brought Poe to the attention of the publisher Lea and Blanchard, who agreed to publish *Tales of the Grotesque and Arabesque*, a collection of twenty-five stories in two volumes.

The book received mixed reviews. While the *Boston Notion* said that the tales "fall below the average of newspaper trash," the *Philadelphia Saturday Courier* proclaimed the tales "wildly imaginative in plot; fanciful in description . . . possessed of rare and varied learning." Despite the attention, the book sold poorly.

In May 1840 Burton put his magazine up for sale and fired

Poe, in part because of their many disagreements and in part because of Poe's drinking. Poe tried to find subscribers to launch his own magazine, the *Penn*, without success. The new owner of *Burton's*, George Graham, started a magazine called *Graham's*, hiring Poe as editor for eight hundred dollars a year. Under Poe's guidance, including his continued reviews and tales, *Graham's* prospered. In just over two years, subscriptions rose from twenty-five thousand to forty thousand. Unfortunately, Poe's salary remained the same.

Poe enlivened *Graham's* with a number of innovative ideas, including a running cipher contest in which he boasted of being able to solve any puzzle the subscribers came up with. Unfortunately, the popularity of the column left Poe with little time for anything besides solving the puzzles. He disbanded the column. Poe published some of his best stories in *Graham's*, including "The Murders in the Rue Morgue," which debuted Poe's inventive detective Auguste Dupin, in April 1841. Auguste Dupin remains one of the most original and well remembered characters in literature. "A Descent into the Maelstrom" was also published at this time.

In spite of his stable position, Poe's financial circumstances remained precarious. Although the inventive Maria Clemm managed to keep her family barely fed on Poe's salary, they were never able to afford adequate food nor pay for warm lodgings. Under these conditions, Virginia, who had contracted tuberculosis, worsened. While singing and playing the piano in January 1842, she began hemorrhaging from a broken blood vessel. Although Virginia's condition would alternately improve and worsen over the next few years, she would never fully regain her health. Poe's response to her illness was an almost obsessive fear of losing her.

Edgar Allan Poe

The year 1842 was memorable for Poe because he met two literary giants of his time, Charles Dickens and Nathaniel Hawthorne. In fact, Dickens offered to help Poe find an English publisher for his works. Although the effort proved unsuccessful, they remained acquaintances throughout Poe's life. Poe corresponded with Hawthorne after he reviewed several of his works in *Graham's*, including *Twice-Told Tales* and *Mosses from an Old Manse* in November 1847. Poe's reviews of Hawthorne's work were always mixed; in his review of *Mosses from an Old Manse*, Poe praised Hawthorne's writing but condemned him for overworking his allegory. Hawthorne responded to Poe's criticism with a letter urging him to return to writing his own tales:

> I admire you rather as a writer of tales than as a critic upon them. I might often—and often do—dissent from your opinions in the latter capacity, but could never fail to recognize your force and originality in the former.

The years 1842–1843 were marked by the publication of some of Poe's best-known stories, including "The Masque of the Red Death," "The Mystery of Marie Roget," "The Gold-Bug," "The Black Cat," and "The Tell-Tale Heart." Poe continued to earn little more than his salary at *Graham's*, however, which, because of Virginia's medical expenses, was woefully inadequate to support the Poe family. Poe resorted to hack writing to supplement his income.

In April 1842 Poe resigned from *Graham's* with a combination of complaints, including "disgust with the namby-pamby character of the Magazine—a character which it was impossible to eradicate.... The salary, moreover, did not pay me for the labor I was forced to bestow." Falling into the despair that plagued him all his life, Poe returned to drinking heavily after his resignation.

In 1843 Poe tried lecturing for fees. An effective speaker, Poe lectured on and recited American poetry and gave a scathing critique of Rufus Griswold's volume *The Poets and Poetry of America*. His lectures proved successful, always delivered to sold-out audiences.

In April 1844 Poe left Philadelphia for New York and another crack at the city that was even then known as a literary and publishing mecca. Poe began writing for the New York *Evening Mirror*, and was appointed its editor in the same year for $750 a year. Poe continued to publish his own pieces, including his poem "Dream-land" in *Graham's* and four stories in other popular journals, "A Tale of the Ragged

Mountains," "The Balloon-Hoax," "The Purloined Letter," which featured Dupin, and "The Premature Burial."

"The Balloon-Hoax," the tale of a magnificent balloon adventure that becomes an outer-space excursion, published in the New York *Sun*, was a sensation on the scale of "The War of the Worlds" radio broadcast over a century later. Poe's description of the public's response:

> On the morning of its announcement, the whole square surrounding the *Sun* building was literally besieged, blocked up. . . . I never witnessed more intense excitement to get possession of a newspaper. As soon as the first few copies made their way into the streets, they were bought up, at almost any price, from the news-boys, who made a profitable speculation.

In November 1845, Poe published his most famous poem, "The Raven." Poe himself felt that he had achieved something wonderful with the poem, proclaiming to friends that he had authored "the greatest poem ever written." Published in magazines throughout the country, "The Raven" made Poe a celebrity, and he was invited to salons throughout New York. In February 1845 Poe's popularity was enhanced when poet James Russell Lowell made Poe the subject of a biographical essay in *Graham's*.

In February 1845 Poe became coeditor of the *Broadway Journal* and was offered one-third of the magazine's profits. Poe reviewed many well-known classic and contemporary authors for the magazine, including Milton, Burns, Lamb, Leigh Hunt, Shelley, Tennyson, and Lowell.

Poe's fame after publication of "The Raven" brought him into contact with poets of the day, including several well-known women poets. Poe struck up a romantic mutual admiration society with one of these poets, Frances (Fanny) Sargent Osgood, in 1845.

Capitalizing on Poe's popularity, Wiley and Putnam published twelve of Poe's stories in the collection *Tales*. *Tales* was praised in reviews in both America and England, and Wiley and Putnam followed its success with a book of Poe's poetry, *The Raven and Other Poems*, in November 1845.

Meanwhile, Poe had gone back to his old habits during his editorship at the *Broadway Journal*, alternately drinking and falling into bouts of irrationality. While coeditor Charles Briggs sought to fire Poe, the financially teetering journal collapsed, and publisher John Bisco sold it to Poe for fifty dollars. Poe unsuccessfully and feverishly sought investors for the magazine; he veered on the edge of a nervous break-down, writing, "[I am] dreadfully sick and depressed . . . I seem to have just awakened from some horrible dream, in which all was confusion and suffering. . . . I really believe that I have been mad."

Part ownership of a journal, the publication of "The Raven," and the popularity of *Tales* and *The Raven and Other Poems* should have brought Poe some financial and profes-sional stability; he instead fell into drunken despair and even deeper poverty than ever before.

In November 1846 Poe published "The Cask of Amontil-lado" in *Godey's Lady's Book*. Virginia's health continued to decline; she suffered, as Meyers explains in his biography of Poe, "irregular appetite, facial pallor, flushed cheeks, unsta-ble pulse, night sweats, high fever, sudden chills, shortness of breath, chest pains, severe coughing and spitting of blood. Each day, as the microscopic organisms gnawed through her tissue and destroyed a bit more of her lung, she found it increasingly difficult to breathe."

With the onset of winter, lacking blankets, food, and heat, Virginia worsened alarmingly; on January 30, 1847, she died at the age of twenty-four, at the same age and of the same disease as Poe's mother. Poe promptly fell into a deep de-pression and drank heavily.

> I became insane, with long intervals of horrible sanity. Dur-ing these fits of absolute unconsciousness I drank, God only knows how often or how much. As a matter of course my en-emies referred the insanity to the drink rather than the drink to the insanity.

Poe turned for solace, and even romantic attachment, to Fanny Osgood, who remained, as she had been since meet-ing Poe, separated from her husband. Although Fanny seems to have enjoyed the relationship, she refused Poe's pleas to marry him.

Poe continued to sink more deeply into poverty and de-spair, but managed to write and publish "Ulalume," his clas-sic poem written in imitation of ululation, or wailing, in December 1847. He also completed the almost incompre-hensible philosophical work *Eureka*. Before seeking its pub-lication, Poe promoted the work in a series of lectures, where his ideas were unevenly received. Despite the luke-warm response, Poe managed to convince George Putnam to publish *Eureka*. Putnam recalled the meeting:

A gentleman with a somewhat nervous and excited manner claimed attention on a subject which he said was of the highest importance. Seated at my desk, and looking at me a full minute with his "glittering eye," he at length said: "I am Mr. Poe.". . . After another pause, the poet seeming to be in a tremor of excitement, he at length went on to say that the publication he had to propose was of momentous interest.

Poe grandiosely envisioned an edition of fifty thousand copies; Putnam wisely brought it out at five hundred—and had a difficult time selling those.

Poe felt unhinged by Virginia's death. He sought to replace her as soon as possible by remarrying, and simultaneously sought the affections of three women—Marie Louise Shew, Annie Richmond, and Sarah Helen Whitman. None of these love interests, except for the remote possibility of Sarah Helen Whitman, was destined to succeed. Marie Louise Shew, the intensely religious nurse to Poe and Virginia, was persuaded by her pastor that the man who had written such a secular book as *Eureka* was neither a suitable mate nor friend. Annie Richmond, though friendly with Poe, was a married housewife with four children. Sarah Helen Whitman, a poet herself, at one point accepted Poe but wisely realized that Poe's erratic behavior was a warning. His zealous attempts to find a wife seem not to have dampened his poetic tendencies, however, as during this period Poe wrote "The Bells" and a second "To Helen." He also completed his well-known essay on poetry, "The Poetic Principle."

In 1849, his attempts at remarriage a shambles, Poe managed to publish "Hop-Frog," "Melonta Tauta," "Von Kempelen and His Discovery," and the poems "Eldorado," "To My Mother," and "For Annie."

In this last year of his life Poe was tremendously restless, shuttling between New York, Philadelphia, Virginia, and Maryland. The rush of events that led up to Poe's death have remained mysterious. On June 29 Poe left New York for a lecture tour in an attempt to earn money to launch his own magazine, which he had named the *Stylus*. The next day, on a stop in Philadelphia, he began to drink and was arrested for public drunkenness. At some point, Poe lost his suitcase. While jailed, Poe began to hallucinate; his frightening visions included Maria Clemm being butchered.

Released from jail, Poe tried to return to New York, but, still delusional, he thought that two men on the train were plotting to kill him and he disembarked, returning to

Philadelphia. He stayed with John Sartain, an artist who had worked with Poe at *Burton's* and had remained a friend. Beginning to recover, Poe located his missing suitcase at the train station on July 10. With borrowed money, Poe was able to get to Richmond for lectures on "The Poetic Principle" on August 17 and September 24 and Norfolk on September 14. While in Richmond, Poe renewed his acquaintance with his childhood love, Elmira Royster Shelton, who had been widowed for five years. Seeing opportunity, Poe tried but failed to convince her to marry him.

On September 27 Poe began the return trip to New York. He stopped in Baltimore, began to drink heavily, and again suffered from hallucinations. No one really knows what happened between September 28 and October 3, when Poe was found semiconscious and apparently desperately ill outside Gunner's Hall, an Irish tavern. The man who found him sent a note to Poe's friend Joseph Snodgrass, describing Poe's condition.

Snodgrass was appalled by what he saw. He believed that the ragged clothes Poe was found in were not his own:

> His hat—or rather the hat of somebody else, for he had evidently been robbed of his clothing, or cheated in an exchange—was a cheap palm-leaf one, without a band, and soiled; his coat, of commonest alpaca, and evidently "secondhand"; his pants of gray-mixed cassimere, dingy and badly fitting. He wore neither vest nor neckcloth, if I remember aright, while his shirt was sadly crumpled and soiled.

Snodgrass further noted that Poe's

> face was haggard, not to say bloated, and unwashed, his hair unkempt, and his whole physique repulsive: The intellectual flash of his eye had vanished, or rather had been quenched in the bowl. . . . He was so utterly stupefied with liquor that I thought it best not to seek recognition or conversation. . . . So insensible was he, that we had to carry him to the carriage as if a corpse. The muscles of articulation seemed paralyzed to speechlessness, and mere incoherent mutterings were all that were heard.

Snodgrass put Poe in Washington College Hospital, where he lingered unconscious for ten hours. He then regained consciousness but was hallucinating and delirious. There was little that could be done for him; Poe died on October 7 and was buried in the Presbyterian Cemetery in Baltimore on October 8. Maria Clemm, who had not seen Poe since June 29, was not notified of Poe's death or funeral.

Various causes of Poe's death have been advanced, including brain fever, brain tumor, meningitis, epilepsy, syphilis, hypoglycemia, and, most recently in 1996, rabies. R. Michael Benitez, assistant professor of medicine at the University of Maryland Medical Center, believes that Poe's symptoms describe a near classic case of rabies. Details such as Poe's refusal to take anything to drink, Benitez argues, may have meant he had difficulty swallowing, a symptom of rabies. The delirium tremens, perspiration, hallucinations, and shouting at imaginary companions are also typical symptoms of end-stage rabies, in which the patient, growing increasingly confused and belligerent, finally dies. Benitez analyzed Poe's case for a clinical conference as an exercise in diagnosing the illness of a hypothetical patient. Although an interesting theory, so many years after his death it is necessarily speculation, and Poe's end remains impossible to explain with certainty.

Immediately after Poe's death, Rufus Griswold, Poe's literary executor and editor, published an obituary in which he intoned that Poe was a literary hack and hopeless drunk who had no friends. Griswold, perhaps harboring vengeful feelings because Poe had attacked him in print, began an immediate assault on Poe's character. Thus began the myths surrounding Poe's life which bring us full circle in this biography.

CHARACTERS AND PLOT

CHAPTER 1: THE DETECTIVE STORIES

"THE MURDERS IN THE RUE MORGUE"

Principal Characters

M. Auguste Dupin: Poe's brilliant, eccentric detective

Aldolphe de Bon (Le Bon): an old friend of Dupin who is accused of the murders

Unnamed narrator: Dupin's sidekick

Plot Summary

The victims of Poe's first tale of ratiocination are Madame L'Espanaye and her daughter, Mademoiselle Camille, both brutally murdered. Madame L'Espanaye's head is severed from her neck when the police find her body in the courtyard. And her body, with many of the bones in her arm and leg shattered, is covered in bruises. Police discover Camille choked to death and stuffed, feet first, up the chimney of her fourth-floor apartment.

Police are baffled by the case in that they cannot ascertain how Madame L'Espanaye's body ended up in the courtyard when her apartment was locked from the inside. Additionally, although the room is in a shambles, two bags of gold, totaling four thousand francs, have been left behind in the middle of the room. Finally, witnesses who heard the women's shrieks in the night claim to have heard two voices in the vicinity of the crime scene. One is the deep voice of a Frenchman, and the other, shriller voice cannot be identified.

When Le Bon, an acquaintance of M. Auguste Dupin, is accused of the murders, the police allow Dupin to investigate the crime. The newspapers have suggested that the crime is insolvable, but Dupin is confident that his own theories about the case will be confirmed. First, Dupin notes that the nationality of the shrill voice cannot be determined as the witnesses heard no discernable words. Next, Dupin discovers that windows in the apartment that appear to be nailed shut work on a spring mechanism, thus allowing for a previously dismissed method of entrance into and exit from the apartment. Additionally, Dupin suggests that the criminal could have gained access to the windows by leaping from the building's lightning rod to the window shutters. Finally, Dupin presents a small tuft of animal hair that the police failed to find clutched in Madame L'Espanaye's hand. He draws a sketch of a handprint imprinted around Camille's neck and leads the narrator to conclude that an orangutan has committed the crime.

At the base of the lightning rod, Dupin finds a ribbon that he believes belongs to a Maltese sailor. He expects the animal thus belongs to a sailor and places an ad in the paper for the man to collect his missing beast. When the man arrives to pick up the animal, Dupin confronts him about the crime. The sailor confirms that he owns an orangutan that escaped from his apartment with a razor on the night of the murders. The sailor followed the animal to the women's apartment and watched in horror from the lightning rod as the ape committed the crime.

"THE PURLOINED LETTER"

Principal Characters
Auguste Dupin: Poe's renowned detective
Monsieur G—: the prefect of police in Paris
Minister D—: the thief
Unnamed narrator

Plot Summary
"The Purloined Letter" is considered Poe's finest detective tale. It lacks some of the gruesome gothic elements of his other tales of ratiocination and is carried, instead, by the concept of rational thinking and logical problem solving. The story opens with the prefect of police paying a visit to Dupin to inform him that a letter has been stolen and is being held for ransom by the thief, Minister D—. The letter is of vital political importance, as the letter writer, the victim, and the thief all work for the government. Wishing to retrieve the letter, the prefect of police has already searched the thief's premises, but he has come up empty-handed. Dupin suggests that the prefect conduct another search of the premises, but

a month later, the police still have not been able to uncover the letter. At this time, the prefect offers fifty thousand francs to anyone who can find the missing letter. Dupin then secures the check from the prefect and promptly supplies him with the letter.

Next, Dupin explains to the narrator how he obtained the letter through the process of deductive reasoning. Poe also introduces here the idea that lost or stolen items can often be found in the most obvious places, an idea that has become formulaic to detective fiction. In this case, Dupin illustrates this theory by noting that to solve the case, he simply paired everything he knew about the thief, Minister D—, with everything he understood about the case. Assuming the minister's style of reasoning, Dupin surmised that he must have hidden the letter, though cleverly disguised, in plain sight. Upon visiting Minister D—, Dupin finds his instincts are correct, and he devises a simple plan of leaving behind his snuffbox so that he may return at a later date and swap the stolen letter with his own facsimile, proving once again that a broad, critical approach to solving cases, one that considers psychological angles, is more effective than focusing solely on physical evidence.

CHAPTER 2: REVENGE, MURDER, AND MADNESS

"THE BLACK CAT"

Principal Characters
   Unnamed narrator: a man who has murdered his cat and his wife
   Pluto: the narrator's black cat

Plot Summary
   The narrator of "The Black Cat" is awaiting execution for the brutal murder of his wife. In the brief hours before his death, he gives an account of the events that led him to commit murder and the evidence that ultimately tipped the police off to his crime.

   The narrator claims that from infancy he had been noted for his docile nature. He was especially fond of animals and had a variety of pets both as a child and later when he married. Of his pets, Pluto, a large pure-black cat, was his favorite, despite the fact that his wife claimed all black cats were witches in disguise. The cat often followed the narrator throughout the day, remaining a faithful companion for several years, until the man's personality began to alter from alcohol abuse. During this period, the man also began abusing his wife.

Returning home drunk one evening, the narrator abruptly grabbed for the cat, who then bit him on the hand. Out of revenge for the slight wound, the narrator gouged out one of the cat's eyes with his penknife. In the morning he was remorseful over his actions and turned to drinking to erase his memory of the deed. The cat slowly recovered, but it fled from the narrator's attempts to befriend it again. Irritated by the cat's behavior, the narrator slipped a noose around the cat's neck and hanged it from a tree. He admits that this act was one of pure perversity. That evening, the narrator was awakened by cries of "Fire!" His house was engorged in flames, and he barely escaped with his wife and servant. When he visited the ruins of his home the next day, a crowd had gathered around the only wall left standing. Upon the wall in bas-relief was the figure of a large cat with a rope around its neck.

The narrator explains that when the fire broke out, a neighbor must have cut down the cat from his tree in the garden and thrown it through his window to alert him of the flames. The cat, he says, was compressed into the freshly spread plaster of his bedroom wall when the other walls fell in upon the home. Lime, the flames, and the ammonia from the corpse of the cat, he suggests, worked to create the image of the cat on the wall. For months, the narrator was haunted by this image of the cat, and he began to mourn the loss of his pet. Soon, however, he came across another cat, all-black like his first, except for a large patch of white on its breast. The cat followed him home from a tavern and made itself at home.

Rather than bonding with the new cat, the narrator disliked it intensely, especially upon discovering that like the former cat, this one also was missing an eye. Although the man did not give it any affection, the new cat followed him around the house, seeking attention. The narrator longed to destroy the cat, but he confesses that he felt a sense of dread in its presence. In the meantime, the patch of white on the cat's breast began to mutate into the shape of a gallows. The change in the pattern had a profound effect on the narrator. He found he could no longer rest, night or day. The cat continued to follow him around, and at night he awoke to find its hot breath on his face. He began, he confesses, to think evil thoughts and to hate all mankind.

Not long after this change in attitude, the narrator and his wife went down into their cellar on a household errand. The cat followed them and caused the narrator to nearly trip and fall down the stairs. In a rage, he raised an axe to the cat, but his attempt to kill the cat was thwarted by his wife. He turned the axe on her instead, burying it deep in her skull. She died instantly. In an effort to conceal his crime, he decided to wall up his wife's body in his cellar, as the dampness of the cellar had prevented a recent plaster job from hardening. The narrator believed he could remove the bricks from a false projection from one wall, insert his wife's corpse, and replaster the wall. The man executed these actions as planned and then turned his attention toward finding and killing the cat.

The narrator was unable to find the cat, however. Soon, the man's neighbors began to inquire after his wife. He answered those queries, but four days after his crime, the police unexpectedly appeared at his home, demanding to search the premises. The officers commenced a thorough inspection, and as they took their leave, the narrator bragged to them about the solid construction of his house. He knocked upon the wall in his cellar with his cane, and his rapping was unexpectedly answered by a wailing cry from within the wall. The officers tore down the wall and discovered the rotting corpse of the narrator's wife, the black cat sitting upon her head.

"THE CASK OF AMONTILLADO"

Principal Characters
Montresor: the narrator
Fortunato: Montresor's victim

Plot Summary
Montresor, the narrator of "The Cask of Amontillado," claims early on in the story that Fortunato has repeatedly insulted him, and he plans to seek his revenge during carnival. Fortunato, however, is unaware of his transgressions and is easily duped into Montresor's well-planned trap.

Aware that Fortunato is a connoisseur of wine, Montresor lures him into his family vaults to sample a rare acquisition of Amontillado. The bells on Fortunato's jester costume jingle as he drunkenly descends into the vaults, creating an ironic sense of gaiety as he moves closer to his own demise. As he continues his descent, the dampness of the vaults causes Fortunato to cough violently, but he is determined to sample the rare wine. Montresor offers him a drink of Medoc wine to ward off the cold and drinks to Fortunato's long life. As the two proceed, Fortunato says he has forgotten the symbols that make up Montresor's coat of arms (another unwitting insult to Montresor and his family). Montresor explains that his family motto, *"Nemo me impune lacessit,"* means "No one assails me with impunity."

When Montresor and Fortunato enter the core of the catacombs, Montresor opens another bottle of wine to ward off the cold. Fortunato drinks from the bottle and tosses it in the air with a gesture symbolic of the fraternal order of Freemasons. Seeing that Montresor does not understand the gesture, he insults him yet again by announcing that Montresor obviously does not belong to the brotherhood. Montresor, however, unfolds a trowel from his cloak and proclaims that he is indeed a member of the masons. Fortunato takes this action in jest, unaware of Montresor's plans for the trowel.

Finally, the men reach a remote area of the catacombs in which Montresor has removed the bones of his ancestors from one of the crypts. He bids the intoxicated Fortunato into the crypt, claiming that the Amontillado is inside. Montresor quickly surprises Fortunato by throwing a link of chain around his waist. He chains Fortunato to the walls of the tomb. Montresor next uncovers a supply of stone and mortar and begins, with his trowel, to wall up the entrance of the tomb. Fortunato struggles with the chains and moans as the effects of the alcohol begin to wear off. As the wall grows higher, Fortunato begins shrieking. Montresor answers these cries with shrieks of his own. Fortunato is silent for a while and then cries out that the evening has all been a fine joke, something the men will laugh about at the palazzo. Montresor, however, does not give up the prank. He sets the last stone in place just after midnight, blocking out the final jingling of Fortunato's bells.

"THE TELL-TALE HEART"

Principal Characters
Unnamed narrator: a man driven to murder out of obses-

sion and madness
    The old man: the narrator's victim

Plot Summary

The first-person narrator of "The Tell-Tale Heart" is not an especially reliable one, for as the tale progresses, it becomes obvious that he is mad. At the start of the story, he confesses that he has killed the old man he lives with, not out of malice or greed, but because of the old man's filmy, pale-blue eye, his vulture eye.

The narrator is so obsessed with the old man's eye that every night at midnight, he creeps to the old man's room, shines his lantern on the sleeping man's face, and hopes to catch the evil eye open. His actions, he would have us believe, are those of extreme caution and planning, the actions of a sane man.

Upon the eighth night of the narrator's stealthy routine, the old man awakens to the noise in his room and calls out into the night. The narrator does not move or betray his presence for an entire hour as he senses the old man's growing fear. Finally, the narrator allows a single ray of light to shine upon the old man's waking eye. The old man's terror must have been extreme, the narrator exclaims, for he could hear the beating of the old man's heart. Fearing that the sound of the heart will awaken the neighbors, the narrator pulls the old man to the ground and smothers him with the mattress.

The narrator next delights in dismembering the old man in the bathtub. He is proud of the fact that the tub catches all of the blood. To finally conceal the body, he next removes the planks of the floorboards and scatters the old man's body parts under the floor. As he completes his task at 4 A.M., the narrator is interrupted by the doorbell. Two police officers introduce themselves and explain that a neighbor has complained about hearing a shriek coming from the house.

The narrator explains that the shriek was his own upon dreaming and that the old man is away in the country. He invites the officers to search the premises and places his own chair on the floorboards directly above the spot where he buried the old man. He answers the policemen's questions calmly until he begins to hear a ringing in his ears. Suddenly, he becomes agitated and speaks in a heightened voice as he recognizes the low, dull, quick sound growing in his ears.

The fact that the police officers do not hear the sound drives the narrator insane, and he can no longer tolerate the incessant beating. "I admit the deed!" he shrieks. "Tear up the planks! here! here!—It is the beating of his hideous heart."

CHAPTER 3: JOURNEYS INTO TERROR

"MS. FOUND IN A BOTTLE"

Principal Characters
The first-person narrator: a seafaring adventurer

Plot Summary
"MS. Found in a Bottle" was the first published work to appear under Poe's own name. The narrator is traveling by ship to the Archipelago Islands when the seas suddenly became eerily calm. Then, he reports, a mysterious foam overcomes the ship and knocks the entire crew overboard, except for the narrator and an old man. For five days and nights the ship pitches forward toward an unknown destination, and on the sixth day of the strange storm everything in sight becomes black.

As the sea foam recedes, a huge black ship appears on the crest of a gigantic wave and bears down upon the narrator's ship. The narrator sees a "sullen glare of red light" emanating from the ship, and he estimates that the ship itself weighs up to four thousand tons. When the two ships collide, the narrator is tossed from his own ship into the rigging of this mysterious vessel. His presence, however, goes unacknowledged by the strange, phantomlike crew of the black ship. In fact, the narrator realizes that no one can see him. At one point, the narrator walks unnoticed into the captain's chamber while the captain is present in order to steal the paper he needs on which to write his manuscript.

At the conclusion of the story, the narrator reports that the ship remains cloaked in the blackness of "eternal night." He discerns ice floes off to the sides of the boat, but he is unable to make out much else in his surroundings. Pulled now by the strong current and undertow toward the South Pole, the ship on occasion is lifted straight out of the sea. As the ship begins to whirl in violent concentric circles, the narrator's tale breaks off. He and his ship presumably plunge into a gigantic whirlpool.

"A Descent into the Maelström"

Principal Characters
Unnamed narrator: A tourist visiting Norway
A Norwegian fisherman: a survivor of the maelström

Plot Summary
"A Descent into the Maelström" is the tall tale of how a Norwegian fisherman survived his journey into a maelström. The story is reported by an unnamed tourist who meets the fisherman during the course of his travels in Norway.

As the story begins, the fisherman has taken the tourist to the top of a fifteen-hundred-foot cliff, from which they can view the maelström. The narrator is nervous about climbing the steep cliff, and the fisherman has to coax him to peer over the perilous edge at the monstrous whirlpool in the ocean below. The vast whirlpool swirls with such violence that it shakes the mountain itself. Its tremendous roar is deafening. The narrator is impressed with the magnitude and force of the whirlpool, and he recounts incredible stories about its turbulent history of destroying ships and sea life, which make the fisherman's story of survival all the more amazing.

While on the cliff, the fisherman describes his journey. He explains that he and his brothers often fished near the maelström, as the catch is plentiful there. On the day of his adventure, however, a hurricane delivered his ship into the mouth of the whirlpool, and he and his brother lost all control over the ship. Due to the unusual light from the storm, the fisherman was able to view the maelström in great detail as he plunged forward over its edge.

The fisherman experienced profound psychological changes as he traveled down through the depths of the whirlpool. He began his journey in terror, but that emotion was soon alleviated as he began to marvel at the whirlpool as a unique and powerful creation of God. In this light, the fisherman was able to remain more calm than his brother, and he became curious and eager to explore his new natural surroundings. Peering further into the depths of the maelström, the fisherman saw a magnificent rainbow he likened to the pathway between time and eternity. Moving eventually toward a scientific understanding of the maelström, the fisherman later discovered that objects of different sizes and shapes

fall differently within the whirlpool. From this new understanding, he gained a sense of hope that he might be able to
survive his ordeal if he could cling to a cylindrical object, but
he was unable to convince his brother of his discovery, and
the brother eventually drowned in the maelström.

Having secured himself to a water cask, the fisherman
leaped overboard and saved his own life. He was rescued by
friends a few hours after the ordeal. He was uninjured, but
his hair, once black, had turned pure white, and his face had
aged beyond recognition.

"THE PIT AND THE PENDULUM"

Principal Characters
Unnamed narrator: a man sentenced to death

Plot Summary
"The Pit and the Pendulum" is a tale of terror and suspense. As the story opens, the narrator is on trial during the
Spanish Inquisition. He is so full of terror over the judges'
reputations for torture that he is unable to focus on his own
sentence as it is handed down to him. He faints and later
awakens in a pitch black chamber. It is clear to him that he
has been sentenced to death, but he has yet to discover what
will be the means of his execution.

Soon the narrator begins to explore his surroundings in
the darkness. Upon feeling his way around the slimy floors
of the dark chamber, he uses his mathematical skills to calculate the approximate measurements of the enclosure.
When he slips on the floor, he also discovers a circular pit in
the middle of the chamber. Had he fallen closer to the gap-
ing hole, he would have fallen, presumably to his death.

After taking account of his surroundings, the narrator
falls asleep again. When he awakens, he discovers that his
captors have provided food and water for him. He drinks the
water, realizing too late that it is drugged. He falls asleep
again, and when he next awakens, he finds himself bound
(apart from one arm up to the elbow) to a low-lying framework of wood. With the aid of dim light that now permeates
the chamber, he also realizes that the walls of the vault are
actually half the size he originally surmised. To his horror,
he also discovers the means of his execution. Directly above
him, a sickeningly sharp blade swings on a pendulum in a
crisscrossing motion. As time passes, the pendulum slowly

descends, moving closer and closer to his body.

Finally, after what seems like days to the narrator, the pendulum descends to a mere three inches above his chest, just ten or twelve strokes away, he calculates, from breaking flesh. Relying on his ability to remain calm and reason through his predicament, he smears what is left of his food on the bandages that bind him. This action entices the many rats of the chamber to gnaw at the bandages and set him free in the nick of time. The pendulum then retreats, making the narrator aware that his captors watch his every move. They retaliate against him immediately. The chamber becomes hotter, heated by a series of engraved demonic images burning red hot on the walls that he suddenly realizes are moving in on him.

Just at the moment when the narrator can no longer stand the heat pressing in on him and he is ready to throw himself into the great pit, he hears a blast of trumpets, the walls recede back to their original positions, and he is saved from his fate by rescuers.

CHAPTER 4: AN ATMOSPHERE OF DEATH

"THE MASQUE OF THE RED DEATH"

Principal Characters
Prince Prospero: a wealthy prince
Stranger: death himself

Plot Summary
"The Masque of the Red Death" takes place during a time of a plague, the Red Death, that has ravaged the narrator's country. The disease is so fatal that its victims succumb to death within thirty minutes of infection. Prince Prospero, however, the wealthy monarch of the country, hopes to elude the Red Death by remaining safely behind the walls of his palace. He invites one thousand friends to join him as he escapes the horror of the plague, and he provides a variety of entertainment for them in his home.

As Prince Prospero's guests make merry at a masquerade ball that winds itself through seven rooms of the palace, the less fortunate people of the country continue to die in the streets. The unnamed narrator of the story describes Prospero's seven rooms in great detail. Colored panes of glass and painted walls lend each of the seven rooms its own unique hue, including blue, purple, green, orange, white, violet, and black. Numerous critics have suggested that the colored rooms may represent the seven stages of man's life, the last stage, represented by the black room, being death.

At midnight, a stranger arrives at the party, wearing the mask of the Red Death. The stranger's mask is that of a corpse, and he incites terror among the other guests. When Prince Prospero encounters the stranger, he orders that the man be seized, but the guests are too frightened to follow the order. The stranger quickly makes his way through each of the rooms, moving headlong toward the black room. Prospero pulls his dagger and races after him, until he reaches the black room. As he approaches the figure, dagger drawn, Prospero suddenly falls over dead, and the guests, upon reaching the black room, likewise fall dead to the ground. No one is able to escape the fate of death.

"THE FALL OF THE HOUSE OF USHER"

Principal Characters
Roderick and Madeline Usher: the last remaining survivors of the Usher family
Narrator: a boyhood friend of Roderick Usher

Plot Summary
Although the narrator has not seen Roderick Usher since boyhood, he sets out to visit him. Roderick has asked for his help in ridding himself of a deep melancholy. The narrator travels on horseback to the House of Usher, a mysterious mansion in the throes of death and decay. He finds Roderick pale as a cadaver.

During the course of his stay, the narrator learns that Roderick and his twin sister, Madeline, both suffer from illnesses stemming from family inbreeding. Roderick professes a morbid acuteness of the senses, and he characterizes Madeline's illness as a gradual wasting away that often causes her to lose consciousness, her body falling into a "cataleptical" state in which she cannot be aroused by outside forces. Currently, Roderick is depressed by Madeline's poor state of health, and he is convinced that the house itself controls his superstitious behaviors.

The narrator tries his best over a period of a few days to relieve Roderick of his melancholy. The men paint and read and play music together. One night, however, Roderick informs the narrator that Madeline has died. He expresses his desire to preserve her body for a fortnight until she is ultimately laid to rest. As the narrator helps Roderick inter Madeline, he discovers a striking resemblance between the two and is told that Roderick and Madeline are indeed twins. The narrator also notices the similarities between Madeline's vault and a painting Roderick had painted, and that the vault rested deep below his own sleeping quarters. Most disturbing, however, is the faint blush on Madeline's cheeks and the lingering smile upon her lips, as the men seal her vault.

After Madeline's interment, Roderick takes to roaming the house in a daze. He grows more ghastly pale and seems to have retreated entirely into his own world. A week after Madeline's interment, a fierce storm brews outside, making Roderick even more agitated and restless. The narrator reads to Roderick to help calm his nerves, but both men become unnerved by sounds within the mansion. Roderick falls into a kind of terrified trance and sways back and forth, staring into the doorway of the room. Roderick professes that with his acute senses he has heard the faint sounds of movement emanating from Madeline's vault, and he fears she was, in fact, returning from the grave.

In the next moment, a gust of wind blows open the doors, and the enshrouded figure of Madeline stands there with blood upon her clothes. She falls inward upon Roderick, and the two fall dead together to the ground. The storm increases outside, and the house of Usher begins to shake violently and crumble. The narrator frantically flees the house as the walls of the mansion come crashing down.

CHAPTER 1

The Detective Stories

READINGS ON
THE SHORT STORIES OF
EDGAR ALLAN POE

Auguste Dupin: Poe's Burgeoning Professional

William Crisman

Poe scholar William Crisman of Pennsylvania State University at Altoona discusses the burgeoning career of Poe's detective character, Auguste Dupin. After the family fortune is lost, Dupin becomes obsessed with recovering his station in society. As he gradually becomes a professional detective, Dupin regains his money and social status through the windfall rewards he receives for solving crimes the police cannot. These large sums allow him to live a life of leisure between cases. Dupin's mysterious methods of detection and his astounding revelations enhance his professional image of clairvoyant showmanship and keep his services in high demand.

Dupin is, of course, not a professional investigator of the movie sort with a sign outside, a receptionist, and a regular procession of clients. He also is not, on the other hand, merely a disinterested puzzle solver, in spite of his claim in "Murders in the Rue Morgue" that his "ultimate object is only the truth." In fact, following the Dupin stories in their self-conscious sequence from "The Murders in the Rue Morgue" through "The Mystery of Marie Rogêt" to "The Purloined Letter" shows the development of an increasing professionalism.

REGAINING LOST RICHES

Such professionalism seems only reasonable given Dupin's background. A member of "an illustrious family" who "had been reduced to such poverty that the energy of his character succumbed beneath it," Dupin would naturally be interested in making money, especially since his tastes in life include buying "very rare" books. . . .

Excerpted from "Poe's Dupin as Professional, the Dupin Stories as Serial Text," by William Crisman, *Studies in American Fiction*, Autumn 1995. Reprinted with permission from *Studies in American Fiction*.

A near hermit in at least the first two detection stories, [Dupin] scorns men "who wore windows in their bosoms," literally shutters his own windows, and adopts a practice of living in near darkness illuminated by "a couple of tapers which . . . threw out . . . only the feeblest of rays." Only with the "advent of true Darkness" does he go into public to perform "quiet observation" without being himself observed. Such a desire is more than the "freak of fancy" that the narrator fatuously sees. It is also not as complicated as George Grella would make it, seeing the love of night as a sign from Poe that Dupin actually is the criminal he pretends to seek. Financial and social embarrassment is the motive here. . . .

That the narrator does not consciously name embarrassment over loss of money and class as Dupin's motive in seeking darkness only signals the narrator's relative lack of insight, an obtuseness long recognized as essential to the sort of "Dr. Watson" figure the narrator represents. As a sign of obtuseness in this case, the narrator explains Dupin's desire to tell his family history as a product of his being French and hence confessional. The narrator does not understand Dupin's compulsive engagement with this past, mortifying fall from financial grace. As John T. Irwin ingeniously shows in his analysis of Dupin's opening "mind reading" act in "Murders in the Rue Morgue," sensitivity to lost class pervades Dupin's every thought, even where class is not at all at the forefront of Dupin's conscious discussion. The mystery stories' culmination in "The Purloined Letter" implicitly allows Dupin the social mobility to associate with kings, queens, and ministers and to regain by association the aristocratic station and fortune he has lost. Shawn Rosenheim points out the parallel between the royal figures in the plot and the face cards in the whist game the narrator celebrates in "Murders in the Rue Morgue": winning entails royalty, and by "The Purloined Letter" Dupin has insinuated himself into a royal flush. . . .

Given this obsession with recovering station and money lost, professionalism on Dupin's part is not surprising. It is not, however, as Terence Whalen would have it, a professionalism that suddenly springs up in "Mystery of Marie Rogêt," making Dupin a figure catastrophically lapsing from Enlightenment "free thinker to hired intellectual." As Christopher Rollason says, Dupin's evolution as professional is "gradual," starting with "Murders in the Rue Morgue," not a sudden plunge. But Rollason joins a line of readers who see the Dupin stories, in [Jacques] Derrida's words, as "drift[ing]" from one to another, or who more radically, like Terry Martin, see no connection between the "Dupins" of the three stories at all.

Services Rendered

If the growth of professionalism is a regularly charted, organizational constant throughout the three tales, the reader would expect some sign of this at the outset, and indeed this sign is there. The first connection between Dupin and the narrator is billed as a monetary exchange. Finding in Dupin a "treasure beyond price," the narrator exchanges for it "the expense of renting" their rooms. Even the narrator's vantage for observing the stories' events is one for which Dupin implicitly barters a piece of his "treasure." Interestingly, over the course of the three stories this fungible rental property, "time eaten" and "tottering" in "Murders in the Rue Morgue," becomes a congenial place of "luxury" with a "back library" in "The Purloined Letter.". . . Dupin has achieved professional success, and the professional detective's office is born, from what is from the start a professional agreement between the narrator and Dupin made in response to Dupin's pain of money lost.

The implied exchange of "treasure" for "expense" seems to give Dupin unconscious incentive to pursue a model of exchange. His interest in the grisly "murders" in the Rue Morgue comes not from some abstract interest in puzzle solving but from the identity of one of the killings' incidental figures. Adolphe Le Bon, a bank clerk, had attended the elder victim to her residence "with . . . 4000 francs"; this same Le Bon, Dupin says, "once rendered me a service for which I am not ungrateful." Given Le Bon's duties the reader has to assume the "service" in question entailed giving or lending money; the investigation into the Rue Morgue murders then is on its way toward becoming detective services rendered for fees paid, though at this early stage the professional arrangement is a very hazy, informal one (service as repayment or compensation for financial favor).

Moreover, in "Murders in the Rue Morgue" Dupin seems to be receiving a lesson in fee structures. When he creates the ruse that he has caught the Corsican's killer ape, the Corsican promises "to pay a reward . . . —that is to say, any thing in reason." Later, newspapers report that on recapturing the animal the Corsican sells it to the zoo "for . . . a very large sum." Dupin always reads the newspapers. The sole form of evidence in "Mystery of Marie Rogêt," in "Murders in the Rue Morgue" the newspapers give Dupin a first inkling of what "any thing within reason" might mean when applied to "rewards."

As might be expected in a genuinely compact series of stories, the first tale provides the hero with learning experiences that inform the series. Burton Pollin points out as peculiar Dupin's remark in "Murders in the Rue Morgue" that observation has become only "of late, a species of necessity" for him. The peculiarity disappears, however, if the story is taken as an early, experimental phase in Dupin's self-education. "Observation," along with other skills and techniques, are developing "of late" as responses to "necessities" in Dupin's mental life.

By "Mystery of Marie Rogêt," set "about a year" after the

DUPLICITY IN POE'S DUPIN TALES

The theme of duplicity, an inherent doubleness, is apparent throughout Poe's Dupin mysteries.

The common theme of the Dupin tales, indeed of many of Poe's stories, is duplicity—the inherent doubleness that seems to lurk in both the material universe and the psyche of man and to which man must respond appropriately if he is to resolve the confusion duplicity occasions. In the particular instance of the Dupin tales, this duplicity is symbolized by the crimes. The very nature of a crime smacks of duplicity, not only in the trickery and deviousness commonly associated with its perpetration and concealment, but also in its insistence upon a reality different from or contrary to those standards and values that label an act a crime in the first place. [Edward H.] Davidson states the case accurately when he notes that "A crime is . . . a disruption of the ostensible order of things. . . . It is an instance whereby 'Accident is admitted as a portion of the superstructure' of the world of things." By intruding into the well-ordered affairs of man, a crime reveals not only the duplicitous reality of existence, but also that man's efforts to circumscribe such reality through artificial constructs that ignore it are not only fruitless, but often actually help to create situations where the confusion duplicity brings about is free to operate. Such is the point of the Dupin tales.

Dennis W. Eddings, "Poe, Dupin, and the Reader," *University of Mississippi Studies in English,* vol. 3 (1982), pp. 128–35.

Rue Morgue case, Dupin's professionalism becomes more apparent. Whereas in "Murders in the Rue Morgue" Dupin's attention had been independently drawn to the killings, in "Mystery of Marie Rogêt" no word of Marie's murder "reached the ears" of Dupin until the Prefect of Police arrives to tell the story, an inattention on Dupin's part that even the narrator finds "strange." No puzzle intrinsic to the murder case draws his attention; nevertheless, without knowing anything about the case, Dupin "accept[s] at once" after the Prefect has "made him a liberal proposition, the nature of which [the narrator does not feel himself] at liberty to disclose." This sum must be high, since the narrator has already felt "at liberty" to report on the general reward of thirty thousand francs for Marie's killer. Robert Shulman suggests that Dupin's concern with money in scenes like this represents wishful thinking in which "the poet surrogate [Dupin] easily wins the gold," thus reversing the state of real-world impoverished "poets." Whatever its symbolic "poetic" significance, Dupin's lost social fortune has created a situation in which the Prefect's "liberal proposition" and not the case has led to Dupin's instant acceptance. That "the cases were not few in which attempt was made to engage Dupin's services" suggests Dupin does not take a case without an extravagant fee.

WINDFALL PROFESSIONALISM

This special sort of payment is probably responsible for the long-standing assumption that Dupin is an amateur and not a professional to begin with. Such a view in fact makes sense if "professional" is taken in its most usual current sense of working for a salary (like a police detective) or an hourly wage (like a private detective). Dupin's professional type appears rare, and its closest analog might be the successful prize fighter who takes the occasional match for a very rich purse. Such a career is certainly not "amateur," but a person on the street would probably think twice before saying the boxer "really" has a job. In keeping with his loss of great fortune, Dupin too takes an occasional case for an exceptionally high price; crime detection becomes, therefore, a "profession," but perhaps not a "job." One sign of the usual job, whether for salary or wage, is to show up regularly on time; Brigid Brophy suggests that Dupin intends his "irregular hours" as violation of an employer's time clock, allowing him "the aristocratic mark of the man who does not have to go out to work next morning." As they hide him from the shame of social declassification, so Dupin's nighttime hours at once affront the keepers of workaday time and perhaps also render him physically incapable of day labor. . . .

"The Purloined Letter" caps this development toward occasional windfall professionalism; as [Sevanne] Woodward observes, in this final installment of the trilogy Dupin comes to replace word games with number games, and specifically the numbers of money, when he insists on the Prefect's fifty-thousand-franc check before turning over the stolen letter. Noticeably, the fictional time between "Mystery of Marie Rogêt" and "Purloined Letter" is longer than that between "Murders in the Rue Morgue" and the Marie Rogêt case. Instead of "about a year," the time has been "several years." The case in the Rue Morgue had been a payback to Le Bon, in itself netting no cash; the Rogêt case, in contrast, had brought a "liberal" payment allowing "several years" of aristocratic otium. In "The Purloined Letter," Dupin is out to make as good a deal or better, allowing him another "several" years before performing service again; on receiving the check for fifty thousand francs, Dupin "examined it carefully" before putting it in his wallet. Interest in examining checks is dramatized in a way that interest in the case, to begin with, is not, at least until Dupin's eventual explanation.

Increasing attention to periodic profit-making also helps explain Dupin's mystifications. Dupin discusses his methods with "no other individual" but the narrator. While allowing Dupin to keep his methods a professional secret, the "Dr. Watson" figure also gives Dupin an opportunity to practice a professional style that will be crucial to his business success, namely creating the impression of magical performance. The generic affinity of Dupin-style detective fiction to the supernatural tale has been occasionally remarked; as Syndy Conger remarks, "magical thinking has not been so much banished as temporarily subdued" in the story of ratiocination. The theoretical introduction to "Murders in the Rue Morgue" says that Dupin's sort of "*acumen* . . . appears to the ordinary apprehension preternatural," an impression that, the narrator suggests, may produce a studied affectation, an "air of intuition." Poe's celebrated remark of August 9, 1846, to Philip Pendleton Cooke that the Dupin stories seem "more ingenius than they are—on account of their . . . *air* of method" may show overmodesty or true self-dissatisfaction, but in the reference to "air" Poe echoes his own narrator and suggests his awareness of "intuition" as practiced technique.

When the "Watson" interlocutor first meets Dupin, Dupin "seemed . . . to take an eager delight" in the "exercise—if not exactly . . . display" of his analytic ability. The narrator's repeated "profound astonishment" at Dupin's ability sends Dupin over the verge of "not quite enjoying" an audience and coaches him in the techniques of mystifying display. The narrator is a perfect trainer in such mystification, since in addition to telling Dupin his abilities are amazing ("I do not hesitate to say that I am amazed and can scarcely credit my senses"), he also harbors an unspoken feeling that Dupin's analysis is supernatural ("I was even more startled than I would have been willing to express"). Since Dupin is in the process of picking the narrator's mind clean, the reader has to assume Dupin is aware of these thoughts the narrator dares not speak.

THE ART OF SHOWMANSHIP

By the time of "The Purloined Letter," the mystification in which Dupin schools himself in "Murders in the Rue Morgue" has developed to the high art that is the signature of detective fiction *à la* Sherlock Holmes: revealing the mystery's solution in a way that is sudden for the client and others but delayed for the detective, who has known the solution for some time. Dupin has recovered the stolen letter long before he reveals or explains the fact; one can imagine that the game he plays to surprise Prefect G—would today bring a review board hearing for a police detective and a punch in the nose for a private detective of a more homely professional stamp. A mark of Dupin's professional type is that he not only can risk the shock revelation but that he needs it to pursue the kind of occasional, windfall work he does.

Terry J. Martin notes an increased emphasis on the immaterial in Dupin's explanation of his problem solving between "Murders in the Rue Morgue" and "The Purloined Letter." This increase is effectively a canny business choice, to play up the clairvoyant showmanship of Dupin's methods. As Grella notes, Dupin's style of professionalism requires "insur[ing] the solidity of his reputation" by startling others "through a brilliantly plausible solution." Dennis Porter also emphasizes the element of startling or amazing the client, citing the body-building metaphor at the beginning of "Murders in the Rue Morgue" as an instance of marvellous performance." The narrator speaks of "exhibiting" powers, as the body builder puts his body on display; the goal, as in the narrator's famous analogy between analysis and the games of checkers and whist, is to amaze others. . . .

The importance of Dupin's "miraculous," exhibitionist revelations may also help more fully explain his desire for only very occasional employment. Part of startling an audience requires that the startling revelation not become commonplace. It is the mark of the Sherlock Holmes parody, not the Sherlock Holmes story, for Holmes to be constantly startling his client with amazing "deductions" every few lines. . . .

Among the other techniques Dupin learns through experimenting with the narrator is the importance of putting an audience to sleep between periods of unspeakable amazement, creating the torpor in which "we . . . slumbered tranquilly." Dupin knows to give his more general public an analogous soporific between rare cases. . . .

The situation in which Dupin's name "had grown into a household word" because he was "regarded as little less than miraculous," then, results from a complex, developing professional technique and derives from an equally complex motive. "Analysis" becomes a professional secret revealed to no one but the narrator, who himself serves as an unwitting coach in the use of analysis to provide mystification and the timing of this mystification to create maximum effect. The motive behind the professionally lucrative image of occasional miracle worker is to recapture in experience a social and financial standing unrecoverable in fact.

Dupin Is a New Mythological Figure

Lothar Černý

Lothar Černý defines Detective Dupin as a modern mythological figure who stands for truth and is opposed to the darkness of ignorance. Dupin's role is to reestablish order and justice and discover the light of truth. This process, to Dupin, is a playful and pleasurable one, because to him truth is essentially simple to find. One need only know where to look for it: on the surface of things rather than in the depths, in darkness rather than in light. Dupin's indirect and imaginative methods establish him as a new mythological figure, someone who works outside of the teachings of philosophy, religious thinking, or the scientific, methodological procedures of the police who call on him to solve their toughest crimes.

Assuming that the figure of the detective is at least implicitly regarded by modern readers and writers as a kind of myth, the answer to the question what makes him so is still an open one. . . .

Firstly, Poe's detective achieves mythical status because he literally stands for truth, traditionally equated with the image of light and opposed to the darkness of ignorance. . . . Secondly, the detective as well as the detective story appeals to readers because the seriousness of the ethical issues involved is held in suspension. It seems as if the activity of detection is primarily an aesthetic one and that the solution of the mystery, though a victory of truth, provides the same kind of satisfaction as the successful completion of a game. . . .

THE DETECTIVE'S ROLE

On the level of the plot—and therefore at the centre of the "myth"—the detective plays a particular role in the struggle be-

Excerpted from "Mythical Aspects of Poe's Detective," by Lothar Černý, *Connotations*, 1995/96. Reprinted with permission from *Connotations*.

tween modern society and the forces of darkness and corruption that continually threaten it. He not only solves the riddle posed by a crime, he also protects or re-establishes order and justice, at times even against their own official representatives. The detective succeeds in restoring order in the "body politic," but his position remains that of an outsider. The extent of his power is limited to a particular case. He never becomes a "ruler" or a policeman. His position is always "ex-centric," at the margin of the social hierarchy, and he is without self-interest. Worldly power or material goods are not his objectives.

Even though he fulfils almost superhuman tasks like the heroes in numerous ancient myths, the detective achieves his real fame not through physical prowess (or any other traditional hero-quality), but above all by his ability to solve the riddle posed by an unexplained crime. His ultimate aim, then, is to serve the truth, to help truth come to light. Poe's Dupin provides the classic formula for this endeavour: "My ultimate object is only the truth." The pathos of this claim to find out the truth is the more obvious as Poe distinguishes this search from the verbal sophistry of the law. Commenting on his companion's advice "to make out his case" Dupin insists: "This may be the practice in law, but it is not the usage of reason." Considering these statements, one might go so far as to say that Poe creates a detective who follows in the footsteps of Plato's philosopher, his interest being in the truth and his ability to see the truth where others look in vain.

The Platonic metaphor of bringing truth to light identifies light and truth in the act of recognition. In Poe, however, a dialectical relationship between truth and light emerges, as Poe's detective explains the limited success and even failure of the Parisian police, notably of their head, Vidocq:

> Vidocq . . . was a good guesser, and a persevering man. But, without educated thought, he erred continually by the very intensity of his investigations. He impaired his vision by holding the object too close. . . . Thus there is such a thing as being too profound. Truth is not always in a well. In fact, as regards the more important knowledge, I do believe that she is invariably superficial. The depth lies in the valleys where we seek her, and not upon mountain-tops where she is found. The modes and sources of this kind of error are well typified in the contemplation of the heavenly bodies. To look at a star by glances—to view it in a side-long way . . . is to behold the star distinctly—is to have the best appreciation of its lustre—a lustre which grows dim just in proportion as we turn our vision *fully* upon it.

. . . On the one hand [Dupin's] criticism is directed towards the absence of any real method, on the other his argument is directed against the futility of Vidocq's efforts. To drive his point home Dupin resorts to images of overlooking or not seeing the truth. As often in Poe, the name provides a clue to the problem. Vidocq's name begins with the root syllable of *videre*, and continues with the root syllable of *docere* betraying its ironical character. Its bearer does not really teach how to see. Vidocq's sheer intensity of seeing even produces blindness to the object "in view."

SEEING THE LIGHT IN THE DARK

The most common failure to see the truth, however, is the result of looking for it in the wrong place; it is not hidden but open to view—as visible as the mountain tops. This is the "philosophical" premise throughout Poe's detective stories. There is a second reason for not seeing the truth. It is not possible to look into the source of light directly. To support his view Dupin also resorts to science, i.e. optics and astronomy where he observes the same law.

The light of the stars "grows dim just in proportion as we turn our vision *fully* upon it." Light is propitious to vision only when looked at indirectly or sideways; "a side-long way" will allow us to see "distinctly." Of Vidocq's intensity of investigation he says: "He impaired his vision by holding the object too close." For an explanation of this error Dupin refers to the light of the stars. Significantly he does not speak of *observation* but of "the contemplation of the heavenly bodies." *Contemplation* leads to associations that go beyond physical perception and points, moreover, to a spiritual and intellectual understanding. What the observation of the physical phenomenon of the star exemplifies, however, is the fact that you cannot look into light itself, that the source of light is visible only indirectly, "in a side-long way." Under these conditions "there is the more refined capacity for comprehension." *Comprehension* is another word that brings the subtext of recognition to the surface. Inversely, the lustre of the star "grows dim just in proportion as we turn our vision *fully* upon it." Looking into the source of light directly may lead to total blindness or, to change the perspective, "it is possible to make even Venus herself vanish from the firmament.". . .

Dupin's "scientific" comparisons typify epistemological principles, or to put it differently, empirical evidence is used to explain the failure to recognise truth: "Thus there is such a thing as being too profound. . . . By undue profundity we perplex and enfeeble thought." The tenor of the whole passage is resonant of epistemological terms like "thought," "truth," "knowledge," "profundity," "comprehension." The detective assumes the scientific pose, but his search *for* truth is related to the old philosophical question *of the* truth. In that search it seems as if science may not be his only nor his most important tool, as the ironical reference to Dupin's use of his glasses would indicate. He only wears his glasses, at the beginning of "The Mystery of Marie Roget," to hide from the Prefect that he is sleeping while the latter prattles on. They even serve as a camouflage in "The Purloined Letter" where Dupin uses them to keep his examination of the details in the room of the Minister unnoticed. The tool of seeing is not used by Dupin to improve seeing in the literal, optical sense, on the contrary it is virtually irrelevant to the seeing with the mind. In terms of finding out the truth, Dupin does not rely too much on science. Taking into account that the narrator in "The Murders in the Rue Morgue" admires Dupin's "ideality" we are reminded of the derivation of Greek *idea* from the verb *idein*, to see, which makes it possible to understand Dupin as a "seer" and that his seeing is identical with recognising the truth of things.

It seems as if Poe is sceptical not only as to the method of the police, but that light as a metaphor of truth comes under attack. . . .

While some of the names Poe gave to the newspapers in his stories—*Le Mercurie, Le Diligence, Le Moniteur*—represent an ironical comment on their claim to reporting the truth, *L'Etoile* and *Le Soleil* invoke the connection between light and truth. For all their pretensions to sun-like or star-like shining, these papers are far from enlightened or enlightening. They are not sources of truth. Dupin speaks of "the dogmatic ignorance of Le Soleil." As newspapers go, their primary interest, as Dupin says about *Le Commerciel* (sic!), is "rather to create a sensation . . . than to further the cause of truth." Neither the light, nor the "gazing" of the papers nor the all too intense inquirires of the Prefect lead to the truth. . . .

Dupin prefers darkness to light even to the extent of creating an artificial darkness. When this choice is explained, however, the reader is due for another surprise. Dupin does not prefer night for sheer opposition to the Prefect's benighted use of daylight but for an absolutely independent, apparently illogical reason. A follower of the "sable divinity," he is "enamored of the Night for her own sake," a fact which leaves the narrator as baffled as the Prefect. The narrator goes so far as to admit that most people, had they known about the life he and Dupin were leading, would have regarded it as mad. In darkness Dupin's mind seems to be most awake and capable of giving its best to "reading, writing, or conversing." In "The Purloined Letter" this connection between intellectual activity and darkness is highlighted in a paradoxical statement:

> "If it is any point requiring reflection," observed Dupin, as he forebore to enkindle the wick, "we shall examine it to better purpose in the dark."

Poe transposes the state of being metaphorically in the dark (about truth) into a real darkness, where only Dupin is able to "reflect" the light of truth in the double sense of the word. The truth shines in Dupin's darkness of night, be it real or artificial. Dupin's darkness, then, is radically different from the Prefect's. In his darkness Dupin sees the light of truth, while the Prefect even in the light of day remains in darkness. Since, however, such a kind of "being in the dark" in clear daylight is felt to be normal in the world of gazettes, he has every right to suspect Dupin of having "odd notions."

THE PLEASURE OF DETECTION

Once the reader follows Dupin into his enlightening darkness, he is in for more paradoxes, for looked at in the dark the problem which baffles the Prefect makes itself known as one whose very intricacy is its simplicity: "the mystery is a little *too* plain" or a "little *too* self-evident." For the Prefect who believes to have reason on his side, this must sound like total nonsense; he is blind for what is evident. For him, the truth of the matter does neither show nor shine. Therefore the Prefect's mind cannot "reflect" the truth. Dupin explains this phenomenon in "The Purloined Letter" by the game of puzzles, in which a word is written "upon the motley and perplexed surface of the chart" in such a way as to make it difficult to be discovered. Words in very large letters which should be most "evident" are, however, most commonly overlooked. In Dupin's view this observation represents an analogy to "the moral inapprehension by which the intellect suffers to pass unnoticed those considerations which are too obtrusively and too palpably self-evident." For Dupin the problem lies not in the particular nature of the truth but in the eye or rather the mind of the beholder. Therefore all the light of the stars would not suffice to make the Prefect recognise the truth, while not even darkness prevents Dupin from seeing it. . . .

Obviously the mystical aspect of Dupin's love of night and his almost mystical ecstasy (when his analytic activity occupies his mind) do not as such constitute a mythical element of his character; they contribute, however, to mark his search for truth in opposition to the method of the police and the speculation of the public in general (represented by the newspapers); and they mark his social eccentricity, i.e., his aristocratic independence from social conventions.

Since, to a large extent, it is the negative way of the mystic which puts him in opposition to the institutionalised everyday world the mystical qualities also help shape the character of the great outsider as a myth, the more so as Poe adds simplicity to the detective's vision of truth. In a society of increasing complexity and incomprehensibility this makes the detective even more of an outsider. To Dupin truth is evident and truth is essentially simple, even playfully so. An element of pleasure pervades the whole process of finding the truth by means of analysis as practised by Dupin:

> . . . I could not help remarking and admiring (although from his rich ideality I had been prepared to expect it) a peculiar analytic ability in Dupin. He seemed, too, to take an eager delight in its exercise—if not exactly in its display—and did not hesitate to confess the pleasure thus derived.

. . . It may be that the principle of pleasure involved in the exercise of analytical detection as an imaginative activity and the readers' participation in this exercise are the reasons for the continuous popularity of the detective story. The fictional detective appeals to our play instinct and we derive pleasure from watching the game. This is, perhaps, why we are not too shocked about the gruesome details Poe has introduced into the genre. Moral issues do not appear to be at stake in his stories. The purpose of playing is the game itself and the effect we derive from it is delight. Dupin is not interested in correcting the wrongs of widows and orphans, or in catching criminals, nor in fighting the forces of evil in the world. If all this really happens it is almost accidental.

> "As for these murders, let us enter into some examinations for ourselves. . . . An inquiry will afford us amusement. . . ."

Here, instead of the word "pleasure" which Dupin uses to describe the exercise of his analytic ability, he uses the word "amusement," thus giving a hint that a more complex kind of pleasure principle seems to be involved. . . .

Dupin's endeavours to find the truth, then, appear in a field composed by the co-ordinates light and darkness, but pleasure and serious play constitute a third dimension which prevents the detective from becoming a mere representation of philosophical or theological ideas. He finds the truth on the surface rather than in hidden depths, not in the brightness of light, but in darkness; his way to the truth is not ponderous seriousness but rather in the nature of a game, and not a difficult one at that. This combination is quite different from the great examples of the history of philosophy and religious thinking, not to speak of the seriousness of science or the methodical procedures of the police. Dupin's way of finding the truth is idiosyncratic and perhaps it is his specific, indirect, playful and imaginative way that makes him a new mythical figure. . . .

Poe's detective looks for truth on the level of a game, but this does not mean that this search becomes trivial. The quest for truth in all its existential and philosophical dimensions which it has acquired in the history of Western philosophy is not eliminated or negated, but present in what I would call a state of suspension—not a suspension of disbelief, of course, but perhaps a suspension of belief. Dupin's claim that his "ultimate object is only the truth" recalls the idea of truth, even though the playful context prevents it from being filled with its strictly philosophical meaning. Even if the truth is nothing else but the correct analysis of how a murder was committed or how the letter was hidden etc. and that crime and punishment are virtually unimportant, the idea comes to light or that justice prevails provides that horizon of ideality which Friedrich Schiller thought the literature of the modern age should provide for its readers. He predicted that it would unite in the manner of playfulness the seemingly irreconcilable opposites, reality and ideality, the world of necessity and the world of freedom. The myth of the detective represents this new combination, rooted in the old but continuous quest for truth, and appealing at the same time to the equally deep-rooted sense of play and pleasure as a result of participating in the fictional endeavours of a detection.

Poe's Detective Tales Employ Both Critical Reasoning and Intuition

Jan Whitt

Jan Whitt of the school of journalism and mass communications at the University of Colorado, Boulder, argues that Dupin approaches criminal cases as both a mathematician and a poet by using both science and intuition. The Dupin stories attest to Poe's belief in the importance of reason coupled with emotion and close observation coupled with an innate understanding of human behavior.

Edgar Allan Poe (1809–49) left the world a collection of poems, essays, tales of terror, and detective fiction, all dedicated to the belief that art must appeal both to reason and to emotion. It is in Poe's three detective stories, however, that Poe best defends the interdependence of logic and intuition in reaching what he unabashedly calls "truth." In a poem Poe wrote when he was about 20, "Sonnet to Science," he reveals an early cynicism about the ascendancy of technological development:

> Science! true daughter of Old Time thou art!
>   Who alterest all things with thy peering eyes.
> Why preyest thou thus upon the poet's heart,
>   Vulture, whose wings are dull realities?
> How should he love thee? or how deem thee wise?
>   Who wouldst not leave him in his wandering
> To seek for treasure in the jewelled skies,
>   Albeit he soared with an undaunted wing?
> Has thou not dragged Diana from her car?
>   And driven the Hamadryad from the wood
> To seek a shelter in some happier star?
>   Has thou not torn the Naiad from her flood,
> The Elfin from the green grass, and from me
>   The summer dream beneath the tamarind tree?

Excerpted from "The 'Very Simplicity of the Thing': Edgar Allan Poe and the Murders He Wrote," by Jan Whitt, *Clues,* Spring/Summer 1994. Reprinted with permission from The Popular Press.

The disciple of Samuel Taylor Coleridge (1772–1834) and the contemporary of Nathaniel Hawthorne (1804–64), Poe was part of a worthy tradition which suspected Science of draining the life and emotion from art by trying to eradicate mystery from the earth (Poe, therefore, accuses Science of dragging Diana from her "car"—the moon—symbol of mystery or inconstancy).

Matthew Arnold (1822–88) also was a contemporary of Poe's who espoused a fear of excessive rationality adopted at the expense of faith and poetry in the modern world. In his famous essay "The Study of Poetry," Arnold wrote of poetry as a force which would complete the role of science in transforming the earth:

> More and more mankind will discover that we have to turn to poetry to interpret life for us, to console us, to sustain us. Without poetry, our science will appear incomplete; and most of what now passes with us for religion and philosophy will be replaced by poetry. Science, I say, will appear incomplete without it.

Arnold also noted the importance of "regularity, uniformity, precision, [and] balance" in writing and in decisions, but he warned against the "exclusive attention to these qualities" because of the "repression and silencing of poetry" that might result. Poetry, obviously, is more to Arnold than verse; for him it was a power capable of unifying humankind as he believed religion once had done.

THE MIND AND THE HEART

Although Poe might have been especially devoted to Coleridge and connected philosophically to Arnold, one also must recognize his link to at least one of his contemporaries in America: Hawthorne. Certainly the spirit of the times in both Britain and America involved a reverence for Science and a fear that humankind had lost its spiritual center. In a series of short stories and novels reminiscent of *Frankenstein* by Mary Wollstonecraft Shelley (1797–1851), Hawthorne analyzes the role of the scientist and physician too devoted to factual analysis. The theme runs through "Rappaccini's Daughter," "The Birthmark," *The Scarlet Letter* and other works and testifies to Hawthorne's fear of the possibilities of a mind separated from the heart. The most damning description of the man of science occurs in the first paragraph of "The Birthmark":

In the latter part of the last century there lived a man of science, an eminent proficient in every branch of natural philosophy, who not long before our story opens had made experience of a spiritual affinity more attractive than any
chemical one. He had . . . persuaded a beautiful woman to become his wife. In those days when the comparatively recent
discovery of electricity and other kindred mysteries of Nature
seemed to open paths into the region of miracle, it was not
unusual for the love of science to rival the love of women in
its depth and absorbing energy.

At the end of the tale, the man devoted "too unreservedly to
scientific studies" kills his wife while attempting to remove
a blemish from her face in a vain search for perfection and
for a symbol of "man's ultimate control over Nature."

Poe proposes later in his career that the analytical perspective of mathematics and the physical sciences is limited,
and in C. Auguste Dupin he unites the critical powers of reasoning and the perception and energy of the heart. Like Coleridge and William Wordsworth (1770–1850), Poe struggled
not to treat scientific discovery as arrogant bluff but to balance it with the longings of the human spirit. Coleridge
writes in Chapter 1 of *Biographia Literaria* that while he
was a student he learned that "poetry, even that of the loftiest and, seemingly, that of the wildest odes, had a logic of its
own as severe as that of science; and more difficult, because
more subtle, more complex, and dependent on more, and
more fugitive, causes." In Chapter 4, he pays tribute to the
"union of deep feeling with profound thought," as does
Wordsworth in the "Preface to the *Lyrical Ballads*":

The knowledge both of the poet and the man of science is
pleasure; but the knowledge of the one cleaves to us as a necessary part of our existence, our natural and unalienable inheritance; the other is a personal and individual acquisition,
slow to come to us, and by no habitual and direct sympathy
connecting us with our fellow-beings. The man of science
seeks truth as a remote and unknown benefactor; he cher-
ishes and loves it in his solitude: the poet, singing a song in
which all human beings join with him, rejoices in the presence of truth as our visible friend and hourly companion. Poetry is the breath and finer spirit of all knowledge; it is the
impassioned expression which is in the countenance of all
science. . . . Poetry is the first and last of all knowledge—it is
as immortal as the heart of man.

Poe remained in sympathy with Coleridge and Wordsworth
as he wrote "The Purloined Letter," "The Murders in the
Rue Morgue" and "The Mystery of Marie Rogêt (A Sequel to

'The Murders in the Rue Morgue')." He leaves the cerebral Parisian police acting from habit and past experience, while his famous detective solves the cases as much through an understanding of the human spirit as through a detached analysis of data. . . .

THE METHODS OF C. AUGUSTE DUPIN

In one of Poe's most popular stories, "The Purloined Letter," the narrator discusses the two previous cases which his friend Dupin solved: "The Murders in the Rue Morgue" and "The Mystery of Marie Rogêt." A visit by the Prefect of the Parisian police activates the plot, as Dupin is immediately set up as superior to his guest. The narrator tells the reader that the Prefect has the unfortunate habit of ridiculing what he cannot understand. The Prefect, he says, "had a fashion of calling every thing 'odd' that was beyond his comprehension, and thus lived amid an absolute legion of 'oddities'." These oddities create for the Prefect an impenetrable jungle in which he struggles and fails to make sense of the sign system. Coming to Dupin for help in recovering a stolen letter, the Prefect admits to his failure without understanding that the cause is his lack of self-perception:

> "The fact is, we have all been a good deal puzzled because the affair *is* so simple, and yet baffles us altogether."
>
> "Perhaps it is the very simplicity of the thing which puts you at fault," said my friend.
>
> "What nonsense you *do* talk!" replied the Prefect, laughing heartily.
>
> "Perhaps the mystery is a little *too* plain," said Dupin.
>
> "Oh, good heavens! who ever heard of such an idea?"
>
> "A little too self-evident."
>
> "Ha! ha! ha!—ha! ha! ha!—ho! ho! ho!" roared out our visitor, profoundly amused, "oh, Dupin, you will be the death of me yet!"

Poe reveals the Prefect's Achilles heel through short sections of dramatic monologue, in which the official reveals more about himself than he intends. Discussing the man who took a letter that contains secrets dangerous to a high-ranking government official, the Prefect assesses his opponent by saying, "Not *altogether* a fool, but then he's a poet, which I take to be only one remove from a fool." The reader thereby understands that the Prefect operates with only half of his capacities; the reader then may choose to identify with Dupin, who confesses in an ironically self-deprecating way that he himself is "guilty of certain doggerel."

The Prefect and the Parisian police searched the thief's apartment for the letter and are now at a loss, although they are certain they have the right man. To the narrator, Dupin explains that the measures the Prefect used "were good in their kind and well executed; their defect lay in their being inapplicable to the case, and to the man":

> A certain set of highly ingenious resources are, with the Prefect, a sort of Procrustean bed, to which he forcibly adapts his designs. But he perpetually errs by being too deep or too shallow, for the matter in hand; and many a schoolboy is a better reasoner than he.

Dupin then tells his friend two parables, the first involving a young boy who wins consistently in a game of marbles. The boy reads the faces of his opponents, reasons, observes, trusts experience—and wins, a feat that his acquaintances attribute to luck. Lacking these abilities, the Prefect is crippled, Dupin suggests. He implicates the Prefect when he describes a group of people who operate from custom alone:

> They consider only their *own* ideas of ingenuity; and, in searching for anything hidden, advert only to the modes in which *they* would have hidden it. They are right in this much—that their own ingenuity is a faithful representative of that of *the mass;* but when the cunning of the individual felon is diverse in character from their own, the felon foils them, of course. This always happens when it is above their own, and very usually when it is below. They have variation of principle in their investigations; at best, when urged by some unusual emergency—by some extraordinary reward—they extend or exaggerate their old modes of *practice*, without touching their principles.

THE MATHEMATICIAN AND THE POET

In a second parable later in "The Purloined Letter," Dupin describes what he calls "a game of puzzles which is played upon a map." In this game, "over-largely lettered signs and placards of the street" escape "observation by dint of being excessively obvious." Through both short narratives, Dupin makes clear to his listener the failure of the Prefect to investigate the nature of the man he seeks to trap, an investigation which is at root a poetic enterprise.

In "The Purloined Letter," Dupin eventually combines the

quantitative skills of the mathematician (respected in the culture) with the qualitative powers of the poet (assumed to be the fool) and finds the stolen letter in the Minister's apartment. The limitations of the mathematical approach are revealed when Dupin says:

> There are numerous other mathematical truths which are only truths within the limits of *relation*. But the mathematician argues, from his *finite truths*, through habit, as if they were of an absolutely general applicability—as the world indeed imagines them to be.

By opening scientific premises to the scrutiny of the poetic mind, Dupin testifies to the importance of the two powers working in tandem. By practicing what he preaches, Dupin at last sees a rack with "five or six visiting cards and a solitary letter" in the Minister's home. "This last was much soiled and crumpled," Poe writes of the letter. "It was torn nearly in two, across the middle—as if a design, in the first instance, to tear it entirely up as worthless, had been altered, or stayed, in the second." The detective finds the letter because he knows the Parisian police have checked every hidden corner on the premises; he deduces that the letter must be in plain sight. In the end he spots the letter by realizing that a soiled and torn letter is antithetical to the Minister's own character, since he is by nature compulsively clean and organized: "The *radicalness* of these differences, which was excessive, the dirt; the soiled and torn condition of the paper, so inconsistent with the *true* methodical habits" of the Minister alerted Dupin. Not only does Dupin gain the 50,000 francs offered by the Prefect for helping to solve the case, but he gains the respect of the police force and the pleasure of having outsmarted the Minister, to whom he sends a personal message by replacing the letter he has retrieved with a letter resembling it.

In "The Murders in the Rue Morgue," Poe holds consistently to the motivating philosophy of his earlier two detective sagas. Once again, the necessity of the analytical mind working with intuition is established early. The world, says Dupin, believes that "the calculating and discriminating powers (causality and comparison) are at variance with the imaginative—that the three, in short, can hardly coexist." However, Dupin says:

> [Although] thus opposed to received opinion, the idea will not appear ill-founded when we observe that the processes of in-

vention or creation are strictly akin with the processes of resolution—the former being nearly, if not absolutely, the latter conversed.

Quite simply Dupin argues, the results "brought about by the very soul and essence of method, have, in truth, the whole air of intuition." The gift of the poet, Dupin believes, is the ability to "observe attentively" and thereby to "remember distinctly."

Using these powers, Dupin finds the unlikely killer of Madame L'Espanaye and her daughter, Mademoiselle Camille L'Espanaye: an Ourang-Outang from the East Indian Islands. The ape had been brought to Europe by a sailor who lost the animal and disappeared after the crime, afraid of his own responsibility in the brutal deaths. Another man has been wrongly accused of the murders, and Dupin sets a trap to find the sailor, reassures him of his innocence if he testifies, and thereby frees the accused. "Murders in the Rue Morgue," which Dupin calls a "riddle," reinforces "The Purloined Letter" by implicating those who cannot see what is too obvious. Dupin said, "It appears to me that this mystery is considered insoluble, for the very reasons which should cause it to be regarded as easy of solution—I mean for the *outre* character of its features." Criticizing a Frenchman for his short-sightedness, Dupin tells the narrator:

> He impaired his vision by holding the object too close. He might see, perhaps, one or two points with unusual clearness, but in so doing he, necessarily, lost sight of the matter as a whole. Thus there is such a thing as being too profound. Truth is not always in a well.

A Marriage of Science and Intuition

For the semiologist who equates a detective and his/her clues with a reader exploring the signs of a text, "The Murders in the Rue Morgue" and "The Mystery of Marie Rogêt" are especially rich. In "The Murders in the Rue Morgue," data are accumulated through interviews with multiple witnesses who speak several languages: Italian, English, Spanish, French and others. The linguistic labyrinth overwhelms the police, since descriptions conflict with one another and facts seem shadowed by the varied perceptions, some of which *must* be wrong. The difference in the languages themselves makes even the cognates problematic, and the nuances and semantic puzzles testify to the basic unreliability of language itself. In "The Mystery of Marie Rogêt," the same artistic effect is gained through the use of multiple newspaper stories in which selected facts are revealed. Dupin must solve both cases by gleaning information from accounts by witnesses and from published newspaper articles without being swayed and without missing the implications of those very accounts and stories. All three cases require that Dupin read varied texts (the Minister's apartment, the Minister himself, the Prefect, the police accounts of the crimes, the newspaper stories, etc.).

In "The Mystery of Marie Rogêt," Mary Cecilia Rogers of New York is murdered and her body is found floating in a river. The case remains unsolved, and Dupin has only newspaper accounts with which to work. Again, the central problem Dupin discovers in the coverage of others is their failure to reconcile the "most rigidly exact in science" (what he terms the "Calculus of Probabilities") with the "shadow and spirituality" of the "most intangible" aspects of the case. Inverting his previous method in "The Purloined Letter" and "The Murders in the Rue Morgue," Dupin solves the crime, saying to the narrator:

> I need scarcely tell you ... that this is a far more intricate case than that of the Rue Morgue, from which it differs in one important respect. This is an *ordinary*, although an atrocious instance of crime. There is nothing peculiarly *outré* about it. You will observe that, for this reason, the mystery has been considered easy, when for this reason, it should have been considered difficult, of solution.

Discovering that the murder was committed by a single person instead of a gang as earlier believed, "the Chevalier's analytical abilities acquired for him the credit of intuition," Poe writes. Dupin analyzes the nature of the gang and explains how the murder must have been committed by a single person who would have had to resort to dragging the body and leaving behind some of the evidence. He then analyzes the nature of the murderer himself, deduces his means of escape, and discusses his findings with the narrator. In all three stories, Dupin attests to the value of the scientific method wedded to the discernment of the human heart; to the value of close observation connected with an understanding of others; the value of perseverance in the face of ridicule and doubt; and to the value of not remaining a slave to one's own favorite approach, an approach that may require modification during another case.

Narrator, Detective, Murderer: The Three Faces of Dupin

George Grella

Author and Poe scholar George Grella finds that Poe's Dupin crime stories "The Murders in the Rue Morgue" and "The Purloined Letter" are full of duplicities that show Dupin in the role of detective, narrator, and murderer. Grella suggests that Dupin and the narrator are, in actuality, the same man. The narrator is simply another facet of Dupin's complex personality. In addition, as a detective, Dupin's methods of investigation are vulnerable to scrutiny, Grella says. It is possible, for example, that Dupin manufactures evidence—he has proven his talent for deception and possesses a dash of habitual charlatanry. Dupin would need no motive to commit these apparently motiveless crimes. He is vain and haughty and enjoys demonstrating his triumphant intellect at the expense of others, especially the Prefect of Police.

It is no more than a truism to assert that Edgar Allan Poe is a deceptive and elusive writer: his poetry, his fiction, his criticism, and, of course, strange and unhappy life all defy final judgment. Like a character in one of his own works, he dwells in an enigmatic twilight, never allowing us to see him clearly or know him fully. When they do not torture critics into alternating spasms of recrimination and panegyric, his best works suggest a multitude of conflicting interpretations. Some of his worst works, on the other hand, despite their tintinnabulating sound effects, appear to have inspired a major literary movement in France. Because of his penchant for satire, paronomasia, puzzles, hoax, and burlesque, it is frequently almost impossible to know just when and how to take him seriously. . . . The problem with Poe has always

Excerpted from "Poe's Tangled Web: A Close Look at Poe's Work Unearths Dark Suspicions Regarding the Identity of His Sleuth, C. Auguste Dupin," by George Grella, *The Armchair Detective*, Summer 1988. Reprinted with permission from the author.

been separating the genius from the slush. To deal with him—to paraphrase Ernest Hemingway—the reader needs a built-in slush detector.

FATHER OF A GENRE

Like his other works, Poe's tales of ratiocination have stimulated a wide variety of interpretation, but both critics and scholars unanimously agree on their merit. Among the most popular of all his stories, "The Murders in the Rue Morgue," "The Mystery of Marie Rogêt," and the "Purloined Letter," have pleased just about every kind of reader, from the expert to the fan; everyone finds them examples of the author performing at the height of his powers, positive proof of his genius. In addition, readers of detective fiction honor him as the creator of the genre and the inspiration for innumerable writers for the next hundred years. No fan of mysteries needs to be reminded of the form's debt to Poe; Ellery Queen sums it up most succinctly in a short essay called "A Ghost Haunting America":

> In *The Murders in the Rue Morgue* (1841), Poe originated the basic pattern of the classic form: the eccentric amateur sleuth and his worshipful stooge; the crime which baffles the police; the motif of the hermetically sealed room; the wrongly suspected person; the evidence fully presented to the reader; and the surprise solution based on brilliant deduction. . . . If Poe had written only that one story, he would still be considered the Founding Father and the Supreme Master. Dorothy L. Sayers has said that *The Murders in the Rue Morgue* "constitutes in itself almost a complete manual of detective theory and practice."

The debt that mystery and detective fiction owes to its great originator has been acknowledged by virtually every critic, historian, and writer of the form.

For more orthodox students of literature, especially those who have devoted much of their lives and careers to serious consideration of Poe's works, his detective fiction offers a certain relief from his most troubling and difficult moments. The detective stories show their author at his sanest and most rational: unlike many of his other tales, Poe's detective fiction appears as a luminous example of his genius rather than his slush. He writes all too infrequently, after all, about a normal and comprehensible human intelligence and even less frequently about the preservation rather than the disintegration of that intelligence.

It is a sad but ineluctable fact that most of Poe's fiction ends in some sort of puzzling catastrophe, preventing any clear or final conclusion. His narrators and protagonists are drunk, drugged, dreaming, or demented: many of the stories deal with what seems to be the subject of "The Raven"—a mind hallucinating brilliantly into madness, darkness, or self-destruction. But the detective stories are relatively calm and rational both in manner and matter. We do not see in them, for example, the unhealthy, hypersensitive Roderick Usher, who entombs his twin sister a bit sooner than he should, nor Montresor, who immures his friend Fortunato for no good reason at all. The narrator is not Egaeus of "Berenice," who presumably practices dental extraction on the corpse of his beloved. He is not the lunatic narrator of "Ligeia," who is overwhelmingly obsessed by his dead wife but somehow cannot remember her last name or where he met her. We do not see the maddened, motiveless, guilt-ridden narrator-murderer of "The Tell-Tale Heart" or "The Black Cat." Instead, the central figure of the stories is a brilliant, superior, ironic student of human behavior, who combines the intuition of the poet with the logical powers of the mathematician. Because the stories demonstrate, in the person of Dupin, the triumph of the intellectual faculties over the elements of chaos, crime, and disaster, they also appear to reflect the rational potential within Poe's frequently irrational and disordered psyche. Thus, the stories delight Poe scholars, critics, and biographers, who can see their man defeating his own unfortunate proclivity for the irrational, and redeeming his own sanity.

THE DUPLICITY OF DUPIN

To read the reactions of Poe scholars to the detective stories is to be reminded of Francis Bacon's description of the "three distempers of learning," viz., fantastical learning, contentious learning, and delicate learning. Joseph Wood Krutch has rather melodramatically stated what has come to be a prevailing view among students of Poe:

> First reasoning in order to escape feeling and then seizing upon the idea of reason as an explanation of his own character, Poe invented the detective story in order that he might not go mad.

Krutch's assertion seems to have found favor among a number of literary scholars, partially perhaps because it so neatly integrates the author's life with his work, a common fascination in Poe studies. Virtually all critics link Poe himself with the character of Dupin; indeed, there is strong evidence that Poe consciously strove for such an identification. Joseph Moldenhauer has found a close relationship between Dupin and the critic/artist Poe; he believes that the detective stories embody Poe's aesthetic and moral views. Strenuously contending a philosophical approach to Poe, Edward Davidson suggests that Dupin "is the ultimate dream of the artist who has nothing more to do but enjoy his art."

One of the most ingenious critics of the detective stories is Richard Wilbur, who glosses Krutch's remark in a remarkable interpretation of "The Murders in the Rue Morgue." Despite Poe's own distaste for allegory, Wilbur, like many another reader, succumbs to the ubiquitous temptation of the allegorical approach in his analysis of the story. He notices the obvious series of duplications—not surprising from the author of "William Wilson," "Ligeia," "The Fall of the House of Usher," and so many other exercises in the art of doubling—in the tale. Quoting the narrator, he points out that Dupin is a "double Dupin," capable of being both "creative, and resolvent." The earwitnesses to the horrible double murder hear two different voices behind the locked door of the victims' apartment, and Dupin himself speaks in both a tenor and a treble voice. Moreover, the initial murder suspect is one Adolphe Le Bon, whose name not only suggests his goodness, but also echoes the syllables and sounds of Auguste Dupin. Dupin confesses a relationship between himself and Le Bon, who, he says, "once rendered me a service for which I am not ungrateful." The similarity leads Wilbur to conclude that Le Bon represents the "humbly virtuous side of Dupin." The curious household of the two victims, Madam L'Espanaye and her daughter, along with that of the sailor and his orangutan, replicates the *ménage a deux* of Dupin and the anonymous narrator; Wilbur decides that the three domiciles are really one, "a single structure which signifies the reintegrated and harmonious consciousness of Dupin."

> The implication is [he goes on to say] that the mastermind Dupin, who can intuitively "fathom" all the other characters of the narrative, is to be seen as including them all—that the other "persons" of the tale are to be taken allegorically as elements of one person, whereof Dupin is the presiding faculty.

Finally, Dupin "uses his genius to detect and restrain the brute in himself, thus exorcising the fiend."

No reader can fail to marvel at Wilbur's ingenuity; allegorical explanations of Poe's works abound, but few are so convincing as his. There remain, however, other explanations of the detective stories, requiring perhaps less fantastic researches and more literal readings than the allegorical critics perform. For one thing, too many critics, grateful for Poe's sanity and Dupin's virtuosity, forget their author's fondness in sensational fiction (beyond Poe) to read detective stories with the spirit of the lover of mysteries. An awareness of Poe's love of hoaxing and some close attention to the texture of the tales themselves help to suggest that there may indeed be less in Poe's ratiocination than meets the eye.

DUPIN AS CULPRIT

Whatever the quality of Poe's invention and the particular excellences of "The Murders in the Rue Morgue" and "The Purloined Letter," both of the stories contain palpable quantities of fudge, some of which has obviously stuck to the fingers of the critics. Once the slush is detected, some surprising results emerge. The murderer of the Rue Morgue is not the "large fulvous Ourang-outang of the East Indian Islands," the purloiner of the letter is not the Machiavellian Minister D——. No: the murderer and the thief are the same man, a brilliant, devious psychotic—the Chevalier C. Auguste Dupin. A close examination will demonstrate the truth of this shocking conclusion.

Both stories instruct us rather pedantically in the method that will follow. The tales may in fact be read as illustrations in narrative and dramatic form of Poe's little lectures on ratiocination, or even as challenges to the reader to take literally the advice offered to understand the action of the tales. In "The Murders in the Rue Morgue," Poe warns us that:

> Deprived of ordinary resources, the analyst throws himself into the spirit of his opponent, identifies himself therewith, and not infrequently sees thus, at a glance, the sole methods (sometimes indeed absurdly simple ones) by which he may seduce into error or hurry into miscalculation.

This advice alludes to the game of checkers but is intended to be applied to Dupin's methods as well, since he is, of course, the "true analyst" of the tale. In "The Purloined Letter," Dupin catechizes the narrator on the subject of the analytical method, drawing from him the statement that such a method "requires the identification of the reasoner's intellect with that of his opponent." Although these precepts seem plausible, they possess what Dupin himself would term a "spurious profundity." We know that he does not solve the murders in the Rue Morgue by identifying his intellect with the ape's; instead, he closely scrutinizes the scene of the crime and infers some rather questionable conclusions. Nor does he identify himself with the Minister D——in "The Purloined Letter" but is, in fact, already identified with him through a number of suggestions in the story. Both D——and Dupin share more than an initial letter; they both integrate the abilities of the mathematician and the poet—a perfect combination for the character of the true analyst, as Poe points out in the earlier story. When the Prefect of Police characterizes D——as "a poet, which I take to be only one remove from a fool," Dupin responds, "I have been guilty of certain doggerel myself." In addition, the Minister D——is the obverse of Adolphe Le Bon—instead of a service, he has done Dupin "an evil turn" in the past, for which the detective desires revenge. It seems apparent that Dupin in the first story does not accomplish the ludicrously impossible task of throwing himself into the spirit of his opponent, the ape, and in the second story need not attempt such a thing at all. He need not identify himself with D——; he is D——.

Dupin's methods of investigation are vulnerable to the scrutiny of the true analyst. He gathers certain clues to the crime in the Rue Morgue entirely hidden from our view, producing them after the fact; since we must depend upon his report rather than our observation, we may question his veracity. For all we know, he may have manufactured the evidence—the rusted nailhead, the clump of orangutan hair (in the later story, "Hop-Frog"; false hair from that beast is manufactured from flax), the convenient bit of ribbon tied in a Maltese sailor's knot (the classic instance of the obscure item of information used to dazzle the dimwitted narrator of detective fiction). Similarly, we never see him in the act of discovering and repurloining the famous letter; instead, once again he recounts to the narrator his investigation and the stratagem by which he replaces it with a duplicate. His tactics are as dubious as is the preposterous idea that a brilliant and unscrupulous politician would hide an important document in full sight of the police. That notorious doctrine of the least likely hiding place, the idea that things are best hidden in plain sight, does not seem to have convinced anyone who has ever locked up anything of value; it seems, instead, another instance of Dupin's talent for deception of the reader, with perhaps more than a dash of his habitual charlatanry.

There are further incriminating evidences of Dupin's complicity in the crimes, especially in the atrocity of the Rue Morgue. The narrator tells us that he and the detective are "enamored of the Night for her own sake" and habitually roam the streets of Paris while saner citizens sleep. Dupin states that both the ape and his keeper climbed the lightning rod to the L'Espanaye apartment, and the narrator comments that "a lightning-rod is ascended without difficulty, especially by a sailor." The detective himself no doubt possesses the agility to climb the rod, and in fact his knowledge of the sailor's knot "peculiar to the Maltese" suggests that Dupin might have some experience of sailing and the physical skills it requires. On the other hand, he may have been assisted in the terrible deed by the nameless, deferential narrator, who appears to adore his eccentric friend to a somewhat unhealthy degree anyway; surely, he wouldn't balk at assisting him in committing the crime that would insure the solidity of his reputation. All the earwitnesses hear two voices inside the L'Espanaye apartment, one speaking in French, the other in some unknown tongue, variously identified as Spanish, Italian, German, English, and Russian. The two voices may have been the narrator expostulating with his friend when he saw the decapitated and mutilated corpses and realized the full horror of his crime. If Dupin acted without an accomplice, they may have been simply the detective talking to himself, alternating between his tenor and treble voices.

The perplexing question of motive leads to further indications of Dupin's culpability, as well as to other, more unsettling questions. One obvious motive for the crimes is mere braggadocio; Dupin is a vain and haughty man who delights in demonstrating his own superiority at the expense of others. His vanity could lead him to commit even the most monstrous of crimes in order to display his triumphant intellect, especially if in so doing he could also embarrass his adversary, the Prefect of Police. The very fact that Dupin takes pains to convince the narrator that the murders in the Rue Morgue were unmotivated throws some suspicion on him: "I wish you . . . to discard from your thoughts the blundering idea of *motive.*" His disturbing summary of the murderer's character makes his care to abolish the thought of motive even more suspect. Imagine a being, Dupin asks, who combines

> an agility astounding, a strength superhuman, a ferocity brutal, a butchery without motive, a *grotesquerie* in horror absolutely alien from humanity, and a voice foreign in tone to the ears of men of many nations, and devoid of all distinct or intelligible syllabification. What result, then, has ensued? What impression have I made upon your fancy?

The narrator, quite understandably, experiences a creeping of the flesh at this description and replies that "a madman . . . has done this deed—some raving maniac." And he is, I fear, correct. Madness, that persistent subject and theme of Poe's fiction, is at the center of this story. Dupin, the murderer-detective, is mad; in view of the reiterated dualities of the story and of his character, his insanity appears to involve a division in his personality, to be of the schizoid variety. Throughout the stories, we are warned over and over of the possibility of Dupin's double nature, not for the allegorical implications which Richard Wilbur notices, but for the purposes of discovering the true character of the detective.

DUPIN AS NARRATOR

The first syllable of Dupin's name suggests both his duplicity and his duplexity. We already know of his two voices. In addition, when Dupin boasts of his ability to interpret the secrets of men's hearts—and proves it by reading the narrator's thoughts—his manner changes, becoming "frigid and abstract," his eyes grow vacant, and his voice rises to that didactic treble. At these moments, the narrator is reminded of "the old philosophy of the Bi-Part Soul" and amuses himself with "the fancy of a double Dupin." Dupin's duality suggests a cloven spirit and a deranged intellect; even his adoring friend admits that the detective's behavior is "the result of an excited, or perhaps of a diseased intelligence." He is indeed, as we are told, both "creative and resolvent"—he commits the crime, then constructs a brilliantly plausible solution. He is specifically associated with Adolphe Le Bon and the Minister D——, who do not "represent" various sides of his personality, but *are* literally aspects of himself; he stands equally related to both for precisely opposite reasons. The divided parts of his personality are linked with the crimes and criminals in the stories and indicated as incriminating evidence over and over again, in a variety of subtle hints for the true analyst to comprehend. Dupin seems hopelessly caught between the rational and irrational elements of his psyche: the two voices overheard in the L'Espanaye apartment demonstrate precisely the horror of that division—the sane Dupin remonstrating in anguish at the bloody deed, the insane shrilly gibbering in utter madness.

There remains for the reader a further step in the process of ratiocination, an inquiry into the character of the narrator, whom most critics ignore or neglect. Few readers, surprisingly, wonder just why the narrator should choose to support the curious and eccentric domestic life of Dupin and endure the accompanying difficulties: the gloomy household, the odd hours, the supercilious manner of his roommate, the constant need to shower appreciation and applause on the analyst, the inability to conceal even his most private thoughts from the inquiring mind of the detective. In a revealing but rather embarrassing confession, the narrator explains his life with Dupin:

> Had the routine of our life at this place been known to the world, we should have been regarded as madmen—although, perhaps, as madmen of a harmless nature. Our seclusion was perfect. We admitted no visitors. Indeed the locality of our retirement had been carefully kept a secret from my own former associates; and it had been many years since Dupin had ceased to know or be known in Paris. We existed within ourselves alone.

This suggestive paragraph opens up yet more startling possibilities in the relationship between Dupin and the narrator—he is not describing two men here, but one. They have, he tells us, "a common temper," implying perhaps that both possess the Bi-Part Soul, and further implying that it is one Bi-Part Soul that unites them. They are not harmless madmen, but a single madman, and far from harmless at that. The narrator is simply another facet of Dupin's complex personality, like Adolphe Le Bon, a more or less humble and ordinary side of the master mind. When he tells the reader that "we existed within ourselves alone," he is speaking absolutely literally, with no allegorical or mystical suggestion, and no deliberate obfuscation of any sort.

The several critics who detect a species of interior allegory of the consciousness in these tales are obviously correct. Unfortunately, however, they fail to explore the works fully enough to discover the obvious, which, as Dupin constantly reminds us, is harder to find than the subtle. Over and over in the tales we are warned to concentrate on the literal and obvious facts, clues, reports, and conclusions. As Dupin tells us,

> there is such a thing as being too profound. Truth is not always in a well. In fact, as regards the more important knowledge, I do believe that she is invariably superficial. The truth lies not in the valleys where we seek her, but upon the mountain-tops where she is found.

The whole of "The Purloined Letter," from its epigraph, *Nil sapientiae odiosius acumine nimio* ("Nothing is more odious to wisdom than too much cunning") to its subject and its conclusion, illustrates the author's incessant concern with examining not the hidden but the obvious. The many readers of Poe who choose to focus on the fanciful and the arcane in the stories are themselves allegorically represented by the Prefect of Police, who, as Dupin points out, is guilty *"de nier ce qui est, et d'expliquer ce qui nest pas"* (of denying that which is, and of explaining that which is not). It seems possible to employ an approach defining each of the characters as facets of Dupin's or Poe's, or the artist's consciousness, but to do so without logically extending the argument is to ignore the multitude of clues we have observed. If we recognize the importance of the narrator's character as part of Dupin's, we can appreciate more fully the true extent of the obvious as Poe presents it. If we realize that Dupin himself is not only murderer and detective, but also narrator of these tales, we can understand more fully the complexity of his personality: only he could combine such worshipful admiration for his own genius with such adroit obfuscation of the truth. Only he could stage such carefully controlled Socratic dialogues between himself and his interlocutor. Only he could so fully examine his own personality, present the reader with a plethora of clues to his true character—all the while instructing us in the methods of analysis—then commit the crimes, their solutions, and these tales, as it were, before our eyes, without ever giving the game away.

Puns, Puzzles, and Wordplay

Poe has baked up quite a quantity of fudge in these stories of detection, as we can see, but there is still at least a little bit more. I, for one, have always been bothered by the title of "The Purloined Letter": why that odd and rather grandiloquent synonym for something as simple as, say, stolen? It has always struck me as a typically Poesque bit of flummery. He may have chosen it simply because it fit his rather juicy and elegant prose style, of course. At the same time, all students of Poe are familiar with his delight in puns, wordplay, puzzles, and ciphers; indeed, he once challenged his readers to send him ciphers, claiming he could solve any one invented. His love of puzzles and games may have led him to select the word for its anagrammatic possibilities. Purloined is a varied but incomplete anagram: it contains the words "Poe" and "Dupin" within it. To put the icing on the cake, it also has within it another of Poe's favorite names, "lenor," without the final "e." Lenore, the reiterated name of the beloved in "The Raven," occurs to remind us of the presence of madness and its link with the narrator of these stories, thus providing another clue to the understanding of the tales. And, of course, if we see that "lenor" lacks the final "e" we then know what the purloined letter literally means—it is the missing letter "e" as well as the item of correspondence, and of course Poe is the culprit here. How fortunate we are that Poe provides us such clues to examine, so that we will not wander, lost, in the intricate labyrinths of our own ingenuity.

Irrespective of this final point, it should be clear by now that, beyond the many contributions he made to detective fiction, Poe bequeathed to serious literature one of the whodunit's most important inventions, the incorporation of the reader into the narrative act. He draws the reader into the story, first by instructing him in methodology, then by presenting a puzzle and its solution. He adds further dimensions by making the reader a half-conscious but fully willing participant in the problem and the solution; in short, he turns the reader himself into the detective, presenting him with the means to abstract the truth from the mixture of hints and deceptions he has so carefully placed before him. His sleight-of-hand has enabled him to befuddle generations of scholars into accepting the charlatanry of Dupin and his exploits and constructing some truly enchanting arguments in support of the author's genius. If the reader, as he is constantly reminded, will scrutinize the surface, the literal level of Poe's stories, however, he can succeed at the detective's task and uncover the real criminal.

Poe gives us everything we need to solve the crime; it is up to us to put into practice the methods of the true analyst and arrive at the truth. That truth, of course, may disturb many readers of Poe and of detective fiction, but it must be faced unflinchingly, with Stoic courage. The Chevalier C. Auguste Dupin is the murderer of the Rue Morgue and the purloiner of the letter. After more than a century of obloquy the innocent ape and the slandered Minister D——can rest in peace. After all those years of subtle deception, the true culprit is at last revealed, through precisely those methods he advises us to follow. We are the real detectives of Poe's stories; acting correctly, we can solve even the most abstruse of them. We need only combine the logic of the mathematician with the intuition of the poet, and keep a sharp lookout for quantities of fudge.

CHAPTER 2

Revenge, Murder, and Madness

READINGS ON
THE SHORT STORIES OF
EDGAR ALLAN POE

Madness and Drama in "The Cask of Amontillado"

Kate Stewart

Kate Stewart of Worcester Polytechnic Institute
claims that "The Cask of Amontillado" is reminiscent
of an Elizabethan revenge tragedy, in which Montresor plays the role of the prototypical villain-hero revenging an insult to his family. The bones of Montresor's ancestors, calling to be avenged, are also
similar to ghosts in Elizabethan tragedy. In addition,
the gruesomeness, terror, horror, and violence of
the tale echo conventions of the Elizabethan era.
Through his adroit handling of the theme of revenge,
Poe elicits a full range of dramatic technique through
his use of sound in the story. Present throughout the
tale, the tinkling bells of Fortunato's costume come
to symbolize Montresor's descent into madness,
ringing eternally in his mind, reminding him of the
horror of his crime.

Even the most nonchalant reader admits that Edgar Allan
Poe was more than a little interested in madness; he may be
less aware, however, that Poe also dabbled in the dramatic
arts. Poe's mix of madness and drama, specifically the substance of revenge tragedy in "The Cask of Amontillado," offers yet another example of his wide-ranging mind and creative propensities. I perceive in Poe's tale a parallel to
Elizabethan revenge tragedy. Pointing out that Woodberry
calls "Cask" "a tale of Italian revenge," Thomas Mabbott
states that such feeling embodies "an implacable demand
for retribution," which Poe accounts for in the beginning of
the tale. As he works out the action and develops the character of Montresor as a revenge-tragedy hero, Poe by means
of sound effects proves himself a master of dramatic tech-

Excerpted from "The Supreme Madness: Revenge and Bells in 'The Cask of Amontil-
lado,'" by Kate Stewart, *The University of Mississippi Studies in English*, vol. 5, 1987.
Reprinted with permission from *Journal X* (formerly *The University of Mississippi
Studies in English*).

nique. As Montresor falls deeper into insanity, the ringing of the bells symbolizes his descent.

ELEMENTS OF ELIZABETHAN REVENGE TRAGEDY

Montresor's first declaration alerts us that revenge is the central motivation underlying the story: "The thousand injuries of Fortunato I had borne as I best could, but when he ventured upon insult I vowed revenge." No one will dispute the motivation, yet scholars question the exact nature of the insult. Proponents of a politico-religious interpretation of the story see the insult growing from the tensions arising between the Catholic and the Protestant, the non-member and the Freemason, respectively Montresor and Fortunato. Certainly these factors contribute to the conflict. The insult is, however, the more basic one found in Elizabethan revenge tragedy: revenging an insult to a family member. Noting the connection between Italian revenge and Elizabethan revenge tragedy, Shannon Burns emphasizes that avenging an insult is Montresor's motivation since the tale focuses on family and Catholicism.

This fact is borne out as Montresor and Fortunato wander through the catacombs. When Fortunato comments on the vaults, his companion replies: "The Montresors . . . were a great and numerous family." Fortunato responds: "I forget your arms." Although on the surface the comment appears benign, Fortunato implies that the family is hardly worth remembering. If the Montresors had at one time been prominent, then Fortunato would surely know something about the coat of arms. Since the men also have a fairly close relationship, Fortunato should remember the arms. Gargano sees that Montresor is the "vindicator of his ancestors" for precisely this reason. He adds that the coat of arms itself signifies Montresor's avenging his injured family.

The ancestral bones of the Montresors offer another parallel to revenge tragedy. Although not a device always employed by revenge tragedians, ghosts frequently appeared— the spirits of family members visiting the protagonist and spurring him to action. *Hamlet* offers a good example: the apparition of the murdered father urges his son to avenge his death. The bones of the Montresors in "Cask" function as do ghosts in revenge tragedy. Piles of ancestral bones must be removed to expose the crypt; therefore, the bones of the insulted Montresors that cover the place of Fortunato's entombment share in the death of the enemy. Later, when he finishes his brickwork, Montresor replaces the bones; consequently the "ghosts" reach out to insure the burial of Fortunato. Unlike the ghosts in Elizabethan tragedies, the apparitions in "Cask" do not appear and reappear. Instead they are ever-present, constant reminders of the family's history. When Fortunato, drunken and proud, sarcastically toasts his friend's ancestors, he underlines his contempt for the family, living and dead—and both the living and the dead are there to avenge that insult.

Several characteristics in "Cask" align with elements of Gothicism: gruesomeness, terror, horror, and violence. Because of their association with murder and death, the bones also contribute to Gothicism in this tale. Aside from their immediate relationship with physical suffering, they produce this effect through sound: they rattle and so reinforce terror. Noting the revival of Renaissance drama in the late 1700s, Clara F. McIntyre sees borrowings—especially in the blood and violence, revenge, madness, and ghosts—from Elizabethan tragedy in the novels of Ann Radcliffe and others.

MONTRESOR IS A PROTOTYPICAL VILLAIN-HERO

Added to these distinct features of revenge tragedy is the presence of the prototypical hero from such drama. Fortunato has gradually victimized Montresor. The victim allows a thousand injuries to pass, and he takes punitive action only when Fortunato insults him. To his listener Montresor emphasizes that he would "at length" be avenged. Avoiding any risks, the protagonist carefully calculates his actions because his being caught and punished could render the vengeance ineffective. The fact remains, though, that Montresor, like a revenge hero, does delay the fulfillings of his plans. His meticulous engineering of the murder over an unspecified, but certainly not a brief, period causes Poe's vengeance-seeker to brood upon his hatred for Fortunato. Because of his constant agonizing, Montresor's plans become obsessive, leading him to insanity.

In their study of the revenge-tragedy motif, Charles A. and Elaine S. Hallett postulate that "the brutal act committed by the revenge is what distinguishes the act of revenge from the act of justice and makes void all of the protagonist's claims to sanity." This statement sheds light on Montresor's actions; his violent act emblemizes his mental condition.

Many critics believe that the protagonist of "Cask" resembles Roderick Usher and William Wilson. Edward H. Davidson views Roderick and Madeline as the mental and physical components of one person. Another divided self, William Wilson, confronts his mirror image. He is enraged by his twin's loathsome traits. Montresor is this same type of divided self. Thus, when Montresor kills his enemy, he commits suicide. Ridding himself of Fortunato, he destroys the hated personality traits within himself. Although in his warped mind he views Fortunato as the enemy, in particular his own, Montresor is clearly the sinister figure. He is the plotter, the murderer. Despite his malevolence, however, he is the protagonist of "Cask." Montresor is, then, a hold-over of the Elizabethan villain-hero.

The evidence is sufficient: the protagonist is a split personality—a madman. Without exhaustive characterization of Montresor, the text proper offers ample evidence of his divided self. After he has determined vengeance, he qualifies: "It must be understood that neither by word or deed had I given Fortunato cause to doubt my good will." Here is the classic description of a dual personality, the man who does not externalize his feelings. Showing an apparent or ironic good will, Montresor inquires after Fortunato's health as they travel toward the latter's death.

BELLS SYMBOLIZE MONTRESOR'S BREAKDOWN

Beginning with the cordial meeting of the two, this journey leads Montresor into madness: "I am on my way to Luchresi." Mabbott interprets the name as meaning "Look-crazy." "Luchresi" recurs, yet the structure of its first appearance is highly significant. The tense of the verb is progressive. On the surface the statement is merely a decoy to lure Fortunato to his death; however, the forward-moving action expressed by the verb structure renders greater meaning. Montresor is on his way to deeper insanity. Even after fifty years of pondering his crime, he finds no peace of mind. In his descent into madness, the murderer remembered vividly the ringing of the bells. The story of the crime might become distorted after so many years, although the haunting sound of the bells in the last scene between pursuer and victim remains with Montresor. Noting that Montresor views Fortunato as his "mirror image," Charles A. Sweet [Jr.] states that, when Montresor hears only the jin-

gling of the bells after he yells "Fortunato," those bells signify the insanity of the protagonist. This final chiming
marks Montresor's complete descent into madness. The
bells sound throughout the story, and each "jingling" fur-
thers the mental breakdown of Montresor.

Recounting his murder of Fortunato, Montresor sets the
stage by describing the evening "during the supreme madness of the carnival season." The atmosphere suggests the
mental state of the murderer. Like the craziness around him,
he verges upon collapse. His long brooding over the method
of repaying his adversary has led him to a state of frenzy as
he sets his plans in motion. Poe dresses Montresor's enemy
as a court jester with "conical cap and bells." Critics see this
garb as one of the ironies in "Cask" since Montresor and
Fortunato have switched places. Fortunato is no longer the
power figure; he is a fool who is now victimized by his former victim. Montresor rises to power before Fortunato the
dupe. The costuming is ironic, to be sure, but it serves a dramatic function. The bells on Fortunato's cap ring time and
again. With each ringing, Montresor slips farther and farther
into his own "supreme madness."

Montresor first mentions the bells as he and Fortunato
enter the catacombs: "The gait of my friend was unsteady
and the bells upon his cap jingled as he strode." Montresor
specifically refers to the bells on three subsequent occasions, but his first remark remains significant because it
demonstrates his keen awareness of this particular sound.
Since they "jingled as he strode," the bells sound more or
less constantly. The faint chimes mark each drunken step
taken by Fortunato. Montresor would be attuned to the incessant ringing; consequently the bells haunt him fifty years
after the crime.

Constantly aware of the bells, he would notice them more
on certain occasions. After one coughing spell: "Ugh! Ugh!
Ugh!" (the hacking itself echoing the repeated sounding of
bells), Fortunato drinks to the departed Montresors. Again
the protagonist hears the bells. Montresor observes of Fortunato as the latter proposes his toast: "He raised it to his lips
with a leer. He paused and nodded to me familiarly, while
his bells jingled." Fortunato's actions indeed seem to be con-
temptuous. Once more the aristocrat goes beyond injury to
insult, and Montresor more intensely desires revenge.

Shortly, Montresor again refers to the bells, after explaining his coat of arms: "The wine sparkled in his eyes and the bells jingled." This statement marks roughly the midpoint of the story. The companions near the place of entombment; Montresor will soon realize his goal. Attaining the prize, though, he will slip into greater unreality. This halfway point signals his halfway point to insanity. When readers note Montresor's third reference to the bells, they should look back to the first: the bells sound at each step. Because of his increasing drunkenness, evident in his glazed eyes, his walk no doubt degenerates from being "unsteady" to staggering. To signify mere unsteady steps the bells would sound with some regularity. By contrast, more halting and unsure steps create a more erratic sound. From soft regular tinkling, they would grow irregular. The bells' more erratic sounds symbolize Montresor's loss of mental stability. Another Poe narrator is likewise lost in "fancy," a word closely associated with illusions and distorted mental activity. When the narrator in "The Raven" begins "linking Fancy unto fancy," he is obviously losing control. Montresor's situation is the same because, the closer he comes to destroying his enemy, the cloudier grows his thinking.

A PLAY WITHIN A PLAY

When the men reach their destination, Montresor chains a stunned Fortunato inside the crypt. This scene functions as the play-within-the-play motif of revenge tragedy because it portrays the culmination of the vengeance. Moreover, despite some verbalizing, the episode conveys a sense of pantomime; nowhere are actions so exaggerated. The Halletts suggest that the play-within-a-play reflects the mental state of the revenger by portraying his "mad act." They further surmise that "this motif brings in a world distinct from that of the real world. The separation is represented visually by the creation of a sealed-off space within which the play can be staged." Montresor sets his "dumb-show" in operation, and again the bells figure significantly. The revenge-hero's work with the chain roughly imitates the sound of bells: metal striking metal. This "bell ringing," however, contrasts sharply to the earlier jingles. The bells on Fortunato's cap would emit a light, cheerful tinkling. On the other hand, the ringing of the chain might be heavy and somber. While the amateur mason goes about his work, he hears the "furious vibrations of the chain." The rumblings of the metal prompt

Montresor to cease his labors and sit down to enjoy the success of his plot. When the chains stop rattling, he resumes.
His labors are interrupted, however, by "loud and shrill
screams." Noticeably affected by these outcries, the protagonist admits that he "hesitated" and "trembled." Regaining
his composure, Montresor answers the yells of anguish, returning scream for scream. Finally silence prevails. The type
of ringing produced by the chains represents Montresor's
going insane; the "mad act" is complete. Surely his trem-
blings and screamings, much on the order of the scenes in
"Tarr and Fether," typify a madman.

After his final exchange with his victim, Montresor hears
the bells ring for the last time. Twice calling "'Fortunato'"
and receiving no response, he hears nothing save the jingling of the bells, which sickens him. He attempts to rationalize his sickness as a consequence of the dampness in the
catacombs. His state results, however, from the awareness
and horror of his sin. Earlier he blamed wine for his declin-
ing mental condition, but he rationalizes again. A victim of a
diseased mind, he hears the ringing of the bells, emblems of
his madness, fifty years after the murder. Gargano states:
"Montresor fails because he cannot harmonize the disparate
parts of his nature, and, consequently, cannot achieve self-
knowledge. Also describing Montresor's failure, Kozikowski
seen the man's revenge as "a shambles, a wreckage of the
human spirit." Recognizing his heinous crime, Montresor
cannot escape the horror of the deed. Revenge, madness,
and bells echo eternally in his head.

"Cask" testifies impressively to Poe's subtle art of net-
working his multiform interests and knowledge into a unified work of art. In its compactness this tale offers the full
range of Poe's talents: his adept characterization, his careful
attention to setting, and his stunning dramatic technique.

In Defense of Montresor

Patrick White

Patrick White is professor of English at Eastern Michigan University. He has published essays in the *James Joyce Quarterly, Shaw: The Annual of Bernard Shaw Studies*, and other journals. White explains that Montresor's act of revenge is a form of patriotic vengeance for the sake of his family name. He is no different, in this light, than a patriot killing for the sake of his country. And like a patriot, Montresor kills Fortunato without guilt, feeling fully sanctioned by his family's symbolic coat of arms for his deed. Thus, the story, White says, is a chilling example of man's capacity for rationalization, made more horrible by the fact that readers, all members of universal humanity, share Montresor's soul.

The usual way of responding to "The Cask of Amontillado" with something like pure and unqualified revulsion at Montresor's dark deed as an act outside the normal range of human behavior has its validity but stops short of the story's ultimate revelation. Wittingly or otherwise, Poe has given us the means of seeing Montresor's act as something other than a demented or Satanic pursuit of revenge. True, the story has been found compelling for generations of readers who see Montresor as a very special case of the human potential for evil. But is Montresor such a special case? I do not think so. He is neither demented nor Satanic. He has his reasons for what he does, and these are reasons we should be able to understand. Therein lies a deeper horror in the story.

MONTRESOR'S FAMILY ALLEGIANCE

In order to understand how Montresor can feel justified in what he has done and be free of any twinge of guilt even fifty

Excerpted from "'The Cask of Amontillado': A Case for the Defense," by Patrick White, *Studies in Short Fiction*, Fall 1989. Footnotes in original have been omitted in this reprint. Reprinted with permission.

years after the event, we must understand how family in general and his own family's motto and coat of arms in particular affect his motivation. One of the puzzles of the story has to do with its location. Does it take place in Italy, as some detail might suggest and as most readers have assumed; or in France, as the name Montresor might suggest? There is no way of answering this question definitively, and perhaps Poe intended it that way. For what is important for Montresor is not that he is French or Italian but that he is a Montresor. His allegiance is to his family in a way that we can understand only by reflecting on our national allegiance. Poe has left the historical setting somewhat indeterminate, but his story seems to take place at a time in the past, before the triumph of nationalism, when an aristocratic family like the Montresors could feel something akin to sovereignty and even assert it openly. Living as we do at a time when the family has ceased to exist as a political unit, we may need to make a special effort to understand Montresor's attitude toward his rights and responsibilities as a member of a noble family. From his point of view, he is acting patriotically, as it were, in seeking vengeance on his family's enemy. It may be easier for us to understand how family could be an object of something like patriotic devotion if we bring to mind that the word "patriot" derives from Latin *pater.* Montresor feels justified in killing on behalf of his "fatherland," his family, in the same way that a citizen or subject of more recent times can feel justified in killing on behalf of his "fatherland," the nation-state.

In a modern nation-state, a family coat of arms and motto can be hardly more than innocent wall decoration, however formidable in content. But for Montresor, with his feudal orientation, they would be capable of imposing the most serious and fearful obligations. That is why Poe sees to it that we are informed of their contents. Fortunato's ignorance of Montresor's coat of arms may be an insult even though the presumed insult cannot provide motivation for the killing. That has already been decided upon. More importantly, however, Fortunato's ignorance serves Poe as an expository device: it provides the opportunity for us to learn the details of Montresor's coat of arms and motto. These details are essential to our understanding of the family imperatives rooted in Montresor's mind as he plans and carries out the killing of Fortunato.

"*Nemo me impune lacessit.*" Montresor's family motto has

been translated, "No one attacks me with impunity." But it can be translated, "No one bothers me in the slightest with impunity." It seems to be an assertion, at the least, of extreme punctiliousness, if not of a kind of mad arrogance. Any kind of injury or an insult of almost any degree would warrant retaliation. Just taking the motto at face value, we might well sense a touch of peculiar family madness here. But what, then, are we to make of the fact that, as has been pointed out, this was the motto of the royal house of Scotland? Whether Poe got the motto by way of Fenimore Cooper or through some other source, he was, it would seem, making some kind of point here, although the point might be lost on a reader unaware of the motto's ultimate origin. For by this one stroke, Poe has conflated royal house and aristocratic family. Is retaliation on behalf of the one, acceptable patriotism; and on behalf of the other, madness? Is extravagant touchiness acceptable in the one and arrogance in the other? Deeply buried in the story though it be, once seen, the fact that Montresor's family motto, seemingly so arrogant and barbaric, is that of a royal house clearly places Montresor's proceedings in a new light.

A particular detail in the motto that is worth noting is that it speaks not of "us" but of *me*. Insofar as we are not aware of the motto's origin, the singular pronoun creates some misdirection. It gives the impression that Montresor is seeking redress as an individual person who has been wronged rather than as a member of a family he feels has been wronged. To do justice to Montresor, we should understand that he is not an individual person seeking redress for personal insult or injury but, rather, an agent of retribution acting on behalf of his family. Since we never get any specifics of Montresor's grievance against Fortunato, we have no way of knowing whether Montresor took the brunt of the perceived offense or not. But the question is moot in the sense that Montresor clearly shows himself to be acting on behalf of family, not self. Even if Fortunato's presumed offense had been directed against Montresor personally, not only Montresor but the entire Montresor family would be shamed by it. To strike one is to strike all.

A SYMBOLIC COAT OF ARMS

"A huge human foot d'or, in a field azure; the foot crushes a serpent rampant whose fangs are embedded in the heel."

The Montresor coat of arms owes little to the traditional symbols of heraldry and would seem to be mostly Poe's invention. However, it may owe something to the American Revolution–era flag depicting a snake and the motto "Don't tread on me." The effect of this collocation of revolutionary-era flag and coat of arms is similar to that of the Montresor motto's being that of the royal house of Scotland. Both connections tend to lend dignity and validity to what might otherwise seem to be the pretensions of the Montresors.

The family motto, emphasizing retaliation, would suggest that the snake in the coat of arms represents the Montresor family. The gold foot is striking the snake—crushing it, as Montresor describes the coat of arms to Fortunato—but not with impunity. As the snake is being crushed, it is biting the heel of the gold foot. The scene seems to illustrate graphically what an enemy of the Montresors can expect. We notice also that even though it is being crushed, the snake still somehow manages a proud and heroic pose: it is "rampant,"

DOUBLE MEANING IN "THE CASK OF AMONTILLADO"

As in much of Poe's work, proper names in "The Cask of Amontillado" carry multiple, allusory meanings that add to readers' delight in the story.

Poe's delight in allusions and word play is evident throughout his works but no more so than in the short story "The Cask of Amontillado" where proper nouns, particularly, are capable of carrying multiple meanings. Fortunato believes himself to be the "fortunate one" in that he has been selected by Montresor to taste of the rare Spanish sherry, but he is also "fated" to die. He should feel "fortunate," according to his murderer's line of reasoning, to be laid to rest among the bones of Montresor's ancestors whose arms he had forgotten and whose descendent he had insulted, and yet he is "fortunate" in that he, unlike his murderer, has rested in peace for fifty years.

The name "Montresor" also has obvious possibilities: his treasures are multiple. His first "treasure" is his family honor, which Fortunato has impugned; his second, the sherry he claims to have in the vault to which he leads his victim; and finally, the new "treasure" he entombs with his ancestors, the body and spirit of his victim which haunt him for fifty years, an ironic treasure, indeed.

Dennis W. Eddings, "Poe, Dupin, and the Reader," *University of Mississippi Studies in English*, vol. 3 (1982), pp. 128–35.

and yet, at the same time, it is ignobly biting its adversary in the heel. The coat of arms suggests that if someone puts its foot on the family, the family will strike back as best it can, as a snake might strike the heel of the foot that crushes its body, and not lose any of its assurance of virtue. The coat of arms suggests that Montresor need feel no obligation to be concerned with chivalry in striking back. It is almost as if the coat of arms, depicting the adversary as a golden foot, shows with prescience the feudal family's fall as concomitant with the rise of capitalism and gives its prospective blessing to a response that need owe nothing to the standards of chivalry. For even though Montresor acts with a sense that what he does is fully sanctioned, he still must act in a covert manner. His family can assert sovereignty openly in its motto and coat of arms, but he knows that the actual implementation of this sovereign power must be muted. And so he carries out the killing of his adversary in secret. The snake "rampant," with whatever convolutions, being crushed by an adversary, must strike his adversary in the heel. Montresor need have no qualms about his covert operation. He has prior and complete sanction for it.

But we may still ask how he can relish his retaliation and why he need inflict the unnecessary cruelty of death by slow suffocation on his victim? In order to see how Montresor can do these things and still feel justified, we need to keep the larger context in mind. He can relish what he is doing because he can feel that what he is doing is right as surely as a soldier in the service of a modern state can take pleasure in the killing he does because he is carrying out a patriotic obligation and being of service to his country. The same context should enable us to understand the cruelty of Montresor's method. Put into terms analogous to those of modern warfare, the method constitutes an atrocity. And anybody who knows anything about warfare knows that atrocities are more the practice than the exception. If we grant Montresor the mentality of a soldier in combat—and it would seem he is possibly entitled to such consideration—we should be able to understand that he would not have to be either demented or Satanic to carry out the killing of Fortunato as he does.

Montresor is so convinced of his right in carrying out his plan of vengeance that he can speak of the killing of Fortunato as an "immolation." We need not go so far as to see him assuming the role of a priest performing the ritual killing of a sacrificial victim, as some commentators on the story have done; but we should be able to understand that, given his family imperatives, he might well be able to see himself as a person carrying out a quasi-sacred duty.

He similarly shows confidence in the rightness of his action in his last words to Fortunato. Fortunato, desperate for his life, pleads, *"For the love of God, Montresor!"* Montresor, with what must strike Fortunato as biting irony, replies, "Yes, . . . for the love of God!" He is doing this terrible thing, not "For God and Country!" but for what comes down to the same thing for him, "For God and family!" We are surely mistaken if we see Montresor's invocation of the divine as blasphemy or reduce it to parody. Montresor is apparently quite sincere in equating the family dictate with a divine commandment.

READERS SHARE MONTRESOR'S SOUL

Montresor's lack of remorse, then, even after fifty years, should not be a wonder to us. He is not an exceptional person. He is not a Hamlet, reluctant to take issue with his family's adversary. He is bright, but not one of the *best* and brightest. He is quite ordinary and conventional. He is loyal, but limited. He has an obligation to his family; he carries it out, with relish, and savors deeply the satisfaction that success in carrying out this obligation brings him. He is coarse enough to have been capable of inflicting unnecessary suffering on his victim and enjoying his victim's distress. He is barely sensitive enough to have felt some passing queasiness during the performance of his deed. But, withal, what he did, he is convinced, was justified. He was carrying out an obligation to his family as he saw it—as he was culturally conditioned to see it. Now, fifty years after the event, he can recount it with pride.

He addresses his account to someone who knows, he says, "the nature of my soul." Who is this listener, this person who is physically present to Montresor as he tells of this incident in his family's history? We have no way of knowing. It is not likely to be his father confessor, for there is no hint of penitence, nor any hint that he feels he has done anything that requires penitence. All we know is that it is someone who, Montresor believes, knows the nature of his soul. This is where we, the reader, come in. Poe achieves another conflation here. For we, as surely as the person physically present, are Montresor's listener. And we, as surely as the person physically present, also know the nature of Montresor's soul. We know it because, whether we like to admit it or not, we share that soul. We, as members of the human community, share it with the royal house of Scotland, with revolutionary-era American patriots, with all members of universal humanity whoever they may be, who anticipating or experiencing a grievance against their tribal unit, whether it be one of formal political autonomy or not, feel justified in holding the right to take direct action against an adversary and in taking action if the provocation occurs. And, sharing that soul which we know so well, we know that the provocation can be slight and the retaliation brutal. And the conscience can be left perfectly clear. The story is a chilling example of man's capacity for rationalization. It is as much a tale of ratiocination as a tale of terror, and all the more terrible for that.

One commentator has claimed that Poe was using Montresor as his alter ego in pursuing vicarious revenge against his literary enemies when he wrote the story. Even if Poe were not doing so, he might still have been able to echo Gustave Flaubert's well-known words, *"Madame Bovary, c'est moi."* Given the nature of Montresor's soul, that he, like us, could know so well, he might still have been able to say, "Montresor, he is I." And we, the gentle reader, might similarly welcome Montresor back into the human community with our horror-stricken hearts.

The Supernatural and Psychological in "The Black Cat"

Fred Madden

Fred Madden is associate professor of English at Ithaca College. Madden explains that in Poe's story "The Black Cat," the narrator's repression of his hatred for his wife is at the root of the interplay between the supernatural and psychological levels of the story. In this story, familiar surroundings become supernatural, adding to the bizarre, uncanny atmosphere of the tale and provoking feelings of uneasiness for readers as Poe uses the tale as a vehicle to explore the complexity of human irrationality.

The interplay between the supernatural and psychological levels of "The Black Cat" is obvious to those who have read, even superficially, in the criticism on the story. On the supernatural level, the narrator attempts to convince the reader that the black cat is the representative of a demonic force "whose craft has seduced (him) into murder." However, psychological readings such as James Gargano's and John McElroy's argue that rampant self-deception and prevarication pervade the tale which, they feel, is motivated by the narrator's attempt to disguise his premeditated murder of his wife. In short, for these readers, the narrator seems to blame everybody and everything including the "spirit of perverseness" for his wife's murder, thereby conveniently exonerating himself of any responsibility.

Essentially, psychological interpretations of "The Black Cat" have found more favor recently in a critical climate which is inclined to view Poe as a trickster or hoaxer who is often interested in undercutting the expectations of his readers. Thus, the first sentence of "The Black Cat" might provide two readings: "For the most wild, yet most homely narrative

Excerpted from "Poe's 'The Black Cat' and Freud's 'The Uncanny,'" by Fred Madden, *Literature and Psychology*, vol. 39, no. 1-2, 1993. Reprinted with permission from *Literature and Psychology*.

which I am about to pen, I neither expect nor solicit belief." A "supernatural" reading of the story would look for the narration to present incredible events or occurrences which seem to be beyond belief. And if Poe had not created a number of hoaxes as for example "Berenice" (written on a bet) or the "Facts in the Case of M. Valdemar" (a hoax on mesmerism), one might be inclined to accept "The Black Cat" as a narrative concerned with the supernatural. But when the narrator says that he can "neither expect nor solicit belief," a more skeptical reader might decide to seek other, more logical, explanations for the events which occur in the story, especially in light of the last sentence in the first paragraph: "Hereafter, perhaps, some intellect may be found which will reduce my phantasm to the commonplace—some intellect more calm, more logical, and far less excitable than my own, which will perceive in the circumstances I detail with awe, nothing more than an ordinary succession of very natural causes and effects." Such a sentence can be seen as a "red flag" which challenges the reader to provide a rational explanation for the events detailed in the story.

SOME HELP FROM FREUD

Obviously, psychological readings like Gargano's and McElroy's attempt to do just that. They find the narrator unreliable and untrustworthy due either to a conscious attempt to represent himself as victim or to an unconscious denial of responsibility for his wife's murder. However, it is possible that Poe did not intend his reader to choose either the psychological or supernatural level to the exclusion of the other—but, rather, to entertain both. The possibility of this double option can be seen in relationship to Sigmund Freud's comments on E.T.A. Hoffmann's story, "The Sandman."

Hoffmann's story is complex. Essentially Nathaniel, the main character, is obsessed by the figure of "The Sandman" whom he identifies with Coppelius, his father's "friend." Coppelius is a terrifying figure for Nathaniel because he has become associated in Nathaniel's mind with "The Sandman" who, according to legend plucks out children's eyes. Nathaniel also comes to believe that Coppelius murdered his father. The story opens with Nathaniel's letter to Lothar, the brother of his betrothed sweetheart, Klara. Nathaniel, now a university student, feels he has once again seen Coppelius disguised as the Italian, Giuseppe Coppola, the sight of whom has brought back Nathaniel's long repressed fears. Coppola seems to be involved in a plot with a Professor Spalanzani to get Nathaniel to fall in love with an automaton named Olympia. Coppola and Professor Spalanzani succeed with their plan until Nathaniel discovers them fighting over the automaton. During the struggle Spalanzani throws the "robot's" eyes at Nathaniel, and because of his childhood trauma and fears, Nathaniel loses his sanity. When he recovers, he finds that Klara has nursed him back to health and is prepared to marry him. However, on an outing when the two climb a tower before their marriage, Nathaniel thinks that he once again sees Coppelius. Enraged into a frenzy, he attempts to throw Klara from the tower. Her brother Lothar rescues her, and Nathaniel, thinking that he sees Coppelius at the foot of the tower, hurls himself to his death.

Freud notices two levels in Hoffmann's story. On the supernatural level, Freud finds Nathaniel, the story's main character, to be "the horrible plaything, of dark powers." On the psychological level, Freud sees that Nathaniel is progressively deteriorating as the result of his fixation "upon his father by his castration-complex." Neil Hertz in his essay "Freud and the Sandman" notes that although these two interpretations might seem contradictory, Freud would no doubt argue that they "are linked to each other as latent to manifest, the castration-complex generates the fiction of the Sandman; the reader, even when he is most convinced of the reality of the Sandman, especially when he is most convinced, senses as uncanny the imminent return of the repressed."

While the first person narrator of "The Black Cat" does not suffer from a castration-complex, he does repress negative feelings for his wife which are then projected onto the black cat. As in Freud's analysis of "The Sandman," the latent and manifest levels of the story interplay so that when the reader is most convinced of the reality of the cat (say, for instance, when the cat howls within the wall to reveal the presence of the wife's body), what the reader is experiencing is "the imminent return of the repressed" in the narrator's consciousness. In actuality, this second black cat (an almost exact duplicate of the first cat down to its missing eye) may exist *only* in the narrator's mind, its howl being the narrator's own.

The narrator's repression of his hatred for his wife is at the root of this interplay between the supernatural and psychological levels in Poe's story. The intimation that the black cats in the story possess supernatural abilities results from the narrator's internal, psychological repression of his hatred, which both erupts in outward manifestations of what the narrator attributes to the supernatural and "*recurs*" to create a feeling in the story similar to the one Freud describes as "uncanny" in Hoffmann's tale. In other words, in "The Black Cat," it is the narrator's repression which drives his narration and is responsible for the disappearance and reappearance of the cats. Because the narrator denies his true emotion, he fabricates a supernatural level which becomes for him the manifest or surface level of the tale and which causes the narrator, like Nathaniel, to see himself as a victim of "dark powers" beyond his control.

AN UNCANNY ATMOSPHERE

Additional means for analysis of the inter-relationship between the supernatural and psychological levels in Poe's story are provided in another section of Freud's essay. This section deals with the German words, *heimlich* and *unheimlich*, which at first glance appear to be antonymous but which for Freud converge on one meaning—the idea of the uncanny. In his essay, Freud quotes the following definition of these two German words . . . from Daniel Sander's *Wörterbuch der deutschen Sprache*:

> *Heimlich*, adj.: I. Also *heimelich, heimelig*, belonging to the house, not strange, familiar, tame, intimate, comfortable, homely, etc. (a) (obsolete) belonging to the house or the family. (b) of animals: tame, companionable to man. As opposed to wild, *e.g.*, 'Wild animals . . . that are trained to the *heimlich* and accustomed to men.' 'If these young creatures are brought up from early days among men they become quite *heimlich*, friendly,' etc. (c) Friendly, intimate, homelike; the enjoyment of quite content . . . II. Concealed, kept from sight, so that others do not get to know about it, withheld from holds . . . Compounds and especially also the opposite follow meaning I. (above): *Unheimlich*, uneasy, eerie, bloodcurdling . . . "*'Unheimlich'* is the name for everything that ought to have remained . . . hidden and secret and has become visible," Schelling . . . *Unheimlich* is not often used as opposite meaning to II. (above).

I have quoted at length because of the definition's peculiar relevance to "The Black Cat's" first sentence: "For the most wild, yet most homely narrative which I am about to pen, I neither expect nor solicit belief." In light of the above definition, the odd juxtaposition of the words "homely" and "wild" seems to point to the fact that Poe may have had the word *heimlich* in mind when composing his story. Although it might be argued that Poe used the oxymoron created by these two words as a means to express the extreme emotion of the narrator, the creation of this particular oxymoron has to be seen as increasingly suggestive when put in relationship to the third and fourth sentences of the story:

> My immediate purpose is to place before the world, plainly, succinctly, and without comment, a series of mere household events. In their consequences, these events have terrified— have tortured—have destroyed me.

Poe's emphasis on the "household" nature of the events which have "terrified" the narrator also seems to imply *heimlich* and its antonym *unheimlich* through the transformation of the familiar ("belonging to the house") and ordinary (*heimlich*) into the eerie and frightening (*unheimlich*). In addition, the final sentence of the first paragraph of the story might also be seen to suggest *heimlich/unheimlich*:

> Hereafter, perhaps, some intellect may be found which will reduce my phantasm to the commonplace—some intellect more calm, more logical, and far less excitable than my own, which will perceive in the circumstances I detail with awe, nothing more than an ordinary succession of very natural succession causes and effects.

Here Poe, through the narrator, is possibly tempting the reader with the notion that fantastic and bizarre (*unheimlich*) aspects of the story can be reduced to the familiar or not strange; in short the *heimlich*.

Related to this uncovering of the ordinary in the fantastic, however, is the peculiar interplay of the first sense of *heimlich* with its second sense, an interplay suggested in the supernatural explanation which the first-person narrator's offers the reader. This "supernatural" explanation can be seen as the narrator's attempt to cover up his true motives which remain "secret" in the second sense of *heimlich*—"concealed, kept from sight, withheld from others."

In working toward a conception of "the uncanny," Freud comments on the strange interplay between the first and second senses of *heimlich*:

> What interests us most . . . is to find that among its different shades of meaning the word *heimlich* exhibits one which is identical with its opposite, *unheimlich*. What is *heimlich* thus comes to be *unheimlich*. . . . In general we are reminded that the word *heimlich* is not unambiguous, but belongs to two

sets of ideas, which without being contradictory are yet very different: on the one hand it means that which is familiar and congenial, and on the other, that which is concealed and kept out of sight.

Freud's comments on *heimlich* have definite relevance for the psychological and supernatural levels of Poe's story. The familiar (*heimlich*) through the narrator's repression becomes the psychologically latent level, secret or concealed (also *heimlich*), while the strange, haunted, supernatural level (*unheimlich*) becomes the manifest or familiar level of the story. Such an inversion of the familiar and the secret, supernatural and surface levels of the story creates much of "The Black Cat's" bizarre, uncanny atmosphere.

In light of the German pair of words, *heimlich/unheimlich*, the black cat can be seen as an externalization of the narrator's hatred of his wife. On the psychological level, the secret and clandestine part of the second sense of *heimlich* is exteriorized in the ordinary and familiar form of the domesticated cat which initially exists in the first sense ("homely") of *heimlich*. But the black cat consequently becomes more than simply a cat since it unconsciously objectifies, for the narrator, his repressed hatred. Thus, the familiar becomes strange and supernatural, and that dislocation creates in Poe's story the feeling of "*unheimlich*" or the "uncanny."

THE LIMITS OF THE RATIONAL MIND

In "The Black Cat," the reader can attempt to disregard the supernatural explanation in order to embrace the psychological only to find that the psychological is indissolvably tied to the supernatural in the surface level of the story through the exteriorization of repressed emotion (in this case the narrator's repressed hatred becomes attached to the first black cat and subsequently recurs with his creation of the second black cat). This exteriorization of repressed emotion "charges" familiar objects with hidden emotion making the familiar unfamiliar, the ordinary extraordinary. The surface level of the story takes on psychological reification and becomes, in the sense of words Poe was fond of, "*outré*" and "singular."

The application of ideas in Freud's analysis of the uncanny does indeed provide strategies useful for interpreting "The Black Cat." The interplay of the psychological and supernatural levels, as well as the relationship between the secret (*heimlich*, Sense II) and the familiar (*heimlich*, Sense I) in stories such as Hoffmann's and Poe's indicates similar processes at work. Still, as suggestive as Freud's discussion of the "uncanny" seems in application to Poe's story, it suffers from important limitations: Freud's theory, *a priori*, is based on the assumption that the rational is capable of explaining the irrational. Neither Hoffmann nor Poe wrote from this premise. Instead, "The Sandman" and "The Black Cat" are stories decidedly aimed at provoking uneasiness in the reader about the limitations of rational thought. . . . The narrator of "The Black Cat" is hopelessly filled with delusions, denials, and self-deceptions which cannot be unraveled by the rational mind. Faced with Hoffmann's and Poe's stories, a reader is likely to get the feeling of the uncanny from the recurrent exteriorization of repressed emotions in the two stories. But, this feeling is only part of the total aesthetic experience framed for the reader. For both writers, beyond the uncanny is the specter of the unknown, an unknown which will never be understood due to the inherent limitations of human faculties.

Poe's creation of an interplay between the supernatural and psychological levels in "The Black Cat" is not solely directed at revealing the narrator's self-deceptions nor in producing a feeling of the uncanny. It is also a vehicle through which he probes the intricacies of human irrationality. And here, not only its similarities to Hoffmann's "The Sandman" need noting, but also its connections to the mainstream of American literature as well. The interplay of psychological and supernatural levels in tales such as Washington Irving's "The Legend of Sleepy Hollow," Nathaniel Hawthorne's "Young Goodman Brown," or Henry James's "Turn of the Screw" suggest the subtle interweaving of the rational and irrational, latent and manifest, conscious and unconscious levels of the human psyche which Poe is also detailing.

In final analysis, Poe provokes a feeling of uneasiness in his reader about the limits of the rational mind and, in doing so, gives the irrational a power which "mainstream" American writers have recognized. Where Freud attempts rationally to analyze the irrational or uncanny, Poe is able to represent the inextricable convolutions which bind the rational to the irrational. In doing so, Poe not only elicits, rather than explains, the feeling of the uncanny, but also reveals the limitations of rational thought.

Comic Design in "The Black Cat"

John Harmon McElroy

John Harmon McElroy of the University of Arizona explores the comic design of "The Black Cat." The key to understanding the humor, McElroy says, is in Poe's use of dramatic irony, the distance between the narrative voice and authorial tone of the story. While the narrator of the story attempts to relieve his responsibility for his crimes, the reader is amused by the obvious flaws of his preposterous accounts. Many readers, however, have been drawn in by the narrator's attempts to gain their sympathy, as he obscures the moral distinctions between the silly and the vile and blames others for his actions.

The story that the axe-murderer tells in the first person in "The Black Cat" is distinctly unfunny from his perspective. He pens his manuscript from a "felon's cell" on the day before his scheduled execution ("to-morrow I die"), having been caught, the second time the police searched his house, in possession of undeniable evidence of his crime (his wife's head-cloven corpse carefully concealed in the cellar) and having been tried on that and other evidence and found guilty of murder in the first degree. He announces a wish to tell a "homely narrative," of "mere household events." But the reader of "The Black Cat" discovers that the story includes, in addition to his murder of his wife with an axe, his maiming and strangulation of a cat and the nearly fatal destruction by fire of the first home he shared with his wife. An ordinary reader, amidst his or her shudders, is likely to feel in reading a tale of so much violence that its only amusing feature is the narrator's unawareness of what properly constitutes a homely narrative.

The reason for categorizing the story as comic is that dra-

Grateful acknowledgement is made to the American Humor Studies Association for permission to reprint portions of "The Kindred Artist; or, the Case of the Black Cat," by John Harmon McElroy, *Studies in American Humor*, vol. 3, no. 2, 1976, pp. 103–16.

matic irony is its *sine qua non* [indispensable condition]. "The Black Cat" has two simultaneous perspectives: the narrative and the authorial. The discovery of these puts the reader at a distance from the narrator's concerns, places the narrator in a garish comic light, and completely dissipates that sympathetic feeling for the narrator which is the inevitable accompaniment of reading "The Black Cat" as if it had only the narrative perspective. The doomed felon appeals to our sympathies as readers. But the joking author, Edgar Allan Poe, appeals to our reason. The joke, as is so often the case in Poe's brand of humor, is intellectual. . . .

Poe constructs a manuscript containing physical anomalies and relies entirely on the kindred artistry of the reader to spot these anomalies as such, and thus to see, beyond any reasonable doubt, the difference between the narrator's assertion of his spontaneity and the proof of his premeditation. In sum, Poe's "The Black Cat" is designed, and can only be read because it was so designed, as a hoax or diddle on sentimental readers who too readily pity criminals proclaiming their innocence of malicious intent.

We may be quite certain of Poe's intention in "The Black Cat" because his well-known theory of the short story consistently emphasizes the importance of each and every detail in constructing the effect that, in his opinion, an author of a short story has to have clearly in mind before beginning the task of composition. Plot serves effect in Poe's theory, and no detail of plot can be allowed to be merely ornamental in a skillfully wrought story. Each has to bear its proper amount of stress in building toward the effect of the whole composition. Therefore, we may be sure, when we find in the text of a short story by Edgar Allan Poe two instances of dead bodies concealed in freshly plastered walls, that such a coincidence must be deliberate parts of a meaningful design.

The reader who thinks and feels that the singularity to note in "The Black Cat" is the narrator's insanity may never make the connection between the narrator's first victim (a pet cat) being immured in a freshly plastered wall and the second instance of the same thing (his immurement of his wife's corpse in another freshly plastered wall). Indeed, it may surprise some who have studied the text of this story that there is such a coincidence in it. Yet it is this detail of two freshly plastered walls concealing the bodies of two victims of the narrator's insanity that unequivocally distinguishes the authorial perspective from the narrative for those who contemplate Poe's design in "The Black Cat" with requisite kindred art.

THE NARRATOR'S LAUGHABLE FLAWS

The dramatic situation of the speaking voice must never be overlooked as being what may be thought of as the stage for the theatrics in "The Black Cat." This situation is that the narrator has been lawfully tried and found guilty of premeditated murder. This stage, or implied framework, is evident in the fact that he has not only been detected in the crime of murder but condemned to die for it. The question inherent in his condemnation for murder in the first degree is, on what evidence did the narrator's jury find him guilty of willfully planned cold-blooded murder? The answer is, on the evidence of the coincidence of fresh plasters and what was concealed in each freshly plastered wall.

The narrator admits to killing a cat (by hanging it "in cool blood"), and the carcass of this cat was immured in a freshly plastered wall behind his bed, the night before the house in which he was then living burned to the ground. But the narrator denies agency for this immurement. He sticks to the cock-and-bull explanation that he first gave impromptu to the crowd of witnesses who saw the immured cat's image in the wall. This explanation obscures the fact of the dead cat's body having been placed *inside* the wall and, as much as possible, the fact that this wall was freshly plastered shortly before the fire. The narrator's explanation of this first publicly known instance of the immurement of a victim of his insanely violent ways is full of tell-tale discrepancies. These make it finally incredible except to someone whose sympathies have been too thoroughly aroused to permit precise observation of its laughable flaws.

The particulars and sequence of details in this explanation are crucial to understanding "The Black Cat." The narrator admits that he hanged the cat in cold blood in the garden of his house. Immediately after this admission he reports the fact of the terrible conflagration that destroyed his house that night, taking particular pains to deny a connection between the hanging of the cat and the conflagration. This denial is itself meaningful because it implies his fear that someone could link these two events, which no one would normally understand as having any common link. It is also important to notice in his description of the killing of the cat his report of extreme remorsefulness over the deed. This emphasis includes the asseveration that he wept while he killed the cat. The narrator thus claims tenderness of heart even while describing the commission of a cruel deed. Also, he claims the forgiveness of both God and the reader for the deed because of his sincerity. Moreover, he claims with laughable dramatic irony that he (not the innocent cat) is the *victim*, specifically the victim of an implacable force he calls "Perverseness." From his perspective the innocence of the cat *caused* him to kill it, as earlier the cat's unoffensiveness had caused him to maim its face.

It is necessary to review the entire sequence of this passage in order to be in a position to see, believe, and discuss its designed meaning. The sequence begins with the narrator's self-justifying idea of perverseness:

> Of this spirit [of Perverseness] philosophy takes no account. Yet I am not more sure that my soul lives, than I am that perverseness is one of the primitive impulses of the human heart—one of the indivisible primary faculties, or sentiments, which give direction to the character of Man. Who has not, a hundred times, found himself committing a vile or a silly action, for no other reason than because he knows he should *not*? Have we not a perpetual inclination, in the teeth of our best judgment, to violate that which is *Law*, merely because we understand it as such? This spirit of perverseness, I say, came to my final overthrow. It was this unfathomable longing of the soul *to vex itself*—to offer violence of its own nature— to do wrong for the wrong's sake only—that urged me to continue and finally to consummate the injury I had inflicted upon the unoffending brute. One morning, in cool blood, I slipped a noose about its neck and hung it to the limb of a tree;—hung it with the tears streaming from my eyes, and with the bitterest remorse at my heart;—hung it *because* I knew that it had loved me, and *because* I felt it had given me no reason of offence;—hung it *because* I knew that in so doing I was committing a sin—a deadly sin that would so jeopardize my immortal soul as to place it—if such a thing were possible—even beyond the reach of the infinite mercy of the Most Merciful and Most Terrible God.

> On the night of the day on which this cruel deed was done, I was aroused from sleep by the cry of fire. The curtains of my bed were in flames. The whole house was blazing. It was with great difficulty that my wife, a servant, and myself, made our escape from the conflagration. The destruction was complete. My entire worldly wealth was swallowed up, and I resigned myself thenceforward to despair.

I am above the weakness of seeking to establish a sequence of cause and effect, between the disaster and the atrocity. But I am detailing a chain of facts—and wish not to leave even a possible link imperfect. On the day succeeding the fire, I visited the ruins. The walls, with one exception, had fallen in. This exception was found in a compartment wall, not very thick, which stood about the middle of the house, and against which had rested the head of my bed. The plastering had here, in great measure, resisted the action of the fire—a fact which I attributed to its having been recently spread. About this wall a dense crowd were collected, and many persons seemed to be examining a particular portion of it with very minute and eager attention. The words "strange!" "singular!" and other similar expressions, excited my curiosity. I approached and saw, as if in *bas relief* upon the white surface, the figure of a gigantic *cat*. The impression was given with an accuracy truly marvellous. There was a rope about the animal's neck.

When I first beheld this apparition—for I could scarcely regard it as less—my wonder and my terror were extreme. But at length reflection came to my aid. The cat, I remembered, had been hung in a garden adjacent to the house. Upon the alarm of fire, this garden had been immediately filled by the crowd—by some one of whom the animal must have been cut from the tree and thrown, through an open window, into my chamber. This had probably been done with the view of arousing me from sleep. The falling of other walls had compressed the victim of my cruelty into the substance of the freshly-spread plaster; the lime of which, with the flames, and the *ammonia* from the carcass, had then accomplished the portraiture as I saw it.

This crucial sequence contains several features that comically reveal the narrator's deliberate interpretation of the evidence against him in order to exculpate himself. His self-serving interpretations here, as elsewhere is his manuscript, occur despite the assertion in his introductory paragraph that "My immediate purpose is to place before the world, plainly, succinctly, *and without comment*, a series of mere household events" (italics added).

Despite his disclaimer, the narrator is obviously not presenting a plain, succinct chronology without comment. Rather, he is busy accounting each step of his way for the unaccountable fact that he, the intrinsically innocent victim, is a convicted felon awaiting execution. He attributes this woeful fact to the spirit of perverseness, and the reader who accedes to the legitimacy of this explanation accepts the narrator's point of view completely. The reader who can muster his common sense will, however, laugh at this idea as it deserves to be laughed at, and laugh, too, at the narrator's preposterous account of how the *bas relief* of the cat with the rope around its neck came to be where it was without the narrator's agency. Throughout his manuscript, the narrator pities himself and appeals for sympathy; the filament of feeling that he spins to trap the reader is his doctrine of the perverseness of human nature.

A DOCTRINE OF PERVERSENESS

The narrator identifies perverseness as a primitive impulse inherent in the nature of man, which moves all mankind, the reader included, "to do wrong for the wrong's sake." He would also have us believe, that, like him, any of us would commit a "vile or a silly action" just for the sake of the wrong and because we knew we should not; and that moreover each of us has done so "a hundred times." The common sense of the reader ought to prompt him to ask the honest question, When was the last time I committed a *vile* action just because I knew it was against the moral law of mankind to do so? The answer will be immediately clear. Far from being universal, such cruelties as gouging out the eyes of small animals or strangling them with halters is rare, although it is quite true that all men and women have at some time probably committed some *silly* act just for the sake of violating one of the lower-echelon social taboos. But the inhibitions of civilized decorums are, thankfully and definitively, too powerful to justify belief in universal vileness motivated by a spirit of perversity, however latent the potential for such "primitive" behavior may theoretically be.

The real point of the narrator's doctrine of perverseness, of course, is to justify his own sadism, and to get the reader to identify with him. The narrator wants the reader to excuse his behavior, not absolutely but comparatively, by seeing it as a type, perhaps extreme, but recognizable, a type of behavior that the reader has himself been guilty of "a hundred times." He instinctively knows that he can have the sympathy of the reader only by obscuring the great moral distinction between silliness and vileness, and by obscuring also the evidence of his own premeditation and planning of mayhem. It would seem that in too many cases he has succeeded.

In reporting his hanging of the cat, the narrator states that what he did would have jeopardized his soul "if such a thing

were possible." This is an important statement. It suggests
that forgiveness is, theologically speaking, due the narrator.
He has established to his credit that his behavior is of a kind
no worse than that of other men, and now he hints to the
reader that God forgives his behavior because fundamental
Christian theology teaches us that God will not condemn the
penitent for their sins. And the narrator was, by his own account, so penitent that he wept while he committed his "cruel
deed" against the cat. The impression left on the reader by
the narrator is that of moral sensitivity and deep regret over
his perversity. He readily admits that what he did was a great
"sin," but he committed it only as the thrall of an implacable
metaphysical force. The innocence of the cat *caused* it. He
personally was sorry all the while it was happening.

With regard to the narrator's account of the fire, we should
notice that there is no apparent need for him to make reference to the *post hoc ergo propter hoc* fallacy in reporting that
the hanging of the cat preceded the fire. This seemingly un-
warranted denial of causality should arouse suspicion.

Specifically, the reader should notice and ponder the significance of the witnessed fact that the one wall of the
burned down house that remains standing has been recently
plastered, and that on it is the perfect image of the cat with
the rope around its neck. The narrator muffles as much as
he can the fact of this fresh plaster by removing the word
"plastering" as far as he can from the tell-tale phrase "recently spread." ("The plastering had here, in great measure,
resisted the action of the fire—a fact that I attribute to its
having been recently spread.") The alert reader will also notice that this is an inner wall ("a compartment wall") and
therefore "not very thick." The location of a thin wall in the
part of the house that would be hottest in a conflagration
calls the reader's particular attention to this wall having resisted the action of the fire.

The morning following the fire the narrator visited the
site and found a gathering of people crowded around this
unique wall, with its bizarre image of a cat with a rope
around its neck. These witnesses to the existence of such a
wall are justifiably exclaiming "'strange!'" and "'singular!'"
Anyone familiar with Poe's famous theory of the short story,
and his requirement that all details have to contribute to the
designed effect of the story, should recognize the authorial
stress that is being placed on the importance of this singu-

lar wall. Poe could hardly have been more accommodating of the reader within the restrictions of his design for "The Black Cat."

The sight of this wall with its cat image fills the narrator with "wonder and terror," as well it might. For it is damning evidence against his pretended innocence of premeditated mayhem. There can be no mistaking the image, because the rope around its neck identifies it as the cat the narrator hanged the day before the fire in a garden adjacent to his house. The narrator perforce admits it is the same cat. His explanation of how its image got where it was on the wall without his agency is the funniest thing in "The Black Cat."

He would have us believe that an onlooker in attendance the night his house went up in flames did the following: perceiving the deadly danger to the house's sleeping inhabitants and spotting the carcass of a cat hanging from the limb of a tree in the garden, this Unknown cut that down and dexterously whanged it through an open window to arouse the people of the house to the fire. But wait, dear reader, there is more: this charitable flinger of cats, according to the narrator's account, hurled the carcass in a nice trajectory so that it landed (thud) and lodged between the narrator's bed (the headboard) and the freshly plastered wall against which it stood, *without waking him.* (It was not the feline fire-alarm that woke him, he says, but "the cry of fire." Never does he claim to *know* that anyone hurled the cat through his bedroom window. He merely supposes, upon "reflection," that this "must have" happened, given the indisputable image of the hanged cat where it is, an image which cries out for explanation as a uniquely baroque detail in an otherwise perfectly commonplace nineteenth-century occurrence: a house-fire.) There is still more, however, to this hypothesis. Once so nicely located between the headboard and the freshly plastered bedroom wall, the hanged cat must then have been pressed, by the action of "falling walls" (gently falling?), *into* the fresh plaster of this "not very thick" interior wall, whereupon the intense heat generated by the fire must have combined with the chemical action of the lime of the plaster in combination with the ammonia in the cat's decomposing carcass to produce the "*bas relief*" image of the cat with the rope around its neck, which the narrator and a crowd of witnesses see the next morning. The reader should be falling off his seat with laughter at this point.

DENYING THE EVIDENCE

In the first place, if all of these suppositions had serially happened, the rope could not have been reproduced because it had no ammonia in its composition. In the second place, had the first part of this happened, up to the part where the narrator supposes falling walls pressing the hanged cat *into* the fresh plaster, the carcass of the cat and the rope would both have been consumed in the fire because the thickness of plaster on an interior wall could not possibly have been thick enough to envelop such objects and keep them from burning up. But all of this is mere quibbling, compared to the great fact that the image is a *bas relief.* That is, it bulges out. It is a *raised* image, bulging from *inside* the wall. The narrator's explanation is thus no explanation at all. It is obfuscation for the sake of exculpation.

From the authorial perspective, the explanation of this *bas relief* of the hanged cat, having "an accuracy truly marvellous," which many witnesses see, and which the narrator must therefore explain, is: after hanging the cat, the narrator cut it down, took it to his bedroom, excavated a hole for it in the not very thick bedroom wall behind his bed, and replastered the wall. That night, the heat of the fire, dehydrating and shrinking the wet plaster, drew it tight over the excavated cavity containing the hanged cat, revealing its image, including the rope around its neck, in *bas relief.* This, and not what the narrator claims, is what must have happened. But the narrator was not willing to admit his agency in immuring the hanged cat.

One strongly suspects that the narrator set the fire which almost proved fatal to the narrator's wife and servant, and, he claims, himself. But there is no definite physical evidence to prove this nonessential point. What the reader does definitely know is that someone put the hanged cat inside the narrator's bedroom wall behind his bed, and then replastered the entire wall, just a few hours before a terrible fire destroyed the house. So short a time elapses between the immuring of the cat and the fire that a still large amount of water in the plastering preserved this wall when all others tumbled down or burned up. Beyond any reasonable doubt the person who hanged the cat is identical with the person who immured the cat and plastered the wall, although any reader remains free to accept the narrator's absurd hypothesis of a Good Samaritan who throws cats as fire alarms, the deft placement of the thrown cat between headboard and wet plaster, the pressure of falling walls, ammonia in a decomposing carcass combining with lime, *et cetera.* This identification of the narrator as the prime cause of the image of the hanged cat is crucial to properly understanding the later explanation that he gives of killing and immuring his wife.

The narrator is not lucky in immuring cats. They keep reemerging in various ways from the walls where he puts them. The second time occurs when he immures his wife's corpse. The live cat that he walls up with her body really is his undoing by making it impossible for him to deny agency for her death. But the narrator is game. He refuses to admit to guilt of willful mayhem. Consistent with his earlier posture of being the victim of the spirit of perverseness, a metaphysical force beyond his control, he finally says of this second cat that it *"seduced me into murder."*

The narrator would have us believe about his wife's death the following account as the complete truth:

> One day she accompanied me, upon some household errand, into the cellar of the old building which our poverty compelled us to inhabit. The cat followed me down the steep stairs, and, nearly throwing me headlong, exasperated me to madness. Uplifting an axe, and forgetting, in my wrath, the childish dread which had hitherto stayed my hand, I aimed a blow at the animal which, of course, would have proved instantly fatal had it descended as I wished. But this blow was arrested by the hand of my wife. Goaded, by the interference, into a rage more than demoniacal, I withdrew my arm from her grasp and buried the axe in her brain. She fell dead upon the spot, without a groan.

What "household errand," the reader should ask, required this husband to take his wife downcellar ("she accompanied me"), especially when the man appears to have had an axe ready at hand. (The indefinite article in the narrator's statement "Uplifting *an* axe . . ." is exquisitely exculpating.) A common household event, a cat getting tangled in the narrator's legs on a steep stairs, is what he would have us believe caused the murder of his wife, which he never intended or planned.

Furthermore, we must query the absolutely perfect condition of this cellar for purposes of concealing a corpse *at the moment of the murder.* With an evident tone of pride, the narrator recounts how he solved the problem of disposing of the corpse *after* the murder. (The question of when he solved this problem, before or after the murder, is, of course, all-important, for if he made preparations to conceal his wife's body, then his story of spontaneous manslaughter falls completely apart.) His description of how he solved this problem occupies a long passage in his manuscript. Having reasoned that he could be detected if he tried to take the body out of the house, he thought of getting rid of the evidence of his felony by dismembering and burning the corpse, or putting it in a grave in the cellar floor, or throwing it down the backyard well, or shipping it away in a box of merchandise. He rejected each of these possibilities in turn, as involving too much risk of detection, and decided finally to wall up the corpse in the cellar. For such a purpose, he says, *he discovered after the murder*, that the cellar was at that particular time particularly "well adapted." Not only does it have a disused chimney, the bricks of which could be "readily displaced," but the whole chimney could be rebuilt with the corpse inside and then plastered over "so that no eye could detect anything suspicious" because at the moment of the murder the entire cellar had "lately been plastered throughout with a rough plaster, which the dampness of the atmosphere had prevented from hardening." Therefore the fresh plaster on the chimney will be indiscernible from the fresh plaster throughout the cellar. How laughable that this could be considered fortuitous! Yet that is what the narrator expects us to believe. Probably the same readers who never notice anything extravagant (given the narrator's craziness) or important about his hypothesis on how the *bas relief* of the hanged cat got on his bedroom wall in his previous residence, without his agency, also go along unquestioningly with the narrator's claim that he discovered how admirably suited the cellar in his second house was for hiding his wife's corpse only *after* he had accidentally killed her.

FEAR OF THE HANGMAN

No matter how much "The Black Cat" may appear to be a variant of "The Tell-Tale Heart" and "The Imp of the Perverse," the resemblance among these stories is superficial. The narrator in "The Black Cat" is *not* riven by any subconscious compulsion to have his crime detected and punished. He is, quite the contrary, full of anxiety not to be detected in it. Evidence of his state of mind with regard to punishment exists in several important details of the story that are perfectly congruent.

For example, the body of the wife is *not* detected the first time the police search the narrator's house. Rather, it is found during a *second* investigation of the house. This detail is as significant as the narrator's careful preparations to hide his wife's corpse by plastering the entire cellar except for the false chimney before he axed her, because the narrator did not expect the police to make a second search: shortly after the murder, within the first three days, "a search" is "instituted." Nothing is found. On the fourth day following the murder a party of policemen come back to the house, "*very unexpectedly,*" and proceed "*again* to make rigorous investigation of the premises."

In light of these details, the question must be asked: if the murderer is riven by subconscious guilt as his sympathizers claim, why did it not compel him to do something to expose his crime during the first search of his house? Furthermore, during the second search, it is only on "the third or fourth" descent of the police into the cellar that the narrator strikes the false chimney with his cane, the place where he immured his wife (in mockery of the inability of the police to find any clue to the corpse's location). His reaction to the cat's shriek resulting from his loud disturbance of the wall shows an immediate, *subconscious* reaction far different from that of someone who wished to be detected in a crime: he staggers backward, clear across the cellar, in surprise and mortal fear at this feline yowl from inside the wall ("Swooning, I staggered to the opposite wall"). The narrator's evident sense of having triumphantly baffled the police in their second thorough search of the house, and their third or fourth investigation of the cellar during this search, turns in a twinkle into a complete debacle. The narrator had forgotten that the cat could stay alive inside the false chimney by feeding off the corpse.

The narrator's subconscious fear of detection and punishment for his contemplated murder of his wife is manifested in more than his reaction to the cat's unexpected yowl from within the wall. He is so afraid of the hangman that he sees a gallows on the breast of the second black cat, the one he walled up with the corpse of his wife; and he says that she pointed it out to him. Indeed there is a strong implication that the two black cats in the narrator's married life are subconsciously surrogates for his hostility toward his spouse, because he is afraid of the consequences of killing her.

Again the narrator has miscalculated, as he did in killing and immuring the first cat. This time he either walled up the cat inadvertently, which is not very likely to have happened to a cat, or he walled up the animal deliberately, thinking it would die in the wall. . . . In either case, the narrator bungled his planned murder. Whether the murderer knew the cat was in the wall is not nearly so important as his startled reaction at its lively cry when he raps the wall. . . .

One should never overlook in reading "The Black Cat" that it is a remembered action and that the narrator is not free to invent episodes. He is only free to rationalize them. What he is not free to invent are the matters of public information at his trial, principally the public knowledge of the *bas relief* of the hanged cat in the freshly plastered wall of his first residence, his wife's corpse immured with another cat in the freshly plastered cellar of his second residence, and probably, too, his history of drunkenness and physical violence against his wife. These are things the narrator has to deal with as best he can to get the reader's sympathy. They are the coordinates, the givens, of the dramatic framework of this fiction as Poe designed it. . . .

In "The Black Cat" we have an application of Poe's theory of partnership in "true originality" between writer and reader, for the thought behind "The Black Cat" is the commonplace truth that wrongdoers tend to put the blame for their action on others or on circumstances. But the form in which this commonplace is worked up by Poe in "The Black Cat" gives the reader who is able to appreciate it the double pleasure of not only being able to agree to a truism but having that truism so originally presented as to create an illusion of having discovered its truth with the author.

Evil Eye: A Motive for Murder in "The Tell-Tale Heart"

B.D. Tucker

Writing for the *Southern Literary Journal*, B.D. Tucker explains how the narrator's hatred of his victim's eye drives him to murder in "The Tell-Tale Heart." The old man's eye is symbolic of the "evil eye," the Cyclops, the single eye on the reverse side of the Great Seal of the United States, or even the eye of God. It is an all-seeing, all-knowing eye, by which the narrator feels threatened and wishes to remain unseen.

Poe's tale, "The Tell-Tale Heart," is one of his most perfectly constructed stories, and a very skillful study of madness. In such a tale it is futile to look for logical motivation, but an author as acute as Poe would, nevertheless, not choose a completely arbitrary point on which the madman's rage would be focused. Yet the tale itself seems to give no clue. The insane narrator specifically says: "Object there was none. Passion there was none. I loved the old man. He had never wronged me. He had never given me insult. For his gold I had no desire. I think it was his eye!"

What was it that caused the eye of the old man to become a fixation, a monomania for the madman, just as Berenice's teeth has been for Egaeus? Since we know hardly anything about the madman himself, we are forced to ask why the author chose precisely this object on which to fix the rage in the character of his creation.

Eyes obviously had a certain fascination for Poe, as we see in the long description of the eyes of Ligeia. According to John Ingram, "Ligeia" was first suggested "by a dream in which a woman's eyes inspired him with the intense emotions which he described in the fourth paragraph of the tale." Marie Bonaparte states that "the eyes which he saw in

Excerpted from "'The Tell-Tale Heart,' and the 'Evil Eye,'" by B.D. Tucker, *The Southern Literary Journal*, Spring 1981. Copyright © 1981 by the University of North Carolina Press. Reprinted with permission from the publisher.

his dreams . . . are those which, in the miniature of Elizabeth Arnold, turn their strange wide gaze upon us and were to make their adorer, Edgar, a fetishist of eyes."

But there were other eyes: not those of a beautiful woman; not those of his adored but forever lost mother, that fascinated Poe, not with adoration but with fear and terror. In one of his earliest poems, "Sonnet To Science," Poe writes of the "peering eyes" of Science, which is a vulture preying "upon the poet's heart." In "The Tell-Tale Heart" the narrator tells us how he opened his lantern slightly so that "a single dim ray, like the thread of the spider, shot from out the crevice and fell full upon the vulture eye." He also states that the old man "had the eye of a vulture—a pale blue eye, with a film over it. Whenever it fell upon me, my blood ran cold; and so by degrees—very gradually—I made up my mind to take the life of the old man, and thus rid myself of the eye forever." Besides the vulture eye, Poe elsewhere gives us the horse's eye which frightens young Metzengerstein, and—most fearful of all—the solitary eye of "The Black Cat."

Superstitions about "the Evil Eye" are, as Thomas Mabbott notes, widespread, but it does not seem to be superstition that preys upon the mind of the narrator. Although he does refer to it once as "his Evil Eye," he does not seem to fear it or suppose that any evil will come to him as a result of it. It seems to be hatred rather than fear that he feels.

The equating of "the Evil Eye" with "the evil 'I'" of the narrator has been noted by several critics and cannot have escaped Poe's attention. Like William Wilson, the madman is killing his own *doppelganger*, and the further identification with his victim is found in his feeling the old man's terror as if it were his own, and his fantasy that he can actually hear the old man's heart in his own heartbeat. Guilt is a major theme of the tale, and the attack on the objectification of the self fits in well.

HATRED OF THE SYMBOLIC SINGLE EYE

It should be noted that Poe speaks only of a single eye. . . . Now it is poetic convention to speak of "the eye" when we mean "the eyes," and we immediately recall, in this connection, Coleridge's *Ancient Mariner.*

> It is an ancient Mariner
> And he stoppeth one of three.
> "By thy long grey beard and glittering eye,

Now wherefore stopp'st thou me?"...

He holds him with his glittering eye—
The Wedding-Guest stood still,
And listens like a three-years' child
The Mariner hath his will.

Yet, while there is no suggestion that the ancient mariner had only one eye, the reader is left with the impression that Poe's old man may indeed have been a one-eyed specter.

When we search for one-eyed prototypes, the Cyclops comes at once to mind, and the extinction of his one eye through the fearful deed of Odysseus is, of course, a kind of parallel. But the resemblance between the frail old man and the Homeric giant is too remote to make this parallel very suggestive. One-eyed Odin is seen as a possible forerunner of the old-man by Marie Bonaparte and Daniel Hoffman, but again there is little to make the connection between the two. For the narrator, who says that he loved the old man, the vulture eye seems to have an existence of its own apart from the old man.

There is another image of a single eye with which Poe must have been familiar. It is on the reverse side of the Great Seal of the United States, and is most frequently seen by Americans today on the one dollar bill in current use. To many people it may seem to have a strange, disturbing, surrealistic appearance.

William Barton of Philadelphia is given credit for this design which was adopted in 1782. The face of the seal shows the familiar American eagle displayed, in a rather fierce pose, facing left, so that only one eye is visible. (It does not look very much like a vulture.) It is rather the reverse side which holds the attention with its mysterious design. A truncated pyramid, consisting of thirteen courses of stone, representing the thirteen original states, is surmounted by an eye, enclosed in a triangle, surrounded by a glory proper. Above the design are the words, "*Annuit Coeptis*" (He/She has approved our undertaking), and below it "*Novus Ordo Seclorum*" (A new order of the ages).

The eye represents, of course, the watchful Eye of Providence, and the triangle is a traditional symbol of the Triune God. What gives this a rather disturbing appearance is that the eye is not merely a symbolical representation of heraldry, but an exceedingly realistic portrayal of a real eye which seems to be looking out with a penetrating and searching stare. One could imagine that for a mentally or emotionally unbalanced person this specter might be frightening, and even terrifying, suggesting a vindictive and avenging judge or father, from whom there is no escape.

A DESIRE TO REMAIN UNSEEN

The idea of an all-seeing eye, peering at one, even during one's most secret moments, is indeed disturbing. Like the narrator of this tale, Poe wished to be the seer, not the seen. If there were exhibitionist tendencies, they were usually suppressed or disguised, although "the Imp of the Perverse," which caused many of his characters to betray themselves, as in this tale, may itself be thought of as a form of exhibitionism. There is something like the voyeur in Dupin, who boasted, "with a low chuckling laugh, that most men, in respect to himself, wore windows in their bosoms."

Certainly the narrator of "The Tell-Tale Heart" shows himself a voyeur and a secret listener, and his lantern with its lid and single ray is itself a symbolic eye. But this voyeur-narrator did not wish to be seen or heard in the dark, and he goes to insane lengths to conceal himself from the old man, whose vulture eye, nevertheless, poses a threat. The power of this orb is suggested in the extraordinary statement that "no human eye—not even *his*—could have detected any wrong." Granted this is a negative statement, it still implies that the old man's eye had exceptional penetration to discover secret sin; and note that this assertion is made after his corpse has been dismembered and all traces of the crime removed.

Though no *human* eye could see the traces of the crime, there was an eye which could. It was the Eye of God, depicted in strange and disembodied aspect on the Great Seal, from whose all-judging surveillance there is no escape. This thought would have been particularly distressing to the narrator and his secret ways. And if the image of the triangle enclosing the all-seeing eye had also come to his mind, it also would have seemed to have had a mysterious and threatening significance.

"The Tell-Tale Heart" Is a Nightmare About Death

John W. Canario

John W. Canario of San Jose State College argues that in "The Tell-Tale Heart" the mad narrator relates a nightmare he has had about death. From this perspective, the old man in the story is the narrator's alter ego, a part of himself for which he has feelings of both love and hate. The "vulture eye" in the story serves as a symbol of the narrator's own mortality. He tries to conquer the eye in his dream, to triumph over death, but he wakes to the sound of his own beating heart and his own mortality.

Hervey Allen observed in a footnote to *Israfel* that the logic of Poe's stories is "the mad rationalization of a dream." This observation is especially applicable to "The Tell-Tale Heart," which becomes fully understandable only when the narrator is recognized as the deranged victim of an hallucinatory nightmare.

Most commentators on the story have praised it either for its powerful evocation of terror or its artistically skillful revelation by degrees of the narrator as a homicidal maniac. Arthur Hobson Quinn's description of the story as "a study of terror" and "a companion piece to 'The Pit and the Pendulum'" exemplifies the first view. E. Arthur Robinson's close analysis of Poe's handling of two psychological themes in the story—"the indefinite extension of subjective time" and "the murderer's psychological identification with the man he kills"—illustrates the second view. Without denying the value of either of these widely held perspectives, I would like to suggest that Poe, on the most subtle level of his artistic aims, intended the tale of the narrator to be recognized finally as a madman's confession of a nightmare about death.

Excerpted from "The Dream in 'The Tell-Tale Heart,'" by John W. Canario, *English Language Notes*, March 1970. Reprinted with permission from the author.

To understand the story as the relation of a dream, one must respond to suggestions of parallel situations and symbolic meanings in the action and imagery. That the narrator is reporting the events of a nightmare rather than actual happenings is not immediately discernible because the narrator himself is unable to separate fact from fancy. However, the hallucinatory nature of the events he relates becomes steadily clearer as he describes his victim and the circumstances of the supposed murder.

THE NARRATOR AND HIS DOUBLE

From the beginning of the story, the narrator's description of his relationship with the old man gradually gives rise to the suspicion that the old man is really an alter ego representing a side of the narrator toward which he feels ambivalent emotions of love and hate. This possibility is initially suggested by the narrator's statement, that he loves the old man and by the fact that he lives in intimate association with him, but it is soon thereafter given more support by other developments. The narrator admits, for example, that he has experienced the same mortal terror as the old man, that he has groaned in the identical manner, and that he has undergone this experience again and again just at midnight, the time which he has chosen for his observations of the old man. Finally, the suspicion that the narrator and the old man are doubles becomes a certainty when the narrator complains of the loudness with which the old man's heart is beating. It is the increasing loudness of this beating heart, expressive of mounting emotion, that precipitates the narrator's leap upon his victim. Significantly, at this instant the murderer and the old man cry out simultaneously.

The discovery that the two characters are doubles raises the question as to what the narrator's desire to kill his alter ego means. The narrator announces very early in his confession that it is not the old man he wishes to do away with, but one of his eyes: "the eye of a vulture—a pale blue eye, with a film over it." The narrator's obsession with this eye soon makes it apparent that he fears it not simply because it is ugly, but because he sees it as an emblem of his own mortality. That the eye is a symbol of death is suggested by its resemblance to the eyes of a corpse, by the fact that it belongs to an old man, and by the narrator's association of it with a vulture.

The identification of the narrator and the old man as doubles establishes that the narrator's account of the manner in which he killed the old man must be the report of a dream: "In an instant I dragged him to the floor, and pulled the heavy bed over him. I then smiled gaily, to find the deed so far done. But, for many minutes, the heart beat on with a muffled sound." In the symbolism of this dream, the old man can be seen to stand for the physical body of the dreamer, and the narrator to represent the mind and will of that body. Thus, the dream, which is hardly plausible as the description of a real murder, really objectifies the speaker's belief that he has destroyed his body and thereby escaped from death.

The narrator's elaborate preparations for the crime also establish that he is obsessed by a fear of death. His excessive concern with time ("it took me an hour," "seven long nights—every night just at midnight" "just at twelve," "a watch's minute hand moves more quickly than did mine," etc.) and his nightly visits to the room of the old man, during each of which he permitted only a single ray of light from his darkened lantern to shine upon his victim's face, are soon recognized as assisting in no practical way the accomplishment of the murder. On the other hand, these preparations, which are proudly held up by the narrator as evidences of his sanity, are really symbolic expressions of his insane conviction that he has indeed escaped from time and mortality through his own cunning.

The story ends with the narrator's anguished discovery that the old man's heart has resumed beating in thunderously loud pulsations, even after his body has been dismembered and stuffed under the floor. What is actually revealed is the narrator's sudden, horrified discovery, at the very moment when his exultation over his fantasy conquest of death is most intense, that he is still mortal. The narrator terminates his confession in mad ravings to three police officers who, having been attracted to the house by its occupant's scream in the night, are only waiting for conclusive evidence of the man's insanity before taking him into custody.

A Link to *Macbeth* in "The Tell-Tale Heart"

Robert McIlvaine

Robert McIlvaine of Slippery Rock State College highlights the allusions to *Macbeth* in "The Tell-Tale Heart." The narrator, for instance, not only refers to his victim's eye as "the damned spot," but also refers to his victim as the "old man," details reminiscent of Lady Macbeth's famous soliloquy. These and other similarities between the works suggest that Poe, consciously or otherwise, was influenced by *Macbeth* when he wrote his tale.

To my knowledge, no commentator on Edgar Allan Poe's short story "The Tell-Tale Heart" has remarked the narrator's reference to the eye of the old man he is just about to kill as "the damned spot." Almost inevitably, it seems to me, these words remind the reader of Lady Macbeth's line, "Out, damned spot!" in her famous sleepwalking scene in *Macbeth* (Act V, Scene 1). In this context it also seems significant that Lady Macbeth's soliloquy which begins, "Out, damned spot!" ends with the sentence, "Yet who would have thought the old man to have had so much blood in him?" I believe that this is the single place in the play where Duncan is referred to as "the old man," the only name given to the murder victim in Poe's story. While Lady Macbeth is not able to wash the imaginary blood off her hands, Poe's narrator seems to have learned from her experience. After dismembering the corpse of the old man he boasts, "There was nothing to wash out— no stain of any kind—no blood-spot whatever. I had been too wary for that. A tub had caught all—ha! ha!" Though Poe's narrator does not imagine that he has blood on his hands, as does Lady Macbeth, or that he sees a dagger or Banquo's ghost, as does Macbeth, he does imagine that he hears the beating of his victim's heart constantly growing louder. This,

Excerpted from "A Shakespearean Echo in 'The Tell-Tale Heart,'" by Robert McIlvaine, *American Notes and Queries*, November 1976. Reprinted with permission from the author.

of course, is what gives him away to the police. Like Macbeth and Lady Macbeth, he is tortured by hallucinations induced by the workings of his guilt-maddened brain.

UNCONSCIOUS INFLUENCE

These striking parallels, and other similarities, suggest that the murder of Duncan by Macbeth and Lady Macbeth was in Poe's mind when he was writing "The Tell-Tale Heart." Since the scene in which Duncan is murdered (Act 11, Scene 11), and Lady Macbeth's sleepwalking scene, are two of the best-known scenes in all of English literature, and since Poe was certainly well-acquainted with Shakespeare's plays, I would suggest that the influence was probably unconscious. Although it seems there are no obvious intentional references to *Macbeth* in "The Tell-Tale Heart," and a reading of "The Tell-Tale Heart" does not immediately suggest kinship with Shakespeare's great tragedy, upon careful examination there are enough significant parallels to make it likely that Poe's tale was influenced by his subconsciously remembered readings of *Macbeth*.

Like Duncan, the old man of Poe's tale is murdered in his bed by a supposed loyal friend who steals in upon him just after midnight. Macbeth is actually Duncan's kinsman, and it is likely that the murderer-narrator of Poe's tale is related to his victim. Poe's narrator sets to work with "dissimulation," saying, "I was never kinder to the old man than during the whole week before I killed him." Similarly, Macbeth treats Duncan with great hospitality and kindness before the murder, telling Lady Macbeth that they must "mock the time with fairest show./ False face must hide what the false heart doth know." Poe's narrator claims, "I loved the old man," and Macbeth at least feigns a "violent love" for Duncan. The narrator of "The Tell-Tale Heart" states that "Passion there was none" in the murder, and Macbeth's murder of Duncan is even more cold-blooded because it is much more rational.

As Macbeth leaves Duncan's chamber he calls to his wife, "Who's there? What ho!" When the old man in Poe's tale is awakened by the sound of the narrator's lantern he cries, "Who's there?" The old man's "fears" keep him lying awake (or so his murderer imagines). Duncan's two grooms (who are themselves later murdered by Macbeth) are awakened, as Macbeth tells his wife, by "their fear," and lie listening and praying in the dark before they fall back to sleep. After the murder, when Macbeth asks his wife if she heard a noise, she replies, "I heard the owl scream and the crickets cry." When the old man awakens after hearing a noise, the narrator of Poe's tale speculates that he is trying to convince himself that what he heard was "merely a cricket which has made a single chirp."

Immediately after the murder of Duncan, when Macbeth and Lady Macbeth are leaving false clues so that the grooms will be blamed for the crime, and washing the incriminating blood from their own hands, they are startled by "a knocking at the south entry." The early morning knockers are Macduff and Lennox, who will discover the guilt of the Macbeths and avenge the death of Duncan. Similarly, just as the murderer in "The Tell-Tale Heart" finishes hiding all signs of the murder, at four in the morning, he hears "a knocking at the street door" by the police who will apprehend him.

Like Macbeth and his wife, Poe's narrator attempts to prove his innocence by his bold and confident actions on the morning following the murder. However, he is not able to hide his guilt indefinitely. His hallucinations, like those of the Macbeths, reveal his guilt to those who witness them. While Poe's narrator is mad from the beginning of the story, Macbeth and Lady Macbeth seem to be gradually driven mad by the guilt of their crimes.

The overall pattern of the two murders seems too close to be attributed to coincidence. This similarity of overall pattern, the general concern with blood spots in both narratives, and the recurrence of the "damned spot" and "old man" from Lady Macbeth's sleepwalking scene in Poe's story, all strongly suggest that *Macbeth* influenced Poe's conception and composition of "The Tell-Tale Heart."

CHAPTER 3

Journeys into Terror

READINGS ON

THE SHORT STORIES OF
EDGAR ALLAN POE

Echoes of Mary Shelley's *Frankenstein* in "MS. Found in a Bottle"

Don G. Smith

Don G. Smith of Eastern Illinois University discusses the similarities between Mary Shelley's *Frankenstein* and Poe's "MS. Found in a Bottle." Smith notes that the phrase "darkness and distance" appears in the final scenes of each work and is used to evoke a mood of desolation. Other parallels between the stories exist in the types of journeys their narrators embark on, their relationship with their respective families, and their desire to have their stories told.

In a discussion of the influence of Mary Shelley's "A Dirge" upon Poe's "To One in Paradise," Muriel Spark asserts that "Poe must have read and admired *Frankenstein*." An examination of common elements in *Frankenstein* and Poe's "MS. Found in a Bottle" suggests that Shelley's novel may have served, along with other sources, as an inspiration for Poe's prize-winning short story. . . .

DARKNESS AND DISTANCE AND OTHER PARALLELS

One important parallel is the appearance of the phrase "darkness and distance" in the final paragraph of both works. Shelley uses it in the novel's final sentence to signify all we know about the ultimate fate of the monster: "He was soon borne away by the waves and lost in the darkness and distance. Poe uses the phrase in the final paragraph of his short story, where it evokes a similar mood of desolation:

> Oh, horror upon horror!—the ice opens suddenly to the right, and to the left, and we are whirling dizzily, in immense concentric circles, round and round the borders of a gigantic ampitheatre, the summit of whose walls is lost in the *darkness and the distance*.

Excerpted from "Shelley's *Frankenstein:* A Possible Source for Poe's 'MS. Found in a Bottle,'" by Don G. Smith, *Poe Studies*, June–December 1992. Reprinted with permission.

Obviously, this suggestive parallel could be coincidental. For example, Poe uses "darkness" and "distance" in close conjunction in "Al Aaraaf" with no apparent debt to *Frankenstein*. Yet textual comparisons reveal other, reinforcing parallels, the strongest of which follow.

Robert Walton, the narrator in *Frankenstein*, is embarking on a journey of discovery to the North Pole. In letters to his sister, Walton reveals that he is driven to these "undiscovered solitudes" in order to learn of the "wondrous power that attracts the needle; and may regulate a thousand celestial observations, that require only this voyage to render their seeming eccentricities consistent forever." He wants to "satiate [his] ardent curiosity with the sight of a part of the world never before visited." Such promise, he says, is "sufficient to conquer all fear of danger and death." Walton continues, "Nothing contributes so much to tranquilize the mind as a steady purpose—a point on which the soul may fix an intellectual eye." Of course, Dr. Frankenstein, whom Walton will rescue near the pole, is also an intellectual whose life's work has been the search for hitherto unknown knowledge. Walton and Frankenstein are similar in other ways. Walton writes his sister, "I have no friend, Margaret: when I am glowing with success there will be none to participate in my joy; if I am assailed by disappointment, no one will endeavor to sustain me in dejection." Walton must be content to commit his thoughts to paper. And Frankenstein, also isolated and without friends, must be content to relate his tale of woe only to a stranger, Walton.

Poe's anonymous narrator mirrors Walton and Frankenstein in several ways. Like the latter, he is "estranged" from both his family and country. Like Walton, he is a man of intellectual temperament, not given to flights of fancy: "Upon the whole no person could be less liable than myself to be led away from the severe precincts of truth by the *ignes fatui* of superstition." Through a series of mishaps at sea, he finds himself aboard a ghost ship on a voyage of discovery toward the South Pole, the opposite of Walton's destination, but a pole nonetheless. As will be seen, both Walton and Poe's narrator share similar attitudes toward the dangers of their journeys.

At a critical point in his tale, Walton reports that his ship is walled in by ice: "I am surrounded by mountains of ice, which admit no escape, and threaten every moment to crush my vessel." With the aid of Frankenstein, he tries to convince the frightened crew to continue north if their ship is freed rather than to retreat for home: "How all this will terminate, I know not, but I had rather die than return shamefully,—my purpose unfulfilled." As he predicts, the promise of discovery does indeed prove strong enough to conquer his fear of danger and death. At the end of Poe's tale, the narrator is trapped aboard a ship in a similar physical environment: "about a league on either side of us, may be seen, indistinctly and at intervals, stupendous ramparts of ice, towering away into the desolate sky, and looking like the walls of the universe." Though he is being drawn amidst these mountains of ice into the grasp of a deadly whirlpool, his curiosity to discover the truth in the face of death parallels that of Walton:

> To conceive of the horror of my sensations is, I presume, utterly impossible; yet a curiosity to penetrate the mysteries of these awful regions, predominates even over my despair, and will reconcile me to the most hideous aspect of death. It is evident that we are hurrying onwards to some exciting knowledge—some never-to-be-imparted secret, whose attainment is destruction.

Both narrators resolve that, if necessary, their stories will be told in spite of their deaths, Walton's through his letters and Poe's narrator's through the manuscript he places in a bottle. Walton is, of course, spared, while Poe's narrator perishes in the whirlpool.

To summarize, the phrase "darkness and distance" evokes similar moods in the final paragraphs of these two works. Their narrators possess similar backgrounds, interests, and temperaments; both are on voyages of polar discovery on ships that become threatened amidst mountains of ice; and both find their fear of death overcome by their desire to discover the truth. There are other major similarities as well, which can be explained partially by the fact that Samuel Coleridge's *Rime of the Ancient Mariner* functioned as a source for both tales, partially by the generic similarities of narratives of polar exploration. But based upon the evidence, closer scrutiny of Poe's knowledge and use of *Frankenstein* seems warranted.

"A Descent into the Maelström" Can Be Read as a Tall Tale

Fred Madden

Fred Madden is associate professor of English at Ithaca College. He has published articles on Ken Kesey, Joseph Conrad, Lewis Carroll, Sherwood Anderson, and others. Madden defines "A Descent into the Maelström" as a tall tale, as evidenced by the narrator's excessive emotionality, the inconsistencies of the old-timer's account of his experiences, and Poe's use of true facts from the *Encyclopedia Britannica* that help dupe the unsuspecting reader into believing the yarn.

In comparison with the attention given many of Poe's tales, criticism on "A Descent into the Maelstrom" is scant. The most definitive articles have dealt with Poe's sources. In recent years, critical commentary has regarded the tale as a serious treatment of the problems of human understanding, possibly with transcendental implications. But the specter of Baudelaire's early, astute assessment of Poe as "a trickster" and the growing critical acknowledgment of the number and variety of Poe's hoaxes, parodies, and burlesques cannot easily be dismissed. Tonal ambiguities and authorial distance make reading much of Poe's canon rife with pitfalls. "A Descent into the Maelstrom" is no exception; its illogicalities and exaggerations, its narrative structure, and Poe's familiarity with the types of humorous stories which appeared in magazines in the late 1820s and 1830s suggest a tall tale in which "the old-timer" deceives a "tenderfoot." Poe's use of the tall tale as a schema for "A Descent into the Maelstrom" may have resulted from an artistic impulse similar to the one which gave rise to hoaxes like "Hans Phaall"—a radical skepticism about the possibility of ever arriving at the truth.

Excerpted from "'A Descent into the Maelström': Suggestions of a Tall Tale," by Fred Madden, *Studies in the Humanities*, December 1987. Reprinted with permission from *Studies in the Humanities*.

"A Descent into the Maelstrom" plays on a number of epistemological factors which distort truth: the excessive emotionality of the "green" first-person narrator's perspective, the numerous inconsistencies in the "old-timer's" account of his experience which masquerades as truth, and Poe's use of verisimilitude to gull the unwary reader.

Resembling the ironic narrators of "A Predicament" or "Berenice," the tall tale's "tenderfoot" in "A Descent into the Maelstrom," is agitated, timorous, and nervous. Poe makes a fool of this romantically excessive narrator, in part by having him listen without objection to the "old-timer's" preposterous story which contains numerous exaggerations, illogicalities, and physical impossibilities. The tale begins with the old-timer asking the narrator to believe "an event such as never happened before to mortal man." Not only that, but the old man presents an improbable and inconsistent self-portrait:

> "You suppose me a very old man—but I am not. It took less than a single day to change these hairs from a jetty black to white, to weaken my limbs, and to unstring my nerves, so that I tremble at the least exertion, and am frightened at a shadow. Do you know I can scarcely look over this little cliff without getting giddy?"

While an extraordinary change of hair color might be possible, the reader is also asked to believe that the old-timer can view a sheer unobstructed precipice of black shining rock, some fifteen or sixteen hundred feet from the crags beneath as a "little cliff." The "old man" who claims to be "frightened at a shadow" carelessly throws himself down to rest at the edge of this cliff so that "the weightier portion of his body hung over it, while he was only kept from falling by the tenure of his elbow on its extreme and slippery edge." Within the first two paragraphs of the tale Poe forces a choice: should the reader believe the old man, who says he is "broken" and "frightened" while nonchalantly perched on the precarious edge of a slippery cliff, or the narrator who is "so deeply excited by the perilous position of [his] companion, that [he] fell at full length upon the ground, clung to the shrubs around [him], and dared not even glance upward at the sky?"

A TOUCH OF TRUTH

This contradictory and bizarre picture of the unruffled "old-timer" and the foolish, terrified "tenderfoot" is followed by Poe's almost word-for-word description of his source material from the 1797 edition of the *Encyclopedia Britannica*. This material serves two purposes. First, it gives the tale "verisimilitude" which, as Constance Rourke says in discussing "Hans Phaall," is an essential feature of the tall tale: "With its carefully prepared verisimilitude even to effects of costuming, with its intense stress on all outward sensation, 'Hans Phaall' [bears] a close resemblance to the more elaborate and finished tall tales of the West, which were scrupulous as to detail." Rourke is right to notice the importance of verisimilitude as a necessary part of the tall tale. But her discussion of "Hans Phaall" does not adequately separate the "tall tale" from "the hoax," a literary form that also promotes the appearance of truth. Here G.R. Thompson's definition seems germane: "A literary hoax attempts to persuade the reader not merely of the reality of false events but of false literary intentions or circumstances—that a work is by a certain writer or of a certain age when it is not, or that one is writing a serious Gothic story when one is not. The laugh of the hoaxer is rather private, intended at best for a limited coterie of followers." In "A Descent into the Maelstrom," Poe is not attempting to convince the reader of "false literary intentions" which will only be understood by "a limited coterie of followers." Instead the tale depends upon a verisimilitude which leads readers to recognize that they are being "sold." This recognition is necessary to understand the darker implications Poe had in mind and to which the motto of the tale alludes.

The second purpose for Poe's inclusion of his source material, which he introduces as an account by "Jonas Ramus" is to provide a means for the astute reader to gauge the exaggerations of the romantic narrator and the prevarications of the old-timer. On the one hand, it appears that the terrified narrator does not trust the old-timer's account: "I could not help smiling at the simplicity with which the honest Jonas Ramus records, as a matter difficult of belief, the anecdotes of the whales and the bears [that were caught in the maelstrom], for it appeared to me, in fact, a self-evident thing, that the largest ships of the line in existence, coming within the influence of that deadly attraction, could resist it as little as a feather the hurricane, and must disappear bodily and at once." Downplaying Ramus's account for its inability to describe the terror of the maelstrom and, at the same time, giving Ramus the tag "honest" creates problems.

Should the reader believe the seemingly understated comments of Jonas Ramus or the exaggerated ones of the first-person narrator?

Furthermore, the reader who questions the narrator's exaggerations in relationship to Poe's sources must also question the "old-timer's" story from the perspective of the source material. One glaring inconsistency between the Encyclopedia's account and the old man's is built up from a passage early in the tale:

> "The island in the distance," resumed the old man, "is called by the Norwegians Vurrgh. The one midway is Moskoe. That a mile to the northward is Ambaaren. Yonder are Islesen, Hotholm, Keildhelm, Suarven, and Buckholm. Further off— between Moskoe and Vurrgh—are Otterholm, Flimen, Sanflesen, and Stockholm. These are the true names of the places— but why it has been thought necessary to name them at all, is more than either you or I can understand."

The listing of the islands creates factual authenticity, but why the old-timer questions the naming of the islands seems obscure until Poe provides two further passages which put the above quotation in a new light. The first passage comments on the impassable channel above Moskoe: "'Between Lofoden and Moskoe,' he says, 'the depth of the water is between thirty-six and forty fathoms; but on the other side, toward Ver [Vurrgh] this depth decreases so as not to afford a convenient passage for a vessel, without the risk of splitting on the rocks, which happens even in the calmest weather.'" Yet the old-timer supposedly fishes in this channel: "'Myself and my two brothers once owned a schooner-rigged smack of about seventy tons burthen, with which we were in the habit of fishing among the islands beyond Moskoe, nearly to Vurrgh.'" A few pages later, when the old man is about to describe the boat's actual movement into the maelstrom, his words recall the above passage: "'You perceive that in crossing the Strom channel, we always went a long way up above the whirl, even in the calmest weather.'" The reader, through the inconsistency between source and story, should begin to see the whopper the old man is telling; the repetition of "in the calmest weather" provides a cue.

THE LIMITATIONS OF HUMAN KNOWLEDGE

Tall tales frequently have a narratorial frame. Botkin calls it "a traditional device." Blair is more specific about the frame: "'a framework' pictures a storyteller spinning his yarn and an audience listening, while within this framework a narrative is quoted directly." Although Blair notes that the tall tale developed along "regional, historical, and fantastical" lines, Poe's main concern in adapting this "traditional device" is epistemological. This emphasis in "A Descent into the Maelstrom" is underscored by the story's opening inscription, which Poe attributes to Joseph Glanville: "The ways of God in Nature, as in Providence, are not as our ways; nor are the models that we frame in any way commensurate to the vastness, profundity, and unsearchableness of His works, which have a depth in them greater than the well of Democritus." Although Woodberry notices that Poe's motto for the story is not an exact rendering of the original, the context in which Glanville presents the passage is crucial. The quotation appears in an essay called "Against Confidence in Philosophy" in a section designated "the CAUSES of our Ignorance, and Mistakes." "Against Confidence in Philosophy" is a reworking of two of Glanville's earlier works, *The Vanity of Dogmatizing* and *Scepsis Scientifica.* Whether Poe knew these other works is not certain, but it is interesting to note that the earlier chapter in both books, out of which the above quotation was derived, was "The cause of the Shortness of our Knowledge, viz. the depth of verity discours't of, as of its admixtion in mens Opinions with falsehood, and the connexion of truths, and their mutual dependence." The passage relevant to Poe's motto is as follows:

> And first, one cause of the little we *know* may be, that Knowledge lies deep, and is therefore difficult; and so not the acquist of every careless Inquirer. Democritus his Well hath a (depth), and Truth floats not. The useless froth swims on the surface; but the Pearl lies cover'd with a mass of Waters. Verisimilitude and Opinion are an easie purchase; and these counterfeits are all the Vulgars treasure: But true Knowledge is as dear in acquisition, as rare in possession. . . . And 'tis the more difficult to find out Verity, because it is in such inconsiderable proportions scattered in a mass of opinionative uncertainty; like the Silver in Hiero's Crown of Gold: And it is no easie piece of *Chymistry* to reduce them to their unmixed selves.

"A Descent into the Maelstrom" might be viewed as an artistic rendering of an attitude, similar to Glanville's, about the limitations of human knowledge. Poe asks the reader to examine the verisimilitude and opinions of his narrators in order to come to the conclusion that both are untrustworthy and that "true knowledge is dear in acquisition." If the reader has been fooled until the last sentence of the tale, the tale does provide further insight into human failings, limitations, and gullibility. Although Glanville did not see himself as a skeptic since he, underneath all his questioning, believed in God, his stance toward knowledge emphasized man's limitations. . . .

Poe's tales often suggest the same sort of opinion of man's infirmities and limitations. His hoaxes, satires, parodies, burlesques, and tall tales result from his sense that we cannot know the truth and we are easily duped by falsehoods. . . .

Seen in the light of Poe's work as a whole, "A Descent into the Maelstrom" is in line with that part of his fiction which concerns our tendency to disguise truth. . . .

EXAGGERATIONS, LIES, AND ILLOGICALITIES

Still, one might argue that Poe is questioning the discrepancy between the inaccuracy of knowledge recorded in books and the local knowledge of the old man's experience. However, the major portion of the tale does not center on this discrepancy but, instead, on the old-timer's improbable and unreliable account itself. In fact, immediately following his claim that he fishes in an area of water, which "in the calmest weather" would not allow passage for his boat (and very probably sink it), the old-timer says, "'In all violent eddies at sea there is good fishing, at proper opportunities, if one has only the courage to attempt it; but among the whole of the Lofoden coastmen, we three were the only ones who made a regular business of going out to the islands, as I tell you.'" The old man's use of "all" in reference to "violent eddies" should alert the reader to a distortion of truth. Any fisher knows that the best fishing at sea occurs in calm waters.

Such a close argument in relationship to the old man's account would not be terribly convincing if it did not begin to reveal an overall pattern of prevarication and exaggeration. The old-timer says he fishes among the islands of Otterholm and Sandflesen "where the eddies are not so violent as elsewhere." In the paragraph before, he had made the point that in "all violent eddies at sea there is good fishing." He goes on to say that once he and his brothers "had to remain on the grounds a week, starving to death, owing to a gale which blew up shortly after [their] arrival." One would think that experienced seamen would keep rations in preparation for the unpredictability of weather. One might also be inclined to question whether fishermen caught in inclement weather would starve in a week or whether they might be saved by the excellent fishing which occurs in "all violent eddies of the sea," which in this instance would be created by the gale.

The old man's string of exaggerations, lies, and illogicalities prefaces his account of the maelstrom: "'It was on the tenth of July, 18—, a day which the people of this part of the world will never forget—for it was one in which blew the most terrible hurricane that ever came out of the heavens.'" This sentence is loaded with exaggerations and inaccuracies. First, his account of the hurricane must be judged exaggerated and certainly not "the most terrible" to ever come "out of the heavens." Second, Norway does not have hurricanes, and the gales they do have occur mainly in the late fall, winter, and early spring. Finally, July 10th is given as the date of the old man's encounter with the maelstrom. Yet from the first of June to the thirteenth of July the sun remains continually visible in Lofoden, located at sixty-eight degrees latitude and within the Arctic circle, something to remember when considering the old-timer's description of the moonlight on the maelstrom.

The description of the hurricane's arrival also seems implausible: "'In less than a minute the storm was upon us—in less than two the sky was entirely overcast—and what with this and the driving spray, it become suddenly so dark that we could not see each other in the smack.'" If Poe had not written hoaxes, parodies and burlesques before and after this tale, one would not be so likely to see humor in his presentation of the old man's continuing account: "'We had let our sails go by the run before it cleverly took us, but, at first puff, both our masts went by the board as if they had been sawed off—the mainmast taking with it my youngest brother, who had lashed himself to it for safety.'" How were the narrator and his brother able to let their sails "go by the run" and the old-timer's youngest brother to lash himself to the mast in less than two minutes—and in the dark?

When the boat actually goes into the maelstrom, the old man says his "self-possession" was restored somewhat since he was out of the direct force of the gale: "'If you have never been at sea in a heavy gale, you can form no idea of the confusion of mind occasioned by the wind and spray together. They blind, deafen, and strangle you, and take away all power of action or reflection. But we were now, in a great measure, rid of these annoyances. . . .'" The old man claims that he is free from annoyance through escaping the deafening gale. But at the beginning of the story, the reader learns that the maelstrom is heard miles in the distance with a noise greater than even "the mighty cataract of Niagara ever lifts up in its agony to Heaven." The old-timer himself reminds us of the maelstrom's noise: "'This mist, or spray was no doubt occasioned by the clashing of the great walls of the funnel, as they all met together at the bottom—but the yell that went up to the Heavens from out of that mist I dare not attempt to describe.'" Surely, the old man also must experience some "annoyance" from the circular motion of the maelstrom since he describes it as proceeding "in dizzying swings and jerks."

Under such distressing circumstances, the old man is able to find "'amusement in speculating upon the relative velocities'" of bodies as they descend in the whirlpool. From this speculation, he arrives at three observations or axioms regarding descending bodies in vortices, all of which are wrong and not attributable to Archimedes as Poe's footnote erroneously suggests. As a result of these faulty observations, the old man straps himself to a water cask and casts himself into the sea. This means of escape is patently ridiculous since a person holding onto or being lashed to a barrel in the water ends up under it. Rather than escaping, the old man would have drowned.

However, in the last paragraph of his story, the old-timer, in a manner characteristic of the tall tale, insists on the veracity of his story: "'The result was precisely what I had hoped it might be. As it is myself who now tell you this tale—as you see that I did escape—and as you are already in possession of the mode in which this escape was effected, and must therefore anticipate all that I have farther to say—I will bring my story quickly to conclusion.'" The "mode" of escape is without doubt the old man's prevarication which is the substance of the tale itself. Although the old-timer seems to make claims for the story's veracity, he also intimates to the astute reader that all he has "further to say" is a lie and can only be viewed as such. But for the less perceptive, the old man finishes with what still might be mistaken for the truth.

THE READER HAS BEEN "SOLD"

After the whirlpool collapses, the old man sees the full moon "setting radiantly in the west." He might be able to see the full moon set during time of the midnight sun in July, but it would not do so "radiantly." After being heaved "down the coast into the 'grounds' of the fishermen" by the mountainous waves which resulted from the hurricane, the old man is picked up by a fishing boat. One might ask what these fishermen were doing for six hours in the "most terrible hurricane that ever came out of the heavens." At any rate, the listener to the old man's story is supposed to accept the fact that the rescuers, who were the "old mates and daily companions" of the old-timer failed to recognize him because his hair turned white during his six hours in the maelstrom and "the whole expression of [his] countenance had changed." If, however, there were any doubt about the reliability of the old-timer, the last two lines of the story, the punch line, clearly demonstrate that the unperceptive listener (or reader) has been "sold": "'I told them my story—they did not believe it. I now tell it to you—and I can scarcely expect you to put more faith in it than did the merry fishermen of Lofoden.'"

Poe must have been aware of early tall tales which appeared in the magazines of the 1830s. As a parodist, he must also have been aware of the formal patterns in the tales themselves. One of the early debates about "A Descent into the Maelstrom" centered on whether Poe might have intended the tale for *The Folio Club* but published it later. The tale was mistaken for an earlier one mainly because of the use of a first person narrator as a "frame" for the story. *The Folio Club* tales were to have a similar frame; each of the fictitious members was to tell a tale. But in the earlier tales Poe's aims were primarily satiric; in "A Descent into the Maelstrom" Poe's ideas and method are more complex.

In a note at the end of "Hans Phaall" Poe described the tone of his tale as "banter." Burton Pollin finds that this comment has wider applications in describing other works by Poe. However, one might go still further by recognizing that a bantering tone is present in a number of Poe's works of fiction which deal with the extent of human fallibility and limitations to knowledge. Poe makes use of popular fictional forms such as the hoax and the gothic tale in order to present variations on his epistemological concerns.

In this context, "A Descent into the Maelstrom" is best understood in relation to the tall tale. This fictional form allowed Poe numerous opportunities to examine fictionally the difficulties hindering a person's search for the truth. Poe played with the reliability of the framing narrator, the veri-similitude of the "old-timer's" story, and the reader's willingness to believe. The narrative frame, attention to verisimilitude, excessive exaggeration, and the ending "punch line" were part of an American tradition that flowered in the 1840s and 1850s. The tall tale questions the reliability of reported experience. Poe uses this form to examine the slippery nature of truth and the elusiveness of knowledge. The nature of such epistemological concerns, however, also furnishes a link between Poe and the darker and supposedly more substantial visions of Nathaniel Hawthorne and Herman Melville, visions which continue in the works of major twentieth century writers. Although some readers wish to separate Poe from the mainstream of American literature, it may be increasingly difficult to do so when the underlying skepticism and epistemology of a story such as "A Descent into the Maelstrom" make themselves felt.

"A Descent into the Maelström" and the Quest for Ideal Beauty

Frederick S. Frank

Frederick S. Frank of Allegheny College describes "A Descent into the Maelström" as the antithesis of the conventional episode of descent in which a Gothic character falls toward madness, horror, or death. Here, the narrator never views himself as a victim during his descent, nor does he define the whirlpool as a deadly power. Rather, his strange experience can be defined as a voyage within God, from which he returns as a prophet of beauty and higher consciousness.

"A Descent into the Maelström" is Poe's presentation of a transcendental idea in reverse Gothic form. Traditionally, the discovery of the transcendental world has been expressed in images of ascent and luminosity rather than descent and darkness. The self-destructive patterns of orthodox Gothicism would seem to be alien to any portrayal of mystic enlightenment, but in the vertical voyage undertaken by the submarine narrator of this aqua-Gothic tale, several norms of the typical descent story are turned against themselves. Here Poe transforms the fatal journey into dark and forbidden places into a quest for ideal beauty. The fatal predicament becomes an opportunity for visionary enlargement because of the aesthetic view the narrator assumes toward the deadly vortex of rushing water. Indulging fully in that attitude which Poe calls elsewhere "a wild effort to reach the Beauty above," he is an outstanding example of the urge which drives certain Poe protagonists to achieve immortality by an annihilation of mortality. The beautification of the horrible, creation through destruction, and the penetration of mortal boundaries might appear to be variations of the suicidal impulse, but taken in terms of paradox these at-

Excerpted from "The Aqua-Gothic Voyage of 'A Descent into the Maelström,'" by Frederick S. Frank, *American Transcendental Quarterly*, Winter 1976. Reprinted with permission from the author.

titudes express a desire for an elevated plane of existence. The conventional episode of descent, which usually takes a Gothic character toward madness, the ultimate horror of horrors, or a death too terrible to imagine, here works in an opposite way and results instead in a heightened vision of the cosmos. The descender never sees himself as a victim nor regards the whirlpool as a deadly agency. Thus we encounter here an exceptional voice among Poe's distressed narrators—an aesthete who is willing to ignore everything but the imaginative possibilities inherent in the fatal experience and who turns a Gothic situation into a dream-flight and mind-expanding excursion.

THE DEEPER HE GOES, THE HIGHER HE RISES

The hero of "A Descent into the Maelström" is a kind of Keatsian quester for beauty who eradicates his ego as he descends into the whirlpool. He is more than ready to die for beauty, to surrender his mortality, in return for one enraptured glimpse of the higher world latent in the horror of the abyss. *He* is nothing; *descent* is all. The physical dynamics of downwardness which normally symbolize a movement toward some absolute horror or chaos in the subterranean recesses of the Gothic world have an inverse significance in this submarine adventure. The deeper the narrator goes physically, the higher he rises metaphysically. The mouth of death becomes the womb of life, and water becomes ethereal as this ordinary Norwegian fisherman undergoes an angelic metamorphosis. As his body is pulled downward into the watery Hades, his powers of aesthetic insight are released and elevated into a transcendental noesis. Self, God, and Nature cease their struggle with one another and merge into a primal unity in the eye of the aesthetic observer. Gothic disaster, however, befalls the voyager's pragmatic brother who, terrified, remains on the surface and clings for dear life to the ring-bolt of the fishing smack only to be drowned, victim of the limits of his imagination. By deliberately choosing death over life, the descender is granted a sea-change by the whirlpool. By his voluntary immersion in the terrible funnel he is changed into an underwater Israfel, a version of Poe's own angel of poetry who dwells in the heaven of ideal beauty. Poe's hero literally died into a new identity and is blissfully suspended in a nautical paradise, face to face with God.

Although the aqua-Gothic voyager is nameless in the story, he might be called "Aquarius," for his incredible adventure and even more impossible survival belong to both sky and water. Like the constellation of the waterbearer, Poe's Aquarius holds an exalted place in the miniature firmament of the Maelström's interior. Poe's insistence upon the whirlpool's likeness to the starry expanse places him within a microcosmic, underwater heaven. His descent dramatizes a transcendental hypothesis that the deepest and loftiest self can be attained only by yielding completely to the mysterious energies of nature.

Poe's contemporary Ralph Waldo Emerson bears out this hypothesis when he resorts to an aqua-Gothic metaphor in his essay "Compensation," where he describes the sort of spiritual equilibrium which Aquarius reaches through his submission to the anthropomorphic force of the whirlpool: "The soul *is*. Under all this running sea of circumstance, whose waters ebb and flow with perfect balance, lies the aboriginal abyss of real being. Essence, or God, is not a relation or a part, but the whole. Being is the vast affirmative, excluding negation, self-balanced, and swallowing up all relations, parts and times within itself." The imagery of this statement moves from surface to subsurface in a plunge from rationality, a directional metaphor highly uncharacteristic of the transcendental imagination but curiously close to the religious theme of Poe's "A Descent."

With total disregard for his superficial self, Poe's Aquarius wills himself to the depths in an absurd gesture of faith in non-rational action. Entering the contracting enclosure of the Maelström in defiance of all laws of reason, he descends into "the aboriginal abyss of real being," thus changing a situation of enlightenment into a situation of release. In a sense, the aesthetic hero exploits the typical Gothic ordeal of living entombment to arrive at a higher notion of self available only to those bold divers who descend from the plane of reason. In his ability to appreciate form itself during the fatal experience, Aquarius breaks through, or transcends, all corporeal barriers to find God at the circle's center.

A STEP AWAY FROM THE GOTHIC TALE

Recent Poe criticism has begun to acknowledge the process of deGothification witnessed in Aquarius's voyage. Even so, the tale has never been ranked at the same level as Poe's most appalling victim stories. Perhaps it owes its inferior status to the fact that it seems to lack the traditional Gothic stimuli found in other tales. Fixtures like the feminine superforce of "Ligeia," contraptions like animated architecture and poisonous chambers, cadaverous resurrections and sadistic murders, and the climactic disintegration of the House of Usher are not found in this submarine extravaganza. But several clever transpositions between the old mode of earthly terror into the new mode of watery terror underscore Poe's strategy of making the Gothic perform a higher function than was its wont. Apparently he aimed at using the deadly turmoil of the Gothic to depict a higher state of consciousness that would arise out of man' s primordial encounter with one of nature's most voracious monsters, the gigantic whirlpool. No doubt Poe wished the reader to apprehend this structural change and to perceive the connection between the underground of the old Gothic and the underwater of the new. Seen in this way, the great Maelström is a fluidic equivalent of the dark pit, crypt, cavern, or cellar of the old Gothic fiction. Aquarius's voice, ascending as it does from the hysterical to the sublime, also takes its place as a fascinating Gothic transposition. . . .

Separated from other story-tellers in Poe by his refusal to treat a potentially Gothic experience Gothically, Aquarius neither slays nor is slain. On the contrary, he uses his aesthetic intelligence to reverse all our Gothic expectations about the act of irrational crossover. Filled with an intuitive confidence in the aesthetic rightness of descent, his tone is much closer to the disembodied voice of Poe's poetry than to the carnally burdened voices of the speakers in the prose tales. Since he is Poe's paradigm for the successful artist—the sensitive observer who can extract the maximum of beauty from the apex of horror—his response to the crisis of the whirlpool stands in juxtaposition to his philosophical opposite among Poe's gallery of lethal voyagers, the unnamed visitor to the House of Usher. . . .

Unlike the analytic explorer of the mysteries of the House of Usher, however, Aquarius exercises his imagination to achieve a perfect psychic coalition between mind and matter. Had Aquarius been the guest of Roderick Usher perhaps there might have been no ultimate collapse of the kingdom of aesthetics and perhaps he would not have "fled aghast" from the catastrophe.

Also, "A Descent into the Maelström" and "The Fall of the House of Usher" both commence at the water's edge. When the Usher narrator gazes protractedly into the dark mirror of the tarn, he glimpses momentarily a residual world of beauty hidden from the conventional rationalist; nevertheless he quickly dismisses this spasm of his imagination, belittling his desire to descend as "a fancy so ridiculous indeed that I but mention it to show the vivid force of the sensations which oppressed me." The real fall in "Usher" is the inadequacy of the narrator's analytic faculty when confronted by the Gothic beauty of the tarn and mansion, whereas the real rise in "A Descent" is the triumphant soaring of Aquarius's imagination to a point where it beholds the divine order and beauty of the universe. He does what in Poe's view the artist must always do—plunges boldly over the edge of the abyss to plumb the depths of horror in quest of a vertiginous beauty found only in the midst of terror. Although he is of a

IRONIC IMAGES OF ENCLOSURE IN "A DESCENT INTO THE MAELSTRÖM"

In "A Descent into the Maelström" Poe's narrator experiences a self-awareness that is ironic when viewed against the numerous images of enclosure that occur during his descent into the whirlpool.

In "A Descent into the Maelström," the main character's boat has been caught up in the whirlpool:

> We were now in the belt of surf that always surrounds the whirl: and I thought, of course, that another moment would plunge us into the abyss—down which we could only see indistinctly on account of the amazing velocity with which we were borne along.

> It may appear strange, but now, when we were in the very jaws of the gulf, I felt more composed than when we were only approaching it. Having made up my mind to hope no more, I got rid of a great deal of that terror which unmanned me at first. I suppose it was despair that strung my nerves.

> It may look like boast but what I tell you is truth—I began to reflect how magnificent a thing it was to die in such a manner, and how foolish it was in me to think of so paltry a consideration as my own individual life, in view of so wonderful a manifestation of God's power. After a little while I became possessed with the keenest curiosity about the whirl itself. I positively felt a wish to explore its depths, even at the sacrifice I was going to make; and my principal grief was that I should never he able to

scientific turn of mind, his sensibilities are the antithesis of those of the Usher narrator. Life and logic are inconsequential once he has gone over the edge of the Maelström. Aesthetic reconnaissance, submarine acrobatics, levitational thrill, and fatal ecstasy become almost immediately the objectives of the downward expedition. Following the lead of the narrator in the earlier aqua-Gothic sketch, "MS. Found in a Bottle," he never hesitates upon the "brink of eternity" but relinquishes his mortality in order to be sucked downward like Poe's earlier diver "to some exciting knowledge—some never-to-be-imparted secret whose attainment is destruction." Poe knows precisely what to do with Aquarius's quest for the higher law of life amidst the concentric circles of death, how to make the cool and critical voice of the diver-artist address the reader matter-of-factly from an aesthetic perspective in an environment that is terrifying. Instead of the subterranean, Poe allows the submarine its chance to

> tell my old companions on shore about the mysteries I would see. These, no doubt, were singular fancies to occupy a man's mind in such extremity—and I have often thought since, that the revolutions of the boat around the pool might have rendered me a little light-headed.

In the last line the character is obviously trying to mitigate the impact of these terrifying "fancies" on his consciousness by attributing his strange desires to the dizzying effect of the revolutions: this is a logical, a highly rational explanation.

However, in reality, the dizzying effect should have made him nauseous or at least blurred his mind, but this does not appear to have been the case. If anything, his mind is clarified and his vision focused. His imagination seems to open: he becomes possessed with curiosity, wishes to explore the depths of the whirlpool, and only regrets that he will not be able to tell his old companions about the mysteries he will see. His attitude parallels that of the narrator in "MS. Found in a Bottle." That is to say, having become enclosed by the walls of water and heading directly into the abyss, both the narrator of "MS" and the main character of "Descent" reach a higher awareness whereby realization of the self is related to cosmic magnificence, and the identity of each becomes aligned to a transcendental concept of reality.

From Leonard W. Engel, "Edgar Allan Poe's Use of the Enclosure Device in 'A Descent into the Maelström,'" *Essays in Arts and Sciences*, vol. 8 (May 1979), pp. 21–26.

function as a Gothic setting and converts the fantasy of drowning found in earlier Gothic literature into his own version or aesthetic euphoria.

Although the transcendental experience is certainly paramount, some attention must be paid to the scientific aspect of Aquarius's outlook. There can be no merger with primal unity or nothingness or any supreme insight into the beautiful oneness of the universe without the coöperation of the analytic faculty which enables Aquarius to triumph over the phenomenal world and to transcend mortality during the descent. The seeker of beauty and the seeker of truth are both embarked on the same quest in Poe. Once Aquarius is overwhelmed with the awe produced by the immense power of nature, he can derive the sort of transcendental epistemology required for the apprehension of beautiful truth contained within the sensory world but visible through the combined application of imagination and scientific reasoning. . . . Therefore, the path to wisdom in Poe depends upon the investigator's willingness to join aesthetic spontaneity with scientific method. The searcher can go nowhere without a proper symmetry of imagination (the spiritual determinant) and scientific deduction (the material determinant). Reason without imagination, as Poe illustrates in the vain quest of the Usher narrator, is superfluous, and imagination without reasoning leads to the dissociation of the personality and madness. . . .

REALIZING A TRANSCENDENTAL SELF

Because his mind is already accustomed to "desperate speculation," plunging and cliffhanging proclivities, and veneration of the inner workings of God's power, Aquarius's acts against reason during the descent place him in the company of other mystics and prophets who have renounced life to find God. Toward mortal considerations Aquarius is indifferent. He has discovered that fear can be overcome by a total resignation to the thing feared. Regarding it as "foolish" to dwell upon "so paltry a consideration as my own individual life," Aquarius commits his body to the deep, a volitional choice that is radically different from mere falling. "Having made up my mind to hope no more," he finds "I got rid of a great deal of that terror which unmanned me at first."

As the descent begins, the opportunity for self-release looms large in his expanding vision. The potential for realizing a transcendental self beyond the confines of his own ego is never greater than when he is on the verge of death, and he meets the challenge which the experience within the whirlpool holds forth. In another earlier sea adventure, *The Narrative of A. Gordon Pym* (1838), Poe had taken his voyager up to the threshold of transcendental illumination and had then broken off the narrative. But in "A Descent" the mortal barrier is crossed and Usher's "kingdom of inorganization" is revealed. Aquarius attains the heavenly eye of the Maelström by being conveyed along Al Aaraaf, as it were, the regions between heaven and hell in the Mohammedan religion which Poe describes in his poem of the same name. Aquarius speaks of the "tottering bridge which Mussulmen say is the only pathway between Time and Eternity" in the midst of his submarine pilgrimage. He understands what the Usher narrator did not with all of his sanity and precaution and sees that if he were to behave practically about his own safety or the safety of his drowning brothers he would somehow be profaning the extreme trial of imagination now being provided for him by God.

Poe's epigraph from the writings of the seventeenth-century theologian Joseph Glanville (1636–1680) confirms the religious motifs which underlie the overt Gothic scenario of "A Descent." It fortifies the plausibility of Aquarius's decision to descend by defending the rightness of absurd action in its statement that "the ways of God in Nature, as in Providence, are not *our* ways." The transcendental theme of the story may also be detected in its cryptic certitude. "*Our* ways" may be construed as rational, self-serving, and non-visionary, whereas the "ways of God in Nature" are above all such hard Aristotelian categories and apprehensible solely through reliance on sensation. According to the clue contained in Glanville, the less the adherence to "*our* ways," the greater the pleasure of the descent. [Critic] Maurice Levy's observation concerning the standard Gothic event of falling from an enormous height casts additional light on Poe's religious purposes in Aquarius's violation of all the canons of reason: "The dream of falling is also, in itself, a dream as old as man, by means of which the dreamer enjoys descending into the deepest part of himself and pretends to be a prisoner in the most archaic levels of his Self." As divulged to Aquarius, the "ways of God in Nature" comprise the supernatural within the natural, the divine within the diabolic, the astral within the earthly, and the spiritual within the material. The great Maelström is a spatial projection of Poe's non-Christian deity.

Poe was later to conclude in *Eureka* that God is material and that man, when reunited with the divine substance, will achieve a perfect unison with the artisan of the universe. This mythic fusion explains the risky and imprudent conduct of Aquarius. What he does with his life is summed up near the close of *Eureka* where Poe declares "that Man, ceasing imperceptibly to feel himself Man, will at length attain that awfully triumphant epoch when he shall recognize his existence as that of Jehovah." Once the possibility of auto-deification is clear to Aquarius, he manages to transcend his restrictive self and enjoys the role of artist-scientist-God. Etherealized and disembodied, he is able to envision the true inward form of the Maelström hidden from the ordinary human observer by its external horror. Within the strange Gothic paradise which Poe provides, Aquarius sees God. With such previous manifestations as the pillar of fire, the voice from the whirlwind, and the burning bush as precedents for God's periodic physicality, Poe's Maelström takes its place as another material revelation of divinity. Emerging from the whirlpool, Aquarius undergoes a transfiguration, having become the prophet of beauty who has looked upon the countenance of deity. The instantaneous whitening of the hero's hair from its raven black hue and the hypnagogic transformation which has come over "the whole expression of [his] countenance" are caused as much by the profound holiness of the voyage within God as by the initial terror of the descent. His higher consciousness is indeed an unexpected aftermath to the Gothic sojourn of premature burial by water.

The Mathematician in "The Pit and the Pendulum"

Rochie Lawes

Rochie Lawes of the University of Mississippi claims that the narrator of Poe's "The Pit and the Pendulum" possesses the training of a skilled mathematician. The narrator speaks in the language of math throughout the story, and his activities expose his familiarity with numerology, number theory, and arithmetic, as evidenced by his practice of counting, numbering, and measuring his surroundings during his confinement.

In "The Pit and the Pendulum," Poe provides few particulars about the narrator. Although imprisoned by the Inquisition, the character offers no clue to his religious beliefs or the nature of his heresy, if any. Although rescued by the French army, he does not specify his own nationality. Of his features, his social or financial position, the story discloses little beyond the obvious implication that he is an educated man, important enough to justify the elaborate nature of his torture. Commentators on the tale have understandably focused on his response to his experience, seeing it, among other things, as a confrontation with the power of blackness; as an encounter with Nothingness by a mind clinging to the rational and practical; as an existential probing of the absurdity of human freedom; as a struggle to maintain an integrated consciousness until a moment of grace; and as a facing of ultimate states of horror, especially utter darkness, which are recalled in the language of the sublime. But however one formulates the narrator's experience, there is one characteristic that he brings to it that has not been emphasized in the literature: he has the manner and perhaps the training of a mathematician.

Excerpted from "The Dimensions of Terror: Mathematical Imagery in 'The Pit and the Pendulum,'" by Rochie Lawes, *Poe Studies*, June 1983. Reprinted with permission.

THE LANGUAGE OF MATH

That the narrator is well-versed in the branches of mathematics studied in nineteenth-century universities, both his vocabulary and his deductive processes attest. While probing for memories of his condition after his initial swoon, he defines the madness into which he feels drawn with a term from the calculus:

> Shadows of memory tell . . . of a vague horror at my heart . . . then comes a sense of sudden motionlessness throughout all things; as if those who bore me (a ghastly train) had outrun, in their descent, the *limits* of the *limitless*, and paused from the weariness of their toil.

With another phrase from the calculus he denotes the passing of time—"a very long *interval* of time" and another *interval* of utter insensibility"—and the movement of the pendulum: "a descent only appreciable at *intervals* that seemed ages."

His familiarity with that branch of mathematics known in varying ages as numerology, number theory, or arithmetic is expressed in his practise of counting, numbering, and measuring: the candles are *seven*; the stages of reviving from a swoon are *two*; the ceiling is *thirty or forty feet overhead*. He counts vibrations of the pendulum: "I saw that some *ten* or *twelve* vibrations would bring the steel in actual contact with my robe." He sees eyes glaring from a *thousand* directions; his release is signalled by a "harsh grating as of a *thousand* thunders." Tortured, imprisoned, and awaiting a terrible death, the narrator repeatedly orients himself by calculating or estimating the measurements of his cell:

> Up to the period when I fell, I had *counted fifty-two paces*, and upon resuming my walk, I had *counted forty-eight* more. . . . There were in all, then, a *hundred paces*; and, admitting *two paces* to the *yard* I presumed the dungeon to be *fifty yards* in circuit.

> . . . the sulphurous light which illumined the cell . . . proceeded from a fissure, about *half an inch* in width, extending entirely around the prison at the base of the walls. . . .

> At length for my seared and writhing body, there was no longer than an *inch* of foothold on the firm floor of the prison.

Lying bound and helpless, he estimates the measurements of the pendulum descending upon him:

> The sweep of the pendulum had increased in extent by nearly a *yard* . . . its nether extremity was formed by a crescent of glittering steel about a *foot* in length from horn to horn. . . .

> *Inch* by *inch*—line by line—. . . down and still down it came!
> . . . Its terrifically wide sweep, (some *thirty feet* or more,) and
> the hissing vigor of its descent, sufficient to sunder these very
> walls of iron. . . . It vibrated within *three inches* of my bosom.

Jean-Paul Weber considers the narrator's fascination with the
pendulum suggestive, not of the character's vocation or avo-
cation, but of Poe's preoccupation with clocks. To Weber, it is
somehow clear that the denouement of the tale symbolizes
some time near five-thirty—approximately five twenty-seven.
The narrator, however, is not speaking for Poe, nor is Poe
speaking through him. The narrator is a fictional character,
created by an author with a general familiarity with mathematics apparent throughout his works, especially, of course,
in *Eureka.* The narrator's concern with the periodicity and dimensions of the pendulum are as suggestive of the character's own mathematical knowledge as they are of an authorial obsession with time. This is a character who presumably
knew that Galileo's pendular studies of the swinging lamp led
to, not from, the use of pendulums in clock-making.

ARITHMETICAL ACTIVITIES

Poe's narrator uses more than the words and contexts of
mathematics to describe his situation; his activities are
arithmetical, as well. Imprisoned, drugged, and terrified, he
is incapable of what he considers dispassionate thinking until, in the "keen, collected calmness of despair," he notes that
"For the first time during many hours—or perhaps days—I
thought." Before this point, however, the narrator has relied
upon his mathematical cast of mind to orient himself; it enables him not only to count, as I have noted, but also to "deduce his real condition," to ascertain the dimensions of his
dungeon, to hearken to the reverberations of the masonry
fragment he has thrown into the abyss, to survey the ceiling
of his prison, and to contrast the downward with the lateral
velocity of the pendulum. These mathematical procedures,
in which he takes a "frenzied pleasure," when allied with
detached "thought," produce the calculation that leads to his
solution of the problem of the pendulum. His joy is a familiar one to all mathematicians: "Nor had I erred in my *calculations* . . . I was *free.*"

   Not only does his vocabulary and manner of reasoning indicate close acquaintance with mathematics; but the prepon-
derant imagery he uses also suggests his particular branch of

mathematical knowledge—the narrator is apparently a geometer. His very absorption with geometric "trifles" is a predominant element in his response to the atmosphere of terror which is his prison, although he remonstrates, "What could be of less importance, under the terrible circumstances which environed me, than the mere *dimensions* of my dungeon?" Indeed, the ideas presented by the geometric progression of his imagery parallel the development of his awareness of the terror.

In his first description of the chamber, linear imagery abounds. The narrator is horizontal; he recalls how the "agony of suspense grew *at length* intolerable," the one-dimensional image is strengthened by the occurrence of the phrase *at length* sixteen times in the tale. The narrator suggests the terror of confinement with such geometric adjectives as *long, tall,* and *measured,* and with the nouns *line, paces,* and *length.* In a typically Poesque pun, he even declares that he "*longed,* yet dared not" to open his eyes.

As linear imagery connotes the narrator's initial, limited awareness of his condition, phrases from plane geometry accompany the first expansion of that awareness. He early notices the flatness of the floor; he defines another plane as his hands explore the wall. Then, to ascertain the dimensions of his dungeon, he proposes to make a circuit and return to his point of origin. In so doing, he becomes aware of "many *angles* in the wall" and is therefore uncertain of the area, confused as to the shape of the enclosure. An astute geometer, he proposes to measure the diagonal, for only thus can he satisfy his "vague curiosity" concerning the extent of his predicament.

CALCULATED TERROR

Tripping on the torn hem of his robe prevents his falling into the loathsome pit, but that fall is not altogether a fortunate one, for it introduces a third dimension: the depth of terror. The narrator realizes that, when his chin rests upon the plane of the prison floor, his lips and forehead, at *"less elevation"* than the chin, touch nothing. His first apprehension of the pit, therefore, is geometric, rather than sensory, for his awareness of the elevation precedes recognition of the significance of the "clammy vapor" and "peculiar smell" that bathe his forehead. Once awakened to the realization of the depth, as well as the length and breadth of his peril, he notices the door overhead, through which his every movement is observed, his every attempt to escape foiled. After a *deep* sleep, which lasts he knows not how *long*, the narrator receives light, and learns that he has been mistaken in his earlier "researches."

A typical mathematician, the narrator's first thought is "to *account* for the error . . . committed in . . . *measurement*." Enlightened as to the size of his dungeon, the geometer's next concern is with its shape. The cell, he determines, is *square;* the pit is *circular*. In temporary possession of at least the three geometrical dimensions of his condition, the narrator continues to observe and calculate. He estimates the *sweep* and the *velocity* of the *pendulum;* he considers its *weight* and *shape*. He *measures* time, though imperfectly, and *counts* the "rushing vibrations of steel." Noting that the "vibration of the *pendulum* was at *right angles* to [his] *length,"* the prisoner eventually contrives the ploy by which the rats free him.

The final torture he understands in starkly geometric terms: the room which was *square* is changing its shape. As he watches, two of the *right angles* become *acute*, and two, consequently, *obtuse*. The cell changes from a *square* into a *lozenge*, or, in the vocabulary of twentieth-century mathematics, a *parallelogram*. The *lozenge* becomes flatter and flatter, its *center* forcing him toward the *circular* pit. Fully cognizant of the size, the shape, the extent, and the depth of the death ordained him, the prisoner is miraculously rescued when the pit is less than an inch from being tangentially inscribed by the walls. The protagonist falls, not into the depths of terror, but into the arms of his savior.

Since Poe does not use words carelessly, this proliferation of mathematical terms with which the narrator understands and describes his situation can be interpreted only as an intentional artistic device. "The Pit and the Pendulum" is a tale of terror, the terror of confinement. For Poe's purposes, the details of incarceration and release are insignificant; the details of imprisonment are paramount. In the tale mathematical imagery is counterpointed against the dark uncertainties of what [critic] Kent Ljungquist calls "a crucible of painful sensations." The narrator's facility with both the language and the concepts of mathematics allows him to grapple with the enormity of his danger, to avoid the disasters prepared for him until help arrives. Since he uses mathematical procedures and skills to find solutions to the problems posed for him by his torturers, since he "busies" himself with calculating the dimensions of his approaches to death and correcting his mistakes when his conclusions seem at variance with new data, Poe's narrator may be in fact as well as in habit a mathematician. If so, then the predominance of geometric over other mathematical imagery suggests that he is a geometer.

Poe's knowledge of enough mathematics to create plausible characters versed in the field is neither unknown nor unnoted. In "The Gold-Bug," the mathematics of cryptography and map-making are significant. In "The Mystery of Marie Rogêt," Dupin refers to arithmetic and the "Calculus of Probabilities" (although not without error). Indeed, as Clarence R. Wylie points out in "Mathematical Allusions in Poe," all of Poe's tales of ratiocination "involve in an essential way, reasoning of a . . . character strikingly reminiscent of the logical structure of the demonstrations of Euclid."

In *Eureka* and in "The Purloined Letter," Poe implies his contempt for the "mere mathematician," noting instead his appreciation of the reasoning ability of those who are, like Dupin and the Minister D——, both poet and mathematician. In the narrator of "The Pit and the Pendulum," Poe has, I believe, offered his readers a sympathetic character who is primarily the mathematician, one whose skills seem a necessary if not a sufficient foundation for dealing with the terrors he faces.

Suffering and Self-Knowledge: The Path to Redemption in "The Pit and the Pendulum"

Jeanne M. Malloy

Jeanne M. Malloy is a visiting lecturer in the department of English at Temple University. Malloy explains the elements of English Romanticism in "The Pit and the Pendulum" to come to a broader understanding of the work. The apocalyptic imagery that presents itself in the story is common in the work of the English Romantic writers Poe admired, and it suggests that, like many of them, he is writing an allegory of the biblical story of mankind's fall and redemption, represented by the narrator's psychological process of loss and restoration. Malloy argues that redemption is found only through suffering and a new understanding of the self.

Part of the terror of "The Pit and the Pendulum" stems from the apocalyptic imagery with which Poe establishes his narrative framework. Condemned to torture and death by the black-robed, white-lipped judges of the Inquisition in the opening scene of the tale, the narrator observes seven candles, which first dissolve in his mind into seven angels wearing an "aspect of charity" and then, disconcertingly, into "meaningless spectres, with heads of flame." The angels and candles allude to Revelation 112–14: "I saw seven golden candlesticks; and in the midst of the seven candlesticks one like unto the Son of man, clothed with a garment down to the foot, and girt about the paps with a golden girdle. His head and his hair were white like wool, as white as snow; and his eyes were as a flame of fire." By beginning the tale with the narrator's trial and death sentence and by couching

Excerpted from "Apocalyptic Imagery and the Fragmentation of the Psyche: 'The Pit and the Pendulum,'" by Jeanne M. Malloy, *Nineteenth Century Fiction*, June 1991. Copyright © 1991 by The Regents of the University of California. Reprinted with permission from the University of California Press.

these events in apocalyptic imagery, Poe heralds the narrator's, and hence the reader's, entrance into a nightmare world of punishment, dissolution, and death, an announcement amply fulfilled by the violence, pain, and horror experienced by the narrator in his prison cell.

BIBLICAL ALLUSIONS

Although its presence is less immediately apparent in the tale, the Book of Revelation also sets forth the promise of salvation, the eternal life granted the faithful. Despite its depiction of the present age as given over to the forces of evil, Revelation proclaims that judgment and the destruction of the world will be followed by the creation of a new heaven and a new earth. Fittingly, then, Poe concludes his tale with blaring trumpets, "fiery walls," and "a thousand thunders," apocalyptic images that describe the narrator's deliverance by General Lasalle as a sort of Second Coming of Christ. Indeed, removed from its allusive context, the narrator's rescue is difficult to account for since, as David H. Hirsch has pointed out, it is neither foreshadowed in the tale nor congruent with its overwhelming oppression. However, in light of Revelation 16.15—"Behold, I come as a thief"—the narrator as well as the reader accepts the unexpectedness of Lasalle's arrival and the narrator's escape.

Poe's allusions to Revelation and several apocryphal books of the Bible have, of course, been recognized by commentators. Hirsch observes that the final paragraphs of the tale neatly counterpoint the first by reversing the narrator's loss of hearing, and then collapse with auditory amplification and expansion. According to Hirsch, "the 'dreamy indeterminate hum' of the opening lines is caught up in the 'discordant hum' of the conclusion; the 'burr of a mill-wheel' is amplified into the 'thousand thunders,' . . . and the collapsing image of the 'blackness of darkness supervened'" is inverted "into the expanding image of the fiery walls rushing outward." Hirsch suggests, moreover, that the "outstretched arm of General Lasalle" represents a "submerged allusion" to Isaiah 59 "where the Lord is portrayed as a warrior clothed in the armor of righteousness who stretches forth his arm to bring salvation."

The problem for critics interpreting "The Pit and the Pendulum" has not been in recognizing Poe's allusions, but rather in determining what to make of them. Hirsch, for example, is uncomfortable with the conclusion that the narrator's deliverance represents "transcendent hope," a judgment he finds "inconsistent with the themes of many of Poe's other stories and . . . a violation of generally accepted beliefs about Poe's thought." Speculating on how Poe might have come to write a tale of spiritual transcendence, Hirsch conjectures that Poe was attracted to the Bible's "language of despair," and that although he apparently intended to write a story about the irrationality and injustice of divine creation, "the dialectic spirit of Biblical apocalyptic [became] operative in the story and the transcendence downward [resolved] into a transcendence upward."

Certainly Poe was interested in the psychology and, consequently, the language of despair, and in these respects, as Hirsch points out, Poe provides an important model for Kafka, Camus, and Sartre. However, the apocalyptic aspects of "The Pit and the Pendulum" and the theme of transcendence they suggest are less "inconsistent with the themes of many of Poe's other stories," less "a violation of generally accepted beliefs about Poe's thought" if one views them in the context of the English Romantic literary tradition rather than as precursors of the twentieth century's literature of the Absurd. . . .

THE ROMANTIC INFLUENCE

According to M.H. Abrams, apocalyptic imagery is one of the most common features of English Romantic literature. In this literature, which typically embodies "a displaced and reconstituted theology, or else a secularized form of devotional experience" the biblical story of the Fall is reconceived as a psychological growth from innocence to painful knowledge redeemed by heightened consciousness and enlarged sympathy. Among the many Romantic works fulfilling the biblical paradigm described above are William Wordsworth's *Prelude*, a "story of the birth, growth, disappearance, and resurrection of imagination"; Samuel Taylor Coleridge's *Ancient Mariner*, a reenactment of the "Christian plot of moral error, the discipline of suffering, and a consequent change of heart"; and John Keats's *Hyperion* and Percy Bysshe Shelley's *Prometheus Unbound*, epic poems of the "fall, redemption, and millennial return to a lost felicity" couched in the classical myth of the loss of the Golden Age. In rewriting the myth of the Fall of Man, the English Romantics frequently express the redemption achieved through imagination and heightened consciousness with apocalyptic imagery derived both directly from their reading of the Bible and indirectly through their reading of John Milton. They are especially fond, claims Abrams, of the images of the new heaven and earth and of the marriage of Christ and his bride. . . . Of course the Romantics, especially Coleridge, were also interested in the more sinister images of the biblical apocalypse. Coleridge derived the harrowing images of the rotting sea, blood-colored water, and the last trump giving up the dead in *The Ancient Mariner* both from the Bible and from biblical commentaries on the apocrypha. . . . In short, apocalyptic imagery permeates the writings of the English Romantics, a point Poe would hardly fail to appreciate. What Poe's adoption of apocalyptic imagery in "The Pit and the Pendulum" intimates is that he, too, is rewriting the biblical story of mankind's fall and redemption as a psychological process of loss and restoration.

One indication that Poe, like the English Romantics, is using apocalyptic imagery as part of a psychological reconception of the myth of the Fall is Poe's association of the divine with infancy and childhood. The first line of "The Pit and the Pendulum" simultaneously establishes the apocalyptic framework and describes the narrator's estrangement from the supernal as a birth trauma: "I was sick—sick unto death with that long agony." Marie Bonaparte, the first critic to comment on the uterine character of the setting, compares the contracting walls at the tale's conclusion to those of "a giant womb" that force the narrator, like an unwilling fetus, "towards the cloacal abyss." As Bonaparte points out, other prenatal aspects of the tale include the narrator's lack of "any reference whatever to feelings of cold, though we are told that the cell is damp, deep underground and that the prisoner, weak with pain and fasting, wears only a 'wrapper of coarse serge,'" and the "constant recurrence of references to sleeping." Accepting the prison cell as an analogue for the womb also accounts for the narrator's failing eyesight and dimmed hearing—"the blackness of darkness supervened" and the "dreamy indeterminate hum" the narrator associates "in fancy" (Poe's pun on "infancy"?) with the "burr of a mill-wheel"—since the sights and sounds of the external world are necessarily indistinct to a fetus just coming to consciousness. Fittingly, the narrator's sight begins to diminish and his hearing begins to deteriorate upon the judges' announcement of his death sentence, pain and death being the necessary corollaries to birth in the biblical paradigm.

Poe's association of the divine with infancy has many precedents in English Romantic poetry. As William Blake's "Songs of Innocence" and Wordsworth's "Intimations of Immortality from Recollections of Early Childhood" show, the English Romantics frequently equate Eden and happiness with childhood and infancy. . . .

THE HUMAN CONDITION IS ONE OF SUFFERING

Like Wordsworth in the "Intimations" ode, Poe associates the divine in "The Pit and the Pendulum" not only with infancy, but also more generally with special states of consciousness. When the narrator of "The Pit and the Pendulum" recovers from swoons or other lapses in consciousness, he experiences not memories of his earlier life but "impressions eloquent in memories of the gulf beyond." These vague perceptions signal to the narrator, as do Wordsworth's "Intimations" human "immortality." And like Wordsworth again, the narrator of Poe's tale insists that although these deeply buried apprehensions cannot be recalled at will, they recur "unbidden" and "after long interval" when one engages in such meditative acts as watching "wildly familiar faces in coals that glow," sniffing "the perfume of some novel flower," or listening to "some musical cadence." In "The Pit and the Pendulum," then, as in numerous works both fictional and critical, Poe is concerned with the theme of human dissociation from the divine and the consequent longing to return to it, an estrangement signaled by "Our birth," which is, to quote Wordsworth, "but a sleep and a forgetting."

If the apocalyptic framework, the birth imagery, and the narrator's comments all suggest that Poe is rewriting the biblical story of the Fall as a Neoplatonic estrangement from the divine, then what is Poe's view of man's earthly existence in "The Pit and the Pendulum"? First, and most obvious, the human condition is one of terrible suffering, although the initial reason for this pain is unspecified. Like Coleridge, who provides no explanation of the mariner's murder of the albatross, and Shelley, who writes that "the deep truth" of evil "is imageless," Poe never discloses the cause of the narrator's imprisonment. The nameless narrator, a sort of Everyman, expresses neither guilt nor remorse for having committed a crime, nor does he resent being unjustly imprisoned. He is simply unconcerned with the justice of his situation, accepting it as a given as must all the heirs of Adam. As James Lundquist succinctly puts it: "The anonymous hero condemned for an unknown, or at least unstated, crime by a mercilous *[sic]* Inquisition apparently represents mankind condemned by a vindictive power for an almost forgotten sin. His sentence is not immediate death but life lived amid horror." Thus the narrator's dilemma embodies, in an intensified form, the general plight of humanity after the Fall, not the aberrations of an individual psyche. Like all human beings in this life, the narrator is suspended in a "Hades" between the certainty of his death and the indefiniteness of its time, place, or circumstance; between his desire for an afterlife and his fear of absolute dissolution.

Although Poe in typically Romantic fashion remains obscure about the reason for the narrator's suffering, his notion of the experience of the Fall is more explicit. Human estrangement from the supernal is experienced as a fragmentation of the psyche, symbolically represented in the tale by the bisecting pendulum, into ego and non-ego, male and female aspects of the mind. The idea that the human psyche has suffered some fundamental fracture is common in the English Romantics' reinterpretation of the Fall. . . .

Poe's allegory of the psyche's "Infernal Twoness" in "The Pit and the Pendulum," however, is predicated on yet another common Romantic assumption, the idea that psychological and spiritual fragmentation is related to the development of consciousness in general and intellect in particular. Although they find heightened consciousness the ultimate key to redemption, the English Romantics typically view the development of intellect as initially divisive because it fosters distinctions between subject and object, mind and nature, reason and instinct. . . . Unsurprisingly, Poe's attitude toward consciousness and intellect in "The Pit and the Pendulum" is similar to those of Wordsworth and Coleridge. That is, the development of the narrator's consciousness promotes rather than eases his sense of isolation and terror. . . . Upon awakening from the swoon induced by hearing his own death sentence, the narrator first experiences the "impressions eloquent of memories of the gulf beyond" mentioned above, and then physical existence, whence he proceeds to sensations of self-consciousness and an awareness of himself in relation to his surroundings:

> Very suddenly there came back to my soul motion and
> sound—the tumultuous motion of the heart, and, in my ears,
> the sound of its beating. Then a pause in which all is blank.
> Then again sound, and motion, and touch—a tingling sensa-
> tion pervading my frame. Then the mere consciousness of ex-
> istence, without thought—a condition which lasted long.
> Then, very suddenly, *thought*, and shuddering terror, and
> earnest endeavor to comprehend my true state.

Apparently "terror" succeeds *"thought"* because with
"thought" the narrator has completely severed "the gos-
samer web of *some* dream" that had linked him through the
unconscious to the supernal. Once dissociated from the divine, the narrator begins a protracted and doomed effort to
"comprehend" his situation by analytical means.

A CRITIQUE OF REASON

The inability of intellect alone to illuminate the human condition is illustrated by the continual frustration of the narrator's rational plans to free himself. His attempt "to deduce"
his situation by examining his plight in light of historically
known precedents results in consternation, not insight. Why
the narrator's life has been spared when victims were in "immediate demand" for an auto-da-fé held "the very night of
the day" of the narrator's trial remains a mystery. The narrator's attempt to comprehend his condition intellectually is
also foiled in his plan to discover the dimensions of his cell,
a plot that fails not because his calculations are incorrect, but
because he is unaware that the cell's walls are flexible. The
narrator is such a good logician, in fact, that he is able to arrive at the perfectly plausible but nevertheless erroneous explanation that he misjudged the cell's size because he lost his
sense of direction and thus supposed "the circuit nearly double what it actually was." Although the narrator claims to
have begun his researches with "little object" except satisfy-
ing a "vague curiosity" and with "no hope" of escape, he
places increasing value on rational planning. His brilliant
and daring yet cruelly disappointed scheme of escaping the
lethal edge of the pendulum by allowing the rats from the pit
to gnaw away the binds he has smeared with his last morsels
of food represents the pinnacle of his intellectual attempts to
control his destiny. In the instant that he feels the bonds
break and escapes from under the pendulum's swing, the
narrator experiences the joy of being *"free."* His elation, however, is momentary. As soon as he makes his declaration he

realizes that he is "Free!—and in the grasp of the Inquisition!" He has been spared "death in one form of agony, to be delivered unto worse than death in some other." The only benefit the narrator gains for all his strenuous effort is his knowledge of the pit, but his discovery of it is "the merest of accidents," not the result of his scheming. Ironically, his attempt rationally to understand and control his destiny brings him to the very edge of sanity. Becoming "frantically mad" as he awaits death by the lethal pendulum, the narrator first struggles to end his life prematurely by pressing himself "upward against the sweep of the fearful scimitar" and then, resigning himself to despair, lays calmly, "smiling at the glittering death, as a child at some rare bauble."

Poe's critique of reason in other tales helps illuminate the narrator's crisis in "The Pit and the Pendulum." Insisting in "Instinct Vs Reason—A Black Cat" that the boundary between reason and instinct is "far more difficult to settle than even the North-Eastern or the Oregon," Poe notes the paradox that man "perpetually finds himself . . . decrying instinct as an inferior faculty, while he is forced to admit its infinite superiority, in a thousand cases, over . . . reason." Even in the tales of ratiocination Poe demonstrates that mere intellect is ineffectual. [Poe's eccentric detective Auguste] Dupin's success is less the result of analytical subtlety and scientific observation than of a synthesis of talents and faculties. "As poet *and* mathematician, he would reason well," says Dupin admiringly of the minister, a double for Dupin in "The Purloined Letter"; "as mere mathematician, he could not have reasoned at all, and thus would have been at the mercy of the Prefect." The problem with the Prefect of police, says Dupin in "The Murders in the Rue Morgue," is that he is "too cunning to be profound. In his wisdom is no *stamen*. It is all head and no body, like the pictures of the Goddess Laverna,—or, at best, all head and shoulders, like a codfish." As J.A. Leo Lemay has shown, all three of Poe's rather strange images above concern a "head-body dichotomy" in which the head, the "citadel of reason," is revealed as useless without a complementary and interdependent part. In "Instinct Vs Reason" Poe calls this complementary principle "instinct" while in the tales of ratiocination he identifies it with creativity and emotion. But however Poe thought about the composition of the psyche at various points in his career, he clearly felt that rationality or intellect was inadequate in itself and therefore had to be balanced by or integrated with some feminine counterpart: instinct, creativity, or "the Moral Sense."

The climax of "The Pit and the Pendulum" is the narrator's confrontation with the pit, a commonly recognized symbol for the unconscious or feminine aspect of the psyche. General Lasalle rescues the narrator only after the narrator is forced to confront the pit he has devoted himself to avoiding ever since his discovery of it: "I tottered upon the brink—I averted my eyes—." By relating the sequence of final events—the narrator's confrontation with the pit and his immediate resurrection—in the images of the Second Coming of Christ, Poe suggests at the tale's conclusion that the narrator achieves a desirable reintegration of his fragmented psyche by being forced to acknowledge the power of the unconscious and the limitations of the intellect. That the narrator dreads the pit, "the Ultima Thule" of horror, is hardly surprising. According to Carl Jung, the confrontation with the unconscious necessary for the integration of the personality exposes one's "helplessness and ineffectuality" by opening the door to the void, "a boundless expanse full of unprecedented uncertainty, with apparently no inside and no outside, no above and below, no here and no there, no mine and no thine, no good and no bad." Hence it is an experience not only of nothingness—"I dreaded the first glance at objects around me. It was not that I feared to look upon things horrible, but that I grew aghast lest there should be *nothing* to see"—but also of formlessness: the bottomless pit and shifting walls. Poe, of course, did not have a psychoanalytic vocabulary. What he did have was an intimate knowledge of the Bible and of English Romantic literature, and he used the biblical apocalypse in a typically Romantic way at the conclusion of the tale: to signal psychological and spiritual redemption achieved through suffering and heightened consciousness. If Poe wanted to save the narrator only so he could tell his tale of torment, he would have no reason to invert meticulously, as Hirsch has shown, the apocalyptic images of the opening paragraph in the final one. What the narrator's rescue by General Lasalle intimates, then, is his psychological transcendence through a reunification of his severed faculties, not orthodox religious transcendence.

In "Frames of Reference for Poe's Symbolic Language," Eric W. Carlson remarks that Poe's philosophy, aesthetics, and epistemology in the tales and poems are often difficult to comprehend because Poe stretches words and phrases "well beyond their denotative and usual metaphoric meanings until they function as motifs and symbols." As Richard Wilbur demonstrates in his discussions of "The Masque of the Red Death" and "The Tell-Tale Heart," one passage into Poe's complex language is the recognition and proper appreciation of Poe's submerged allusions. When viewed in the context of English Romanticism (to Poe the most important high-culture literary tradition), "The Pit and the Pendulum" reveals itself as a meditation on the fragmentation resulting from humankind's estrangement from the divine and on the redemption achieved through suffering and self-knowledge. By exploring the human condition through devices common to Romantic literature, Poe created an image of suffering palpable enough to terrify generations of readers.

CHAPTER 4

An Atmosphere of Death: "The Masque of the Red Death" and "The Fall of the House of Usher"

READINGS ON
THE SHORT STORIES OF
EDGAR ALLAN POE

Allegorical Meaning in "The Masque of the Red Death"

H.H. Bell Jr.

H.H. Bell Jr. of the U.S. Naval Academy claims that the seven rooms in "The Masque of the Red Death" are symbolic of the seven decades of a person's life. Poe emphasizes their allegorical meaning through the use of symbolic color schemes in each room. Death itself is also symbolized through the ticking of the great black clock that can be heard in each room of the abbey but is more ominously present at the final stage of life, that seventh, black room that has no means of escape.

If after reading it, one concludes that "The Masque of the Red Death" is nothing more than another of Poe's rather numerous explorations of the general theme of death, then there is little that may be said about its meaning other than that it is a rather good example of grim and ironic humor. However, to the student who inclines his attention toward the allegorical overtones of the work, other possibilities as to its meaning present themselves. It is the writer's belief that the story becomes more interesting, as well as broader in scope, when one concentrates on these allegorical elements.

Examining the text of the work, we discover that Prospero is a feelingless ruling prince. To the discerning reader there is also implicit within the text a strong suspicion that this man is probably insane, for we are told that "Prince Prospero was happy and dauntless and sagacious" even though half the people in his kingdom had been killed by the Red Death. This would hardly be the reaction of a ruler who is in contact with his environment. This same man, motivated by a morbid fear of death, selfishly decides to commit the Hawthorne-like sin of alienation by isolating himself from most of his

Excerpted from "'The Masque of the Red Death': An Interpretation," by H.H. Bell Jr., *South Atlantic Review*, November 1973. Reprinted with permission.

subjects by retreating with a thousand light-hearted friends into a castellated abbey to escape the Red Death. Assuming that death, even the one that Prospero is trying to escape, is the wage of sin, there would be little allegorical objection to having Prospero seek refuge in an abbey—a monastery.

THE SEVEN DECADES OF LIFE

While in this state of isolation, as it were, from the majority of his subjects, he entertains his carefully selected guests at a masked ball in the seven rooms of his imperial suite; and from the way that Poe treats these seven rooms, it may be gathered that he views them as the allegorical representation of Prince Prospero's life span. The fact that he does view them thus is further enhanced by his placing the first room in the eastern extremity of the apartment and the last room in the western extremity. These directions are time-honored terms which have been used to refer to the beginning and the end of things—even of life itself.

Since Poe appears to attach so much importance to these rooms, since he devotes so much time to describing them in general, and, furthermore, since he dwells in particular and at great length upon their color and their layout within the abbey, a diagram of them as the writer imagines they might be situated is appended to this article with the hope that it may prove helpful to the reader.

As was noted above, the imperial suite consists of seven rooms, and if it is assumed that the entire suite allegorically represents Prospero's life span, then it is logical to assume that the seven rooms allegorically represent the seven decades of his life, which according to the Bible is the normal life span of man—three score and ten. It has also been noted above that there is a possibility that Prospero is insane, and some weight is given to this suspicion when one learns that this personage's life had been conditioned by his love of the bizarre, and when one learns that the seven rooms which represent his life present a different aspect from that of those rooms which would allegorically represent the life span of another—and perhaps normal—person.

Prospero's apartments were "irregularly disposed" and full of turns which prevented one's seeing from one end to the other. Despite the turns, however, one may infer from Poe's words that they were arranged more or less in a line. That they had a closed corridor on either side of them is definitely known. Likewise it is known that these closed corridors extended the full length of the apartments. In other words, the imperial suite or life span of Prospero is enclosed or embraced by two closed corridors or, if you will, by two unknowns. These two unknowns could very well be thought of as the unknowns of birth and death which in effect enclose or embrace the life of any man.

Poe is careful to point out that in many such palaces "such suites form a long and straight vista" with nothing to hinder one's view from one end to the other; and he is equally careful to point out that this is not true of Prospero's apartments. These he says are crooked and winding with a sharp turn every twenty or thirty yards that prevented one's seeing very far into or through them. By emphasizing the fact that Prospero's apartments differ from similar apartments owned by other people, Poe may well be trying to indicate that Prospero's life differed from that of most people—that it is more crooked and winding, more tortured and stress ridden than the lives of others which are straighter and perhaps calmer.

Each of the seven rooms, with the exception of the last one, has two Gothic windows and two doors. It does not appear that the seventh room—the room of death—would need two doors. An entrance way alone would be sufficient for this one. As for the Gothic windows, each of them has a fire brazier behind it in the closed corridor, and the effect of the fire shining through the colored glass of the windows was productive of "a multitude of gaudy and fantastic appearances." Since the only light in any of the rooms was that of the fires sifted through the stained glass windows, the effect would very likely be an eerie one indeed, productive of "delirious fancies such as the madman fashions." Prospero then perhaps comprehends his life only in terms of the glimmerings of light (knowledge) that emanate from the unknowns of birth and death, and he sees his life as something of a mad drama. At least this line of reasoning provides a *raison d'être* for the closed corridors and the fire braziers. Otherwise they may just seem to be there as extraneous and more or less irrelevant items.

SYMBOLISM IN COLORS

Poe has so much to say about the colors found in the seven rooms that it is difficult, if indeed not impossible, to think that he meant nothing by them. It has been suggested above that the seven rooms probably represent the seven decades of Prospero's life, and proceeding on this assumption, it is logical to conclude that the color in any given room may be related to Prospero's physical and mental condition in that decade of his life.

Admitting that color symbolism can be rather vague at best, there nevertheless appears to be enough evidence in the text of the story to warrant certain pertinent conclusions concerning Poe's use of such symbolism here. The first room, for example, is located in the eastern end of the apartments, and it is colored blue. The symbolism regarding Poe's use of the direction east here is rather obvious, and the color blue may be related to the same beginnings and origins that "East" stands for by thinking of it in the sense that it is the residence of the unknown or the unexpected—i.e., such as when we speak of something coming as a bolt out of the blue. Since blue may thus be associated with the unknown, by extension of meaning it may reasonably be associated in this instance with the beginning of life, which is unknown also.

The second room, says Poe, was purple—a color worn by those who have achieved something in the world or in society. Again, by extension of meaning, one may think of this color as being representative of that period in Prospero's life when he has accomplished a little something in life—perhaps moving into maturity.

The third room is colored green, and the writer doesn't think that it requires too much imagination to associate this color with that which is verdant, with that which is full of life and vigor—indeed with a man who is in the prime of his years.

The fourth room is orange and quite easily suggests, at least to the reader focusing on color symbolism, the autumn of life. Prospero could well be considered here to be beyond his prime, but by no means old yet.

The fifth room is white, and if we follow the same train of thought it would suggest the silver or hoary haired period of old age.

The sixth room is violet, a color that is emblematic of gravity and chastity. It appears that it would not be too much to assume that this room then represents the gravity and the soberness of extreme old age as well as the more or less enforced chastity that goes along with it.

Poe tells us that the seventh room is black, a color easily and most often associated with death; but, as if this were not enough, he tells us that this room is the most westerly of all, and the association of conclusions, ends, and death itself with "West" are too numerous to mention.

DEATH'S VICTORY

Most of the dancing and gaiety in the apartment took place in the first six rooms, for as Poe says "in them beat feverishly the heart of life." We are also told that "there were few of the company bold enough to set foot within" the seventh room—the room of death. Also it is to be noted that in the seventh room was to be found the great black clock, which seemed indeed to be more than a clock and to do more than a clock does. It would appear from the way he writes that Poe meant for the clock to count off periods of life—not mere hours. It is perhaps for this reason that he capitalizes the word "Time" at this point in the story and thus personifies it. This is also very likely why all the maskers stop when the clock strikes off the hour. They think not in terms of an hour having passed but rather in terms of just so much of their lives as having passed. Lastly, let it be noted that the clock of death, though it is heard in all the rooms, is heard best in the seventh or room of death.

Enhancing the possibility of considering Prospero insane, Poe indicates that the rooms were filled with dreams such as those a man with a tortured mind might have. He says that in the rooms "there was much of the beautiful, much of the wanton, much of the bizarre, something of the terrible, and not a little of that which might have excited disgust." Amid these revelers and amid these fantastic dreams there appears at the stroke of midnight a masked figure representing death. That there may be no mistaking its identity, Poe clothes it in the "habiliments of the grave" and causes it to wear a mask which resembles the face of a corpse.

Prospero is very angry at the intrusion and asks, "Who dares insult us with this blasphemous mockery?" He also commands his guests to "seize him [the figure] and unmask him—that we may know whom we have to hang at sunrise from the battlements!" It should be noted that Prospero was standing in the blue room when he uttered these words—in that youthful period of life when a man is braver toward death than he is later on, when it is closer upon him.

In his anger Prospero rushes toward the figure of death with the intention of stabbing him to death—irony of ironies!

In doing so he runs through every room in the apartment—
through every period of life—only to be stricken dead in the
seventh room when he catches up with his intended victim.
Since Prospero is standing in the blue room when he sees the
figure representing death, and since one knows that it is impossible to see very far into this apartment because of its
windings, one may conclude that the figure of death is in either the first or second room. Allegorically this could very well
mean that one becomes aware of death at a very early age.

Lastly, it might be pointed out that Prospero in his last
fateful, headlong rush at death is probably acting from a
self-destructive urge—attracted to that which he at the same
time mortally fears. In any event, with Prospero's death
comes the death of all in the apartment and the tale ends
with the morbidity that is so typical of Poe—the victory of
death over all.

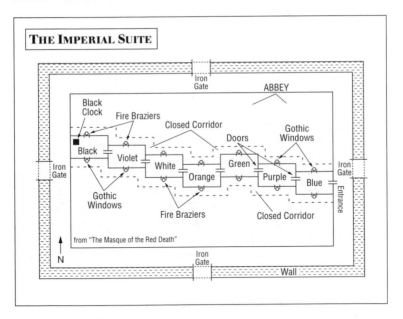

"The Masque of the Red Death" Is a Fable of Nature and Art

Kermit Vanderbilt

Kermit Vanderbilt is a professor of English at San Diego State University. Vanderbilt defines Prospero in "The Masque of the Red Death" as an artist-hero, a man of taste who employs his imagination to re-create the beauty of nature's elements inside his place of refuge. Although Prospero strives to create immortal beauty, his struggle, which echoes the conflict in Shakespeare's *The Tempest*, is between his art and nature's opposing forces of darkness. His imagination fails him in the end, and he is defeated by death's dominion over all.

The intended effect and meaning of "The Masque of the Red Death" have challenged and eluded Poe critics over the years. Readings of the tale have advanced Poe studies by offering valuable glimpses into Poe's fictional world; but none has achieved a satisfactory account of the story in all of its significant parts. An approach to Poe's meaning overlooked up to now has been a study of "The Masque" in the immediate context of Poe's esthetic ideas in 1842. Interpreted in the light of Poe's developing esthetic theory in this crucial year, the story, which appeared in the May issue of *Graham's Magazine*, becomes somewhat more than a tale of horror on the coming of Death. The hero Prospero, who bears an interesting resemblance to his namesake in Shakespeare's *The Tempest*, appears to be not a fear-crazed ruler but instead an exact portrait of Poe's artist-hero, and "The Masque of the Red Death" becomes a fable of nature and art. . . .

The month before "The Masque of the Red Death" appeared, Poe explored the contention between the artist and the limits imposed by mortality. The occasion was a review

Excerpted from "Art and Nature in 'The Masque of the Red Death,'" by Kermit Vanderbilt, *Nineteenth Century Fiction*, March 1968. Copyright © 1968 by The Regents of the University of California. Reprinted with permission from the University of California Press.

of Henry Wadsworth Longfellow's recent poetry. In this essay, which later would be enlarged as "The Poetic Principle," Poe defined the poet or creator of Beauty as a man of "taste" rather than of "pure intellect" or "moral sense." He concerns himself not with temporal duty or earthly truth but with supernal beauty. He is thereby superior to the rest of mankind. They delight in the "manifold forms and colors and sounds" of things-as-they-are, and in the conventional record of nature fashioned by the imitative craftsman. But the true artist strives to create rather than imitate, and his vision therefore transcends mere nature. His "burning thirst" for supernal beauty, a passion approaching even to madness, is related to "the *immortal* essence of man's nature." In making this "wild effort to reach the beauty above," the artist rearranges and transforms material reality:

> Inspired with a prescient ecstasy of the beauty beyond the grave, [the imagination] struggles by multiform novelty of combination among the things and thoughts of Time, to anticipate a portion of that loveliness whose very elements, perhaps, appertain solely to Eternity.

PRINCE PROSPERO IS AN ARTIST-HERO

The next month in "The Masque of the Red Death" Prince Prospero will exactly match this description of the artist-hero. When he isolates himself and one thousand knights and ladies of his court during the pestilence, the Prince is not following the dictates of a judicious "intellect" or a dutiful "moral sense." The Prince, as Poe notes, is a man of "taste." Though his courtiers conceive the adventure to be a well-planned escape from the Red Death itself, the Prince has motives of another order. Objective nature outside having been ravaged by the plague, Poe's hero will employ his taste and imagination to create a symbolic equivalent of nature's elements—a combination which can transform earthly reality into the artist's liberating vision of immortal beauty.

The colors of the Prince's bizarre suite, together with their ordering from east to west, establish the leading clues to Prospero's subjective world. Poe does not seem, at first, to insist that the colors are meaningful. He sketches the seven rooms with fairly rapid strokes, seemingly to illustrate that the Prince is "gaudy," "bizarre," "wanton," and "fantastic" in his artistic predilections:

That at the eastern extremity was hung, for example, in blue—

and vividly blue were its windows. The second chamber was purple in its ornaments and tapestries, and here the panes were purple. The third was green throughout, and so were the casements. The fourth was furnished and litten with orange—the fifth with white—the sixth with violet. The seventh apartment was closely shrouded in black velvet tapestries. . . . The panes here were scarlet—a deep blood color.

Prospero's suite, arranged from east to west, with the first apartment blue and the seventh black, connotes generally the daily cycle of nature and Shakespeare's seven ages of man, as more than one critic has remarked. No one, however, has taken Poe's art seriously enough here to confirm that the pattern is deliberate and precise. Yet Poe in the same issue of *Graham's* had reviewed Nathaniel Hawthorne's *Twice-Told Tales* and set down his requirement that in the tale "there should be no word written, of which the tendency, direct or indirect, is not to the one pre-established design."

A meaningful symmetry does develop precisely in Prospero's seven-room suite. The middle or fourth room, for example, is orange, the warmest color in Poe's spectrum, and analogous to midday. Returning to the cold, blue eastern room, one recognizes the image of dawning human life. It is succeeded by the purple room—an infusion of blue with the warmer tone of red—suggesting perhaps the quickening of life. The third room of green connotes growth, aspiration, youth; and the orange room, corresponding to the high noon of existence, becomes the harvest or fulfillment of human labor and ambition. The next room is white, at once all-color and no-color, a sudden and chill contrast which evokes decline, old age, decomposition, and approaching death. Or as Poe put it in "Tamerlane": "Let life, then, as the day-flower, fall / With the noon-day beauty—which is all." After the white apartment comes the next-to-last room of violet, a bluish blue-red colder than the corresponding purple of the second room, and prefiguring imminent death in the seventh room. In this western room, the blood-colored panes depict, of course, the dread effects of the plague, and the black tapestries represent death itself. And most prominently stands the massive ebony clock against the western wall. Its "dull, heavy monotonous clang" pervades the entire suite and further marks the ravages of time in each of the seven stages of earthly mortality.

If Prospero's suite is a metaphor of nature and mortality, one naturally asks why the Prince, apparently bent on escape from death, should have patterned his suite after the very reminders of mutability, decay, and the Red Death. The previous essay on Longfellow has suggested the answer. Poe is writing a fable of the imagination striving to control and transform the corrosive elements of nature and to gain, through immortal beauty, the artist's triumph over death. Prospero has designed an imperial suite to embody, first of all, the cycle of natural life, including what Poe had termed in the Longfellow review "the things and thoughts of Time." Next, he has created the "multiform novelty of combinations" which will permit him to move through and beyond the confinements of nature, time, and finite reality. The suite, with its windings, its stained-glass windows, closed outer corridors, artificial illumination, and bizarre embellishments—its "multitude of gaudy and fantastic appearances"—represents Prospero's imaginative re-ordering of actuality. He has created a setting which can evoke the magic and unearthly visions of the liberated sensibility. These enclosed apartments, both singly and together, define the magic circle which Poe earlier had termed "the circumscribed Eden" of the poet's dreams.

ECHOES OF SHAKESPEARE

Prospero's elaborate masque provides the main drama of Poe's tale. As in Shakespeare's *The Tempest*, the masque also climaxes the struggle between the hero's art and nature's opposing forces of darkness. In fact, the illuminating parallels between the two works, while they may not prove that Poe consciously used Shakespeare's play as a source, do suggest at least a way to read Poe's climactic action in the tale. Shakespeare's Prospero, it will be remembered, succeeds in controlling a savage island and turning it into a land suffused with idyllic greenness and ethereal music. To achieve this triumph of his art over barbaric nature, Prospero frees Ariel from a cloven pine where he had been imprisoned by the "earthly and abhorred commands" of the witch-hag Sycorax. So liberated from the destructive element of earth, the delicate Ariel becomes the spiritual quality of nature which unites with the powers of Prospero's art to create a landscape of paradisal beauty. Ariel helps to preserve Prospero's island dominion, though he reminds his master that this magic service will presently end.

Prospero's island rule, then, is precarious, and made more

so by his chief enemy Caliban, the bestial offspring of Syco-rax. Caliban embodies the withering threat of destructive na-ture to the artist's imagination. Shakespeare brilliantly con-denses this antagonism toward Prospero's higher powers by giving Caliban's curse on his master: "the red plague rid you, / For learning me your language."

The climax of Prospero's reign occurs in the masque which he conjures in the fourth act. During the dance of nymphs and reapers which follows Ceres' song of harvest abundance, Prospero grows distracted and petulant. He breaks off the masque. His imagination has failed him, his worldly fears of Caliban's "foul conspiracy" have returned, and as a result of both, he gives in to a despairing vision of cosmic dissolution. In this decline of imagination, Shakespeare's artist-hero con-fronts utter reality and admits, in effect, that man's creative art cannot transcend the life-threatening forces of hostile na-ture. In particular, he concedes his failure either to elevate or to vanquish Caliban: "This thing of darkness I / Acknowledge mine." At the end, he owns that his liberation from darkness, death, and the limits of earth must arrive from a power greater than his own:

> Now I want
> Spirits to enforce, art to enchant
> And my ending is despair,
> Unless I be reliev'd by prayer,
> Which pierces so that it assaults
> Mercy itself and frees all faults.

Poe's Prospero also meets the ultimate challenge to his art as he stages his bizarre masque "while the pestilence raged most furiously abroad." The Prince's "guiding taste," once again, dictates the colors and effects. Like Shakespeare's hero, also, Poe's Prospero gives character to the masquer-aders themselves. And their character is such stuff as dreams are made of. They are no longer people, but have be-come, instead, "a multitude of dreams": "And these—the dreams—writhed in and about, taking hue from the rooms, and causing the wild music of the orchestra to seem as the echo of their steps." Prospero has combined light and color, arabesque sculpture, wild music, and the rhythms of the dance to create his dreamland, out of space, out of time. Only the measured, hourly chiming of the ebony clock threatens to dissipate the fantasy; but this brief, contrapun-tal note of reality also emphasizes, by contrast, the prevailing "glare and glitter and piquancy and phantasm" of Prospero's conjured assembly of spirits:

> The dreams are stiff-frozen as they stand. But the echoes of the chime die away—they have endured but an instant— . . . And now again the music swells, and the dreams live, and writhe to and fro more merrily than ever, taking hue from the many-tinted windows through which stream the rays from the tripods.

Like Shakespeare's hero, Prospero has controlled the movements of his visitors, transcended the limitations of nature, and approached the threshold of supernal beauty. But at the midnight hour, the figure of the Red Death—the counterpart of Caliban—appears at the masque.

PROSPERO'S DEFEAT

Prospero's failure is first signaled not by the imminent threat of death, but by his troubled reaction to its appearance. His convulsion and anger indicate the failure of imagination even before he waves his hand to end the masque. His fearful command to his courtiers, "'Uncase the varlet that we may know whom we have to hang to-morrow at sunrise from the battlements,'" is both impotent and utterly mundane, the conventional reflex of a petulant, earthly ruler. The world, in short, is finally too much with him. The mummer of Death strides majestically past him and through the seven apartments (Poe once more underscores the exact sequence of the polychromatic décor) in symbolic triumph over each stage of earthly life and over Prospero's art and aspiring imagination. As in *The Tempest,* Ariel has taken leave and Prospero alone must confront his mortality and ultimate defeat. While the courtiers shrink from the grim figure, Prospero acknowledges this thing of darkness to be his own. In a self-destructive charge, he pursues the spectre of death westward into the seventh apartment. And predictably, death gains his midnight victory in the western room where the dread clock and macabre appointments had been the artist's ultimate challenge to his powers of imagination.

Prospero's defeat becomes inevitable within the precise logic which supports Poe's esthetic fable. And it suggests one last parallel to *The Tempest.* Anticipating the return of Caliban, Shakespeare's Prospero can no longer prolong his masque. Instead, he entertains a vision of cosmic dissolution and offers the dispiriting prophecy that

the great globe itself
Yea, all which it inherit, shall dissolve
And, like this insubstantial pageant faded,
Leave not a rack behind.

Poe repeats this cataclysmic vision of destructive nature and triumphant death. The outer and inner worlds of his defeated hero fade, and the final curtain lowers to the measured and fateful cadence of Poe's closing rhetoric:

And the life of the ebony clock went out with that of the last of the gay. And the flames of the tripods expired. And Darkness and Decay and the Red Death held illimitable dominion over all.

In "The Masque of the Red Death" Life Itself Is Death

Joseph Patrick Roppolo

Joseph Patrick Roppolo is professor of English at Tulane University. His essays primarily explore New Orleans' stage history and Poe's fiction. Roppolo suggests that in "The Masque of the Red Death" images of blood or the pulse of life ironically serve as reminders of death. Another ironic image appears in the persona of the story's intruder, the stranger "shrouded" in the "habiliments of the grave." He is not, Roppolo says, the plague or even death itself, but people's own fearful misconception of death.

In Poe's imaginative prose, beginnings unfailingly are important. "The Masque of the Red Death" begins with these three short sentences:

> The "Red Death" had long devastated the country. No pestilence had ever been so fatal or so hideous. Blood was its Avatar and its seal—the redness and horror of blood.

On one level, the reader is introduced to a disease, a plague, with hideous and terrifying symptoms, a remarkably rapid course, and inevitable termination in death. But Poe's heaviest emphasis is on blood, not as sign or symptom, but as avatar and seal. A seal is something that confirms or assures or ratifies. The appearance—the presence—of blood is confirmation or assurance of the existence of the Red Death or, more broadly, of Death itself. As avatar, blood is the incarnation, the bodily representation, of the Red Death. It is, further, something god-like, an eternal principle, for in Hindu myth, the word "avatar" referred to the descent of a god, in human form, to earth. Further, "avatar" can be defined as "a variant phase or version of a continuing entity." A second level thus emerges: blood represents something in-

Excerpted from "Meaning and 'The Masque of the Red Death,'" by Joseph Patrick Roppolo, *Tulane Studies in English*, 1963. Reprinted with permission.

visible and eternal, a ruling principle of the universe. That principle, Poe seems to suggest, is death.

But is it? The Red Death, Poe tells us, "had long devastated the country." And then: "No pestilence had ever been so fatal"—surely a remarkable second sentence for a man so careful of grammar and logic as Poe. Is or is not the Red Death a pestilence? And does the word "fatal" permit of comparison? I should like to suggest that here Poe is being neither ungrammatical nor even carefully ambiguous, but daringly clear. The Red Death is not a pestilence, in the usual sense; it is unfailingly and universally fatal, as no mere disease or plague can be; and blood is its guarantee, its avatar and seal. Life itself, then, is the Red Death, the one "affliction" shared by all mankind.

For purposes of commenting on life and of achieving his single effect, Poe chooses to emphasize death. He is aware not only of the brevity of all life and of its inevitable termination but also of men's isolation: blood, the visible sign of life, is, Poe says, "the pest ban which shuts him out from the aid and sympathy of his fellow man." In the trap of life and in his death, every man *is* an island. If there is a mutual bond, it is the shared horror of death.

PROSPERO CANNOT SHUT OUT DEATH

Out of the chaos that has "long devastated" his dominions, Prince Prospero creates a new and smaller world for the preservation of life. A kind of demi-god, Prospero can "create" his world, and he can people it; but time (the ebony clock) exists in his new world, and he is, of course, deluded in his belief that he can let in life and shut out death. Prospero's world of seven rooms, without "means [either] of ingress or egress," is a microcosm, as the parallel with the seven ages of man indicates, and its people are eminently human, with their predilection for pleasure and their susceptibility to "sudden impulses of despair or frenzy." In their masquerade costumes, the people are "in fact, a multitude of dreams," but they are fashioned like the inhabitants of the macrocosmic world. Many are beautiful, but many also are bizarre or grotesque. Some are wanton; some are "arabesque figures with unsuited limbs and appointments"; some are terrible, some are disgusting, and some are "delirious fancies such as the madman fashions" (and Prospero, the demi-god, for all his "fine eye for colors and effects," may indeed be mad). But all of them are life, and in six of the seven apartments "the heart of life" beats "feverishly." And even here, by deliberate use of the word "feverishly," Poe links life with disease and death.

The seventh apartment is not the room of death; death occurs in fact in each of the rooms. It is, however, the room in which the reminders of death are strongest, and it is the room to which all must come who traverse the preceding six. Death's colors, red and black, are there; and there the ebony clock mercilessly measures Time, reminding the revelers hour after hour that life, like the course of the Red Death, is short.

When the clock strikes the dreaded hour of twelve, the revelers become aware suddenly of the presence of a masked figure which none has noted before:

> The figure was tall and gaunt, and shrouded from head to foot in the habiliments of the grave. The mask which concealed the visage was made so nearly to resemble the countenance of a stiffened corpse that the closest scrutiny must have had difficulty in detecting the cheat. And yet all this might have been endured, if not approved, by the mad revellers around. But the mummer had gone so far as to assume the type of the Red Death. His vesture was dabbled in blood—and his broad brow, with all the features of the face, was besprinkled with the scarlet horror.

Poe does not indicate in which room the awareness of the masked figure occurred first, but Prince Prospero sees this blood-sprinkled horror in the blue, or easternmost, room, which is usually associated with birth, rather than with death. The figure moves then through each of the apartments, and Prospero follows, to meet his own death in the room of black and red.

Not once does Poe say that the figure is the Red Death. Instead, "this new presence" is called "the masked figure," "the stranger," "the mummer," "this spectral image," and "the intruder." He is "shrouded" in "the habiliments of the grave," the dress provided by the living for their dead and endowed by the living with all the horror and terror which they associate with death. The mask, fashioned to resemble "the countenance of a stiffened corpse," is but a mask, a "cheat." And all this, we are told, "might have been borne" had it not been for the blood, that inescapable reminder to life of the inevitability of death. The intruder is, literally, "The Mask of the Red Death," not the plague itself, nor even—as many would have it—the all-inclusive representation of Death.

There is horror in the discovery that "the grave-cerements and corpse-like mask!" are "untenanted by any tangible form," but the horror runs more deeply than the supernatural interpretation allows, so deeply in fact that it washes itself clean to emerge as Truth. Blood, Poe has been saying, is (or is symbolic of) the life force; but even as it suggests life, blood serves as a reminder of death. Man himself invests death with elements of terror, and he clothes not death but the terror of death in garb of his own making—"the habiliments of the grave"—and then runs, foolishly, to escape it or, madly, to kill it, mistaking the mummer, the cheat, for death itself. The fear of death can kill: Prospero attempts to attack the masked figure and falls; but when man's image of death is confronted directly, it is found to be nothing. The vestments are empty. The intruder in "The Masque of the Red Death" is, then, not the plague, not death itself, but man's creation, his self-aroused and self-developed fear of his own mistaken concept of death.

THE FATE OF THE UNIVERSE

Death is nevertheless present, as pervasive and as invisible as eternal law. He is nowhere and everywhere, not only near, about, and around man, but in him. And so it is, at last, that, having unmasked their unreasoning fear, the revelers acknowledge the presence of the Red Death. One by one, the revelers die—as everything endowed with life must; and, with the last of them, time, which is measured and feared only by man, dies, too.

Poe might have stopped there, just as he might have ended "The Raven" with the sixteenth stanza. The narrative is complete, and there are even "morals" or "lessons" for those who demand them. But, as Poe says in "The Philosophy of Composition,"

> in subjects so handled, however skilfully, or with however vivid an array of incident, there is always a certain hardness or nakedness, which repels the artistical eye. Two things are invariably required—first, some amount of complexity, or more properly, adapation; and, secondly, some amount of suggestiveness—some undercurrent, however indefinite, of meaning.

To achieve complexity and suggestiveness, Poe added two stanzas to "The Raven." To "The Masque of the Red Death" he added two sentences: "And the flames of the tripods expired. And Darkness and Decay and the Red Death held illimitable dominion over all."

"Let there be light" was one of the principles of Creation; darkness, then, is a principle of Chaos. And to Poe Chaos is synonymous with Nothingness, "which, to all finite perception, Unity must be." Decay occurs as matter "expels the ether" to return to or to sink into Unity. Prince Prospero's world, created out of a chaos ruled by the Red Death, returns to chaos, ruled by the trinity of Darkness and Decay and the Red Death. But, it will be remembered, Prince Prospero's world came into being *because of* the Red Death, which, although it includes death, is the principle of life. In Chaos, then, is the promise of new lives and of new worlds which will swell into existence and then, in their turn, subside into nothingness in the eternal process of contraction and expansion which Poe describes in "Eureka."

There are "morals" implicit and explicit in this interpretation of "The Masque of the Red Death," but they need not be underlined here. Poe, who had maintained in his "Review of Nathaniel Hawthorne's *Twice-Told Tales*" that "Truth is often, and in very great degree, the aim of the tale," was working with a larger, but surely not entirely inexpressible, truth than can be conveyed in a simple "Poor Richard" maxim; and in that task, it seems to me, he transcends the tale (into which classification most critics put "The Masque of the Red Death") to create a prose which, in its free rhythms, its diction, its compression, and its suggestion, approaches poetry.

The ideas that were haunting Poe when he published "Eureka" were already haunting him in 1842, when he published "The Masque of the Red Death," and what emerged was not, certainly, a short story; nor was it, except by the freest definition, a tale. For either category, it is deficient in plot and in characterization. Instead, "The Masque of the Red Death" combines elements of the parable and of the myth. Not as explicit or as pointedly allegorical always as the parable, "The Masque of the Red Death" nevertheless can be (and has been) read as a parable of the inevitability and the universality of death; but it deals also with the feats of a hero or demi-god—Prospero—and with Poe's concepts of universal principles, and it has the mystery and the remoteness of myth. What Poe has created, then, is a kind of mythic parable, brief and poetic, of the human condition, of man's fate, and of the fate of the universe.

The Enclosure Motif in "The Fall of the House of Usher"

Leonard W. Engel

Leonard W. Engel of Quinnipiac College describes Poe's use of the enclosure motif in "The Fall of the House of Usher." From the opening of the tale to its conclusion, images of enclosure provide a dramatic focus on both plot and character development and contribute to the mood of pervading gloom. Entering the ultimate enclosure, the house itself, the narrator embarks on a journey into madness and self-revelation, from which he is reborn into new life.

That Poe realized the potency of the enclosure in fiction is clear from his essay "The Philosophy of Composition," where he refers to it as a "close *circumscription of space.*" It is, he writes, "absolutely necessary to the effect of insulated incident;—it has the force of a frame to a picture." Decidedly, Poe is speaking of the importance of an enclosure on the plot, or incident, of a narrative, but I believe it has a significant influence on character in his tales as well. For one thing, it serves to separate the character from the real world, isolate him physically, and intensify his mental experience. For example, in "The Fall of the House of Usher," the series of enclosures obvious from the opening scene in the tale to its conclusion, contributes to the mood of gloom pervading the narrator's consciousness and leads directly to the dominant enclosure—the House itself, which the narrator will soon enter and from which he will barely escape. In short, Poe's use of the enclosure device chronicles the narrator's journey from reason to madness in addition to providing the artistic focus and unity of impression that were such a fundamental part of his theory of the short story. . . .

Excerpted from "The Journey from Reason to Madness: Edgar Allan Poe's 'The Fall of the House of Usher,'" by Leonard W. Engel, *Essays in Art and Sciences*, May 1985. Reprinted with permission.

THE MOOD OF GLOOM

The first sentence, "During the whole of a dull, dark, and soundless day in the autumn of the year, when the clouds hung oppressively low in the heavens, I had been passing alone, on horseback, through a singularly dreary tract of country, and, at length found myself, as the shades of the evening drew on, within view of the melancholy House of Usher," and the description that follows is highly suggestive of a tightly closed, virtually airtight box. The narrator's next words, ". . . with the first glimpse of the building, a sense of unsufferable gloom pervaded my spirit," a masterful stroke by Poe, emphasizes not only the dominance of the House and the mood of gloom, but deepen the effect of confinement on the narrator, as though he were on the verge of suffocation. Thus in the first two sentences, Poe artfully describes, in the following order, the climatic conditions, the time of year, the countryside, the time of day, and finally the House itself. The movement is from the general to the particular, culminating with the House, and leaving the narrator with powerful and ominous feelings.

A sensitive man of reason, he makes a concerted effort to dispel the gloom by trying to objectify the scene, to detach himself from it and describe it logically, perhaps even reduce the House to a mere house, but he is unsuccessful. He rearranges the particulars of the scene, descending from his horse to gaze into a black tarn by the house. What he sees shocks him more because all the images are now grotesquely inverted. The "lurid" black water, of course, foreshadows the dramatic conclusion of the tale. Despite his disturbing feelings, however, the narrator faces the inevitable, ". . . in this mansion of gloom I now proposed to myself a sojourn of some weeks." Clearly, he is a man whose head rules his heart, and he is able to put his feelings of depression aside and accept his situation, at least for the present.

After this lengthy introduction, uncommon in most of Poe's tales but quintessential in this one, establishing the mood of gloom, Poe has the narrator ride over a short causeway—the threshold of the House—and enter the Gothic archway. "A valet, of stealthy step," he relates "thence conducted me, in silence, through many dark and intricate passages in my progress to the *studio* of his master." From this point on, the narrator's sense of responsibility, sense of self, diminishes, and his actions are more and more controlled by those around him. For example, he is "conducted" by the valet "through many dark and intricate passages" and is "ushered . . . into the presence of his master." This description, consistent with the singular mood of gloom, has about it a sense of further isolation from the world the narrator has recently left. He is entering a labyrinthine unknown, symbolized, of course, by the House. As [critic] Roy Male has remarked, "The narrator is 'ushered into' Roderick's room." "The name of the house and its occupants," Male concludes, "is in keeping with the story's province: the threshold between mind and matter, reason and madness, life and death."

The narrator's journey *does* symbolically suggest a movement from "reason to madness." [Critic] Daniel Hoffman has astutely pointed out that "'Usher' is a terrifying tale of the protagonist's journey into the darkest, most hidden regions of himself." I believe that Poe uses the House, with its numerous chambers and passageways, to reinforce the mysteriousness of this journey and to dramatize the stages or levels of awareness he passes through, or loses touch with, as he moves from the rational, safe, secure world to the irrational world of Roderick and Madeline.

AN OPPRESSIVE SENSE OF ENTOMBMENT

The narrator's description of Roderick's room, with its remote angles and recesses and "air of stern, deep, and irredeemable gloom," substantiates this view, and the changes he sees in Roderick are shocking. "Surely, man had never before so terribly altered," the narrator exclaims, "in so brief a period, as had Roderick Usher! It was with difficulty that I could bring myself to admit the identity of the wan being before me with the companion of my early boyhood."

In the following passage, Poe reveals the changes in Roderick's psychological identity through his "struggle with the grim phantasm, FEAR." Roderick, the narrator relates,

> . . . was enchained by certain superstitious impressions in regard to the dwelling which he tenanted, and whence, for many years, he had never ventured forth—in regard to an influence whose suppositious force was conveyed in terms too shadowy here to be re-stated—an influence which some peculiarities in the mere form and substance of his family mansion, had, by dint of long sufferance, he said, obtained over his spirit—an effect which the *physique* of the gray walls and turrets, and of the dim tarn into which they all looked down, had, at length, brought about upon the *morale* of his existence.

The key words here connote confinement and point toward the concluding phrase, "the *morale* of his existence." Not only has Roderick's physical identity been affected by the atmosphere of the House, these images suggest deeper, more complex changes as well. In effect, Usher's psychological identity is in the grip of "FEAR," and the enclosure has provided the impetus for his obsession.

Even Roderick's art is filled with images of enclosure. An oppressive sense of entombment pervades the narrator's description of one of the pictures Usher has painted, "A small picture presented the interior of an immensely long and rectangular vault. . . . This excavation lay at an exceeding depth below the surface of the earth. No outlet was observed in any portion of its vast extent, and no torch . . . was discernable; yet a flood of intense rays . . . bathed the whole in a ghastly and inappropriate splendour." Undoubtedly, this passage describing Roderick's picture foreshadows Lady Madeline's premature burial in the vault beneath the House. Furthermore, in one of Roderick's poems, "The Haunted Palace," the narrator notes a reference to past glories being ". . . but a dim-remembered story/Of the old time entombed."

Enclosures are everywhere, and the more the narrator immerses himself in Roderick's life, the more he senses the overwhelming gloom he noted in the initial paragraph. In "The Haunted Palace," he relates, "I was . . . the more forcibly impressed with it . . . because I perceived, and for the first time, a full consciousness on the part of Usher, of the tottering of his lofty reason upon her throne." The narrator perceives Usher's awareness of his own irrationality, and the line "Of the old time entombed," might symbolize Roderick's perception of the entombment of his reason.

SEPARATION OF SELF

Remarkably, what the narrator *fails* to perceive is the beginning of his own psychological deterioration. When Roderick tells him of Madeline's death and of his intention to preserve her corpse, "(previously to its final interment) in one of the numerous vaults within the main walls of the building," the narrator regards it "as at best but a harmless, and by no means an unnatural, precaution," especially since the family burial ground is at a distance from the house and exposed to grave robbers.

The body having been encoffined, we two alone bore it to its rest. The vault in which we placed it (and which had been so long unopened that our torches, half smothered in its oppressive atmosphere, gave us little opportunity for investigation) was small, damp, and entirely without means of admission for light; lying, at great depth, immediately beneath that portion of the building in which was my own sleeping apartment.

Before leaving the vault, they have a last look at the deceased. "The disease which had thus entombed the lady in the maturity of youth, had left, as usual in all maladies of a strictly cataleptical character, the mockery of a faint blush upon the bosom and the face, and that suspiciously lingering smile upon the lip which is so terrible in death. We replaced and screwed down the lid, and . . . made our way, with toil, into the scarcely less gloomy apartments of the upper portion of the house." Poe clearly indicates they are burying a living person, but the narrator for all his astute reasoning elsewhere in the tale fails to discern this most crucial of facts.

Poe has from the beginning used enclosures as a means of creating setting, influencing the mood of the narrator, and intensifying the mystery, and the cumulative effect of them on the narrator results in an increasing awareness of Usher's situation. But, at the same time, the narrator appears to lose perspective in other areas, such as the mystery surrounding Madeline. After his initial glimpse of her on the evening of the day he arrived, he does not see her again until he and Roderick convey her to the vault and seal her up. His lack of curiosity about her is amazing; he does not ask to see her while she is ill, nor does he mention her name to Roderick, and he unhesitatingly accepts Roderick's explanation for temporarily entombing her. One would, at the very least, expect some sort of ceremony accompanying Madeline's death; after all, she was held in respect in the region for she was known as "Lady Madeline." But the narrator apparently sees nothing wrong with the proceedings and does not even question the "faint blush" upon her bosom and face. One wonders if this sane man from the outside world, this model of objectivity and rationalism, Roderick's touchstone with reality, is not beginning to lose his own bearings.

I believe this is exactly what Poe wants his readers to infer, and he indicates this change most forcibly when the narrator is gazing at the face of the living Madeline and rationalizing about her appearance and the nature of the malady in pseudoscientific jargon. The climactic loss of his old self in this scene, in point of fact, his identity, what [critic] Sam Girgus calls his "separation of self from his body—" his disembodiment or transcendence, occurs while the narrator is in a vault under the House; this seems to be the major event toward which Poe's language and imagery have been directed.

A SLOW DESCENT INTO MADNESS

In the days following Madeline's burial, the narrator's continuing loss of self is evident as he absorbs more of Roderick's mood. He states, "It was no wonder that his [Roderick's] condition terrified—that it infected me. I felt creeping upon me, by slow yet certain degrees, the wild influences of his own fantastic yet impressive superstitions." In the final awful scene, Poe intensifies the narrator's mental and emotional deterioration almost entirely in terms of physical enclosure. About a week after the burial, the narrator relates, he experiences "the full power" of these wild influences. He cannot sleep and, struggling up, peers "within the intense darkness of the chamber [listening] . . . to certain low and indefinite sounds."

Rationally, the narrator knows there is no cause for alarm, but emotionally he is terrified. He tries, unsuccessfully, to attribute his feelings to the room with its strange trappings and thus explain them away. It then crosses his mind that the room may be affecting him in some unknown way and thereby be a possible explanation for his emotional confusion. But because of his scientific bias, he dismisses this as unreasonable, and he is left with an inexplicable situation, which further agitates him because he is unaccustomed to it. The room thus serves as a continuing metaphor for his breakdown, but Poe skillfully keeps that breakdown in the shadow of Roderick's, which, indeed, is climaxed by the return of Madeline.

Poe further intensifies the moment by describing the unnatural weather conditions and metaphorically correlating the mind of the narrator with the tempest outside. He had done this in the opening scene, it will be recalled, when he suggested the narrator's vacillating mental state by describing the low hanging clouds. Now he describes the storm in all its fury as Roderick, who has run to the narrator's apartment in an extremely distracted state, hurries to one of the casements and throws it open: "The impetuous fury of the

entering gust nearly lifted us from our feet. . . . The exceeding density of the clouds . . . hung so low as to press upon the
turrets of the house . . . [and] gaseous exhalation . . . hung
about and enshrouded the mansion." Thus the storm outside
mirrors the turmoil and confusion in the minds of Roderick
and the narrator.

This passage also suggests that Roderick, who has not
moved from the interior of the house, has not even gone near
a window since the narrator arrived, now wishes to be released from its influence. Ironically, it is the narrator who
closes the window and induces Roderick to sit and listen to
one of his favorite romances, the Gothic "Mad Trist," which
the narrator begins to read. This is a reversal; up to this
point Roderick has been the initiator of the action, first re-
questing the narrator to visit him, then gradually leading
him into deeper involvement with his activities.

Significantly, the events of the eerie narrative, the narrator reads, foreshadow those which will occur in the room
very shortly. More important, the act of reading the emotionally explosive "Mad Trist" to the highly unstable Roderick at this critical moment is either to overlook or become so
desensitized to present reality that his own thinking and
feeling processes are dangerously disconnected. It indicates
the narrator's further withdrawal from self, for he seems to
sense no incongruity between his action and the reality
around him. Even mad Roderick recognizes the gravity of
the situation for just before Madeline appears, he jumps to
his feet and shouts at the narrator––*"Madman! I tell you
that she now stands without the door!"*

ESCAPE FROM THE ENCLOSURE

It seems certain Roderick has been tacitly pleading with the
narrator for some kind of recognition, some understanding
of the seriousness of their plight. He has come to the narrator's chamber at a late hour and in a disturbed state and has
thrown open the window in the middle of a raging storm not
merely to be soothed, sat down, and read to as though he
were a child. His frustration is reflected by the shrieking at
the narrator and twice calling him *"Madman!"*

As I have argued, I believe that Poe has used the enclosure
to indicate the levels of awareness the narrator is no longer
capable of perceiving. The device chronicles the stripping
away of the narrator's old, controlled, self where his finely

honed mind has been dulled by the exigencies of the moment, becoming less aware of crucial, empirical facts. However, at the climatic moment of the tale the device also awakens him to the horror of what he has been witnessing. When
he sees the "enshrouded" figure of Madeline, "trembling and
reeling," enter the room and fall on Roderick, enclosing him
under her and bearing him "to the floor a corpse, and a victim to the terrors he had anticipated," he finally comes to
himself as though awakening from a bad dream:

> From that chamber, and from that mansion, I fled aghast.
> The storm was still abroad in all its wrath as I found myself
> crossing the old causeway. Suddenly there shot along the
> path a white light, and I turned to see whence a gleam so un-
> usual could have issued, for the vast house and its shadows
> were alone behind me. The radiance was that of the full, set-
> ting, and blood-red moon, which now shone vividly through
> that once barely discernible fissure, of which I have before
> spoken as extending from the roof of the building, in zigzag
> direction, to the base. While I gazed, this fissure rapidly
> widened—there came a fierce breath of the whirlwind—the
> entire orb of the satellite burst at once upon my sight—my
> brain reeled as I saw the mighty wall rushing asunder—there
> was a long tumultuous shouting sound like the voice of a
> thousand waters—and the deep and dark tarn at my feet
> closed sullenly and silently over the fragments of the "House
> of Usher."

The narrator leaves the chamber, flees the house, crosses
the causeway, removes himself from the shadow of the
house, which is so sharply defined by the light from the
"blood-red moon," and apparently feels no oppressive
clouds, as he had in the first scene, for they have been dis-
pelled by the change in climatic conditions. In other words,
he extricates himself from all the enclosures to which he has
been systematically and inevitably drawn. In point of fact,
the entire "House of Usher" is at once destroyed, enclosed so
to speak, by "the deep and dank tarn" at his feet.

These events have suggested a number of interpretations,
but to me one thing they undoubtedly imply is that the attempt to lose one-self, or bury one's identity and assume an
identity foreign to one's nature, must prove an extremely dangerous undertaking. Fatally fascinated with the language and
imagery of enclosure, the narrator finally recognizes that he
cannot lose contact with his deeper self, cannot separate his
thoughts and feelings, and still remain sane. This sudden revelation comes just in time to allow him to make a harrowing

escape from the house with his identity, relatively intact. In effect, what he experiences is a symbolic "burial"—a journey to the edge of madness, to the brink of destruction—and a "resurrection," a "rebirth" of sorts and a chance for another life.

Similar to his other tales where the enclosure plays a dominant role—in "William Wilson," for example, Poe marks the narrator's journey to self-revelation, which in this story means self-destruction, with a series of carefully wrought enclosures—the device provides dramatic focus for both plot and character, greatly heightening the artistic merit of "The Fall of the House of Usher."

"The Fall of the House of Usher": A Rational Interpretation of Terror

I.M. Walker

Writing for the *Modern Language Review,* I.M. Walker of Manchester takes issue with earlier critics' dismissal of "The Fall of the House of Usher" as marred with elements of the fantastic or gloomy German mysticism. The legitimate sources of realistic terror have been overlooked, Walker says, and these are based on true principles of human nature and conduct. These sources of terror can be traced to the opening image of the sinister tarn, a symbol of desolation and decay that surrounds the House of Usher. In addition, the gases and odors rising from the tarn are said to contain febrile miasma, an agent capable of causing physical illness and mental derangement in those who inhale it.

Early in September 1839 Edgar Allan Poe sent the issue of *Burton's Gentleman's Magazine* containing 'The Fall of the House of Usher' to James E. Heath, the minor novelist and playwright, and former editor of the *Southern Literary Messenger.* While Poe's accompanying letter to Heath is lost, it is clear from Heath's reply of 12 September that Poe had approached him about the possibility of the tale being reprinted in the *Messenger.* Although Heath admired Poe's skill as a writer and praised his abilities as a critic, both he and [editor] Thomas White were distinctly unenthusiastic about what they considered to be the 'German' subject matter of 'The Fall of the House of Usher':

> He [White] doubts whether the readers of the Messenger have much relish for tales of the German school, although written with great power and ability, and in this opinion I confess to you frankly, I am strongly inclined to concur. I doubt very much whether tales of the wild, improbable and terrible class, can ever be permanently popular in this country.

Excerpted from "The Legitimate Sources of Terror in 'The Fall of the House of Usher,'" by I.M. Walker, *Modern Language Review,* vol. 61, no. 4, October 1966, pp. 585–92. Reprinted with permission from *Modern Language Review.*

Heath publicly re-stated these views in a notice of *Burton's Gentleman's Magazine* in the October 1839 issue of the *Messenger,* where Poe is complimented on his 'affluent and splendid' imagination, but brought to task because of his devotion to 'Germanism': 'We also predicted that Mr. Poe would reach a high grade in American literature, but we also thought and still think, that he is too much attached to the gloomy German mysticism, to be a useful and effective writer. . .'. In order to illustrate his argument Heath singled out 'The Fall of the House of Usher' as a tale written with 'great power' but marred by 'Germanism'.

Poe did not allow these criticisms of his work in general and 'The Fall of the House of Usher' in particular to pass unanswered, and in his 'Preface' to *Tales of the Grotesque and Arabesque* (1840) he replied to the false notion ' . . . which has induced one or two critics to tax me, in all friendliness, with what they have been pleased to term "Germanism" and gloom'. Evidently with Heath's charges in mind, he went on to state in forthright and unambiguous terms that the terror he wrote about was not fantastic or 'German', but was realistic and based upon true principles of human nature and conduct:

> If in many of my productions terror has been the thesis, I maintain that terror is not of Germany, but of the soul—that I have deduced this terror only from its legitimate sources, and urged it only to its legitimate results.

Poe's defence of his work in this 'Preface' has too often been underestimated by his critics, and this is nowhere more apparent than in the considerable body of critical commentary on 'The Fall of the House of Usher'. It has been generally recognized that the tale concerns the disintegration of Roderick Usher, but the 'legitimate sources' of terror about which Poe stated he was writing have been largely neglected. . . .

THE SINISTER TARN

The opening scene contains the ingredients of a conventional Gothic melodrama: the solitary rider, passing through 'a singularly dreary tract of country', is oppressed by 'a sense of insufferable gloom', when, as evening draws on, he approaches the lonely, dilapidated, and melancholy House of Usher. The climax of the scene occurs when the rider reins his horse at the brink of 'a black and lurid tarn that lay in unruffled lustre by the dwelling', and experiences 'a shudder more thrilling than before' as he sees in the silent black waters 'inverted images of the grey sedge, and the ghastly tree-stems, and the vacant and eye-like windows'. Although the gloom of this scene undoubtedly prepares the reader for the melancholy happenings at the House of Usher, the black tarn is not simply part of an elaborate Gothic décor. Poe's theory and practice of the short story were conditioned by his belief in unity of form and effect, a unity in which every element in the tale must contribute to the *dénouement*. In his famous review of Nathaniel Hawthorne's *Twice-Told Tales* he declared: 'In the whole composition there should be no word written, of which the tendency, direct or indirect, is not to the one pre-established design'. 'The Fall of the House of Usher' concerns the total disintegration of Roderick Usher, and in accord with Poe's theory of the unity of a work of art, the sinister tarn which so appals the narrator in the first scene, contributes actively to Usher's destruction.

The black tarn is associated with imagery of desolation (grey sedge) and decay (rotting trees), as well as with the house itself, which, as the poem 'The Haunted Palace' makes quite clear, operates throughout as a symbol of Roderick Usher. An emblematic statement of the relationship between the house-man symbol and the tarn is made when the narrator sees them joined together by a crack in the structure of the mansion, the crack representing the imminent collapse of Roderick Usher's ruined personality:

> Perhaps the eye of a scrutinising observer might have discovered a barely perceptible fissure, which, extending from the roof of the building in front, made its way down the wall in a zigzag direction, until it became lost in the sullen waters of the tarn.

The relationship between Roderick Usher and his physical surroundings, and the influence which these surroundings of the decayed house and the stagnant tarn have exerted on his life and the lives of his ancestors, is recognized and meditated upon by the narrator early in the tale:

> . . . while running over in thought the perfect keeping of the character of the premises with the accredited character of the people, and while speculating upon the possible influence which the one, in the long lapse of centuries, might have excercised upon the other.

The narrator also observes what he calls an 'atmosphere' around the house and tarn, which he rightly believes to have noxious qualities:

> . . . about the whole mansion and domain there hung an at-
> mosphere peculiar to themselves and their immediate vicin-
> ity—an atmosphere which had no affinity with the air of
> heaven, but which had reeked up from the decayed trees, and
> the grey wall, and the silent tarn—a pestilent and mystic
> vapour, and leaden-hued.

Poe is using the word 'atmosphere' in this passage in a special physical sense that is rarely used to-day, and which the
New English Dictionary defines as 'a gaseous envelope surrounding any substance', and quite distinct from the air. The
narrator is careful to point out that the 'atmosphere' he sees
surrounding the house and tarn 'had no affinity with the air
of heaven'. The popular *Cyclopaedia* compiled by Abraham
Rees supplies a nineteenth-century usage of the word that is
close to Poe's: 'ATMOSPHERE of solid or consistent Bodies,
is a kind of sphere formed by the effluvia, or minute cor-
puscles emitted from them'.

It is not only the narrator, however, who can recognize the
influence which this pestilential 'atmosphere' has on Roderick Usher, for Usher himself is in the agonizing position of
being able to follow the progress of his own disintegration,
while being powerless to prevent it. He tells the narrator of
the deleterious effect which his physical environment has
had on his life:

> —an effect which the *physique* of the grey walls and turrets,
> and of the dim tarn into which they all looked down, had, at
> length, brought about upon the *morale* of his existence.

Roderick Usher has a firm belief in the sentience of inor-
ganic matter, and significantly he sees the reason for this belief in the 'atmosphere' arising from the stagnant tarn and
decayed house. Moreover, he states clearly that the 'atmosphere' has been responsible not only for the strange characteristics of his family, but for his own pitiful condition also:

> Its evidence—the evidence of the sentience—was to be seen,
> he said (and here I started as he spoke,) in the gradual yet
> certain condensation of an atmosphere of their own about the
> waters and the walls. The result was discoverable, he added,
> in that silent, yet importunate and terrible influence which
> for centuries had moulded the destinies of his family, and
> which made *him* what I now saw him—what he was.

On the night of the catastrophe the noxious 'atmosphere' is particularly dense, and gathers around the house like a shroud:

> But the under surfaces of the huge masses of agitated vapour,
> as well as all terrestrial objects immediately surrounding us,
> were glowing in the unnatural light of a faintly luminous and

distinctly visible gaseous exhalation which hung about and enshrouded the mansion.

The narrator realizing the dangers of this 'atmosphere' warns Usher away from the open window, telling him '. . ."the air is chilling and dangerous to your frame"', and rightly suggesting that the foul airs "'. . . have their ghastly origin in the rank miasma of the tarn."'

THE EFFECTS OF FEBRILE MIASMA

It was accepted as a scientific fact at the time that odours and gases arising out of foul water or decayed matter were the causes of physical and mental illnesses. Thomas C. Upham, for example, the highly esteemed American philosopher and psychologist, wrote in his *Elements of Mental Philosophy:*

> There is another gas, the FEBRILE MIASMA, which is found, on being inhaled, to affect the mind also, by first affecting the sanguineous fluid. But this gas diminishes instead of increasing the volume of blood; as is indicated by a small contracted pulse, and an increasing constriction of the capillaries. As in the case of the nitrous oxide gas, the mental exercises are rendered intense and vivid by the febrile miasma; but the emotions which are experienced, instead of being pleasant, are gloomy and painful. The trains of thought, which are at such times suggested, and the creations of the imagination are all of an analogous character, strange, spectral and terrifying.

It is known that Poe was a keen student of current scientific opinion including medicine, and it is extremely unlikely that he could have written with such convincing realism and accuracy about madness and crime, had he not been familiar with the opinions of 'mental philosophers' then in vogue: men like Benjamin Rush, Isaac Ray, and Thomas Upham. Although *Elements of Mental Philosophy* is not mentioned by Poe in his writings, he was in all probability acquainted with the work which had an international reputation, and which had been published in several American editions by 1839. With his passion for scientific fact and his interest in abnormal mental states, Poe would have been likely to turn to systems of contemporary psychology in the same way that modern writers have turned to Freud and Jung. Moreover, in Poe's day medical science and psychology were far less technical than they are to-day, and information regarding both mental and physical diseases was readily available to the intelligent layman, not only in the original works of the scientists, but also in popular journals and encyclopaedias. The practice of reviewing medical works in journals of a general cultural interest would suggest that these works had a far wider appeal than to the immediate medical profession, and this is borne out by the extensive sales of medical works throughout the time Poe was writing. Poe was certainly aware of the accepted medical opinion that gases arising from stagnant water or decayed matter could be a danger to health, since he mentions this on more than one occasion. In 'King Pest' the luminous and pestilential 'atmosphere' arising from the deserted and decaying city is similar to that seen by Roderick Usher and the narrator on the night of the catastrophe, and ten years later in an essay on 'Street Paving', he suggested that an objection to wooden paving could lie in the possibility of '. . . injury to the public health from miasmata arising from the wood'.

There is a close resemblance between what Thomas Upham and other authorities said about the effects of miasma on the human mind and constitution, and Roderick Usher's deranged mental and physical condition. The letter which the narrator receives calling him to the House of Usher betrays Roderick's derangement: 'The MS. gave evidence of nervous agitation. The writer spoke of acute bodily illness— of a mental disorder which oppressed him'. Thomas Upham pointed out that 'febrile miasma' produced a diminished blood supply and a slow pulse in those exposed to its vapours, and the results of such an exposure can be observed in Usher's physical appearance. The narrator speaks of the 'wan being' before him, and is horrified by his 'cadaverousness of complexion', and the 'ghastly pallor of the skin'.

Throughout the tale Usher is in an acute state of terror arising from undefined causes:

> To an anomalous species of terror I found him a bounden slave. "I shall perish," said he, "I *must* perish in this deplorable folly. . . . In this unnerved—in this pitiable condition—I feel that the period will sooner or later arrive when I must abandon life and reason together, in some struggle with the grim phantasm FEAR."

This state of terror can also be traced back to the stagnant tarn and its miasmic 'atmosphere'. Mental philosophers including Thomas Upham postulated that effluvia arising from decayed matter could produce serious mental and emotional disturbances in those exposed to them. John MacCulloch, the eminent Scottish doctor, in a standard and authoritative work on miasma, describes an irrational state of terror produced by miasmata, which is remarkably similar to Usher's condition:

> Despair and fear, analogous passions, are, rather than anger
> and its modes, the two great mental affections of hypochon-
> driasis; and hence it is that fear chiefly, often attends the
> paroxysm of this obscure remittent. This however is true of
> marsh fevers generally, whether remittent or intermittent,
> and under all the modes of these diseases. So remarkable in-
> deed is this mental condition, fear, in the disorders of this na-
> ture, that in some parts of the Mediterranean where these
> fevers are endemic, the only name by which they are known
> to the common people, is Scanto; fear or fright.

MacCulloch also observed that miasma could produce an
adverse effect upon the 'intellectual faculties':

> The conditions of the intellect then which I would here re-
> mark, are those of torpidity on the one hand and excitement
> on the other; the first consisting in an inability to think,
> sometimes attended by confusion of thought, and the other in
> an excessive flow or crowding of ideas, necessarily, in many
> cases, attended also with similar confusion.

The narrator recognizes in Usher precisely similar states of
alternating excitement and depression, as well as the confusion of thought mentioned by MacCulloch: 'In the manner of
my friend I was at once struck by an incoherence—an inconsistency: . . . His action was alternately vivacious and sullen'.

Thomas Upham, in the passage previously quoted from
Elements of Mental Philosophy, said that in those affected by
the 'febrile miasma', the 'creations of the imagination' would
be 'strange, spectral and terrifying'. The same adjectives
could be used to describe exactly Roderick Usher's peculiar
artistic compositions. His music is distorted by a 'morbid
condition of the auditory nerve', and he plays 'a certain singular perversion and amplification of the wild air of the last
waltz of Von Weber'. In his 'fantastic' impromptu poem 'The
Haunted Palace' Usher writes about the break-up of his own
mind, while his 'phantasmagoric' painting could be accurately described as 'strange, spectral and terrifying':

> A small picture presented the interior of an immensely long
> and rectangular vault or tunnel, with low walls, smooth,
> white and without interruption or device. . . . No outlet was
> observed in any portion of its vast extent, and no torch, or
> other artificial source of light was discernible; yet a flood of
> intense rays rolled throughout, and bathed the whole in a
> ghastly and inappropriate splendour.

The poem, the music, and the painting are all compulsive revelations of Usher's emotional and intellectual derangement.

A STUDY OF MENTAL DERANGEMENT

Following the entombment of Madeline, Roderick's disintegration accelerates. His physical appearance is more spectral and startling than ever: 'The pallor of his countenance had assumed, if possible, a more ghastly hue', and his mental derangement has obviously become extreme. Moods of 'mad hilarity' alternate with periods of silent vacancy, and terror has taken complete possession of his mind: 'The once occasional huskiness of his tone was heard no more; and a tremulous quaver, as if of extreme terror, habitually characterized his utterance'.

But what is perhaps more surprising is what happens to the narrator after Madeline's entombment. His seemingly detached and rational earlier attitudes for the most part disappear, and his mind begins to submit to the power of Roderick's mad fantasies: 'I felt creeping upon me, by slow yet certain degrees, the wild influences of his own fantastic yet impressive superstitions'. What happens to the narrator after Madeline's death is not altogether unprepared for earlier in the tale, for despite his façade of rationalism, he has shown signs of an imaginative and highly impressionable mind. His first sight of the House of Usher had affected him with a sense of gloomy foreboding quite beyond rational explanation: 'I know not how it was—but, with the first glimpse of the building, a sense of insufferable gloom pervaded my spirit'. Similarly his feelings when he first sees Madeline Usher are impressionistic and irrational:

> While he spoke, the lady Madeline (for so was she called) passed slowly through a remote portion of the apartment, and, without having noticed my presence, disappeared. I regarded her with an utter astonishment not unmingled with dread— and yet I found it impossible to account for such feelings.

On the night of the catastrophe the narrator experiences the same depression and terror which had oppressed Roderick throughout the tale, and it becomes obvious that his mental balance is being disturbed by his environment, and by Roderick's madness. He cannot sleep, and tries in vain to 'reason off' the depression which has taken hold of him: 'But my efforts were fruitless. An irrepressible tremour gradually pervaded my frame; and, at length, there sat upon my very heart an incubus of utterly causeless alarm'. Even before Roderick comes to his room the narrator is in a state of extreme terror, which is an extension of Roderick's own condition:

> Overpowered by an intense sentiment of horror, unaccount-
> able yet unendurable, I threw on my clothes with haste (for I
> felt I should sleep no more during the night), and endeavoured
> to arouse myself from the pitiable condition into which I had
> fallen, by pacing rapidly to and fro through the apartment.

Madeline's escape from the tomb seems at first to be real
because the narrator believes it and tells about it in such a
compelling and dramatic manner, but on close inspection
doubts occur about the reality of the whole episode. Roderick claims to hear Madeline's feet on the stairs and outside
the room, but it must be remembered that his senses are deranged, and he also makes the impossible claim to have
heard her 'first feeble movements' in the coffin many days
before. Considered from a realistic viewpoint Madeline's
resurrection is incredible, and what Roderick and the narrator believe they see is an illusion, which, in Thomas Upham's words, ' . . . happens at the moment to be so distinct,
as to control their belief and impose itself upon them for a
reality'. We learn that before her death Madeline suffered a
long and distressing illness that wasted her body, and this
being so, she could hardly be in a condition to break out of
her coffin eight days after being entombed. Moreover, her
body is buried 'at great depth' in a vault beneath the house,
which had been lined with copper, to keep out damp from
the tarn. This vault had at one time been used 'for the worst
purposes of a donjon-keep' and is equipped with a copper
lined door of 'massive iron'. More recently it had been used
as a powder store, and its copper lining, while evidently unsuccessful as damp-proofing (it is 'small, damp . . .'), kept
out both light and air. Further, Poe is careful to point out that
the coffin lid is screwed down and the iron door bolted
when the narrator and Roderick leave the vault. Even if
Madeline does revive in her coffin it is impossible to believe
that after eight days in the tomb she could emerge alive.

   The reading of 'The Mad Trist' which prefigures Madeline's appearance is necessary both to sustain the tension of
the tale, and to precipitate the catastrophe. When Roderick
comes to his room mad through fear, the narrator reads 'The
Mad Trist' in the naïve hope that ' . . . the hypochondriac,
might find relief (for the history of mental disorder is full of
similar anomalies)'. But Roderick's madness is beyond the
stage when such diversions can help, and ironically instead
of distracting Roderick, the reading heightens his alarm and

terror. For a brief period the narrator retains enough fragments of his reason to resist Roderick's hallucination, and realizes that the 'cracking and ripping sound' which he hears while reading how the knight broke into the hermit's dwelling is due to the coincidence of an electrical storm outside: 'It was, beyond doubt, the coincidence alone which arrested my attention'. To Usher's deranged mind, however, the supernatural happenings in 'The Mad Trist' and the sounds of the storm suggest only one meaning—that Madeline has risen from her tomb and is about to destroy him. In this fantasy the narrator eventually acquiesces, overwhelmed by the reality of Usher's terror, and completely unnerved by the sounds of the storm and his grotesque surroundings.

Madeline's return from the tomb has been accepted as a literal fact by Poe's critics, though most of them have avoided committing themselves on the problem of exactly how Madeline achieves her resurrection. It is a tribute to Poe's skill as a writer that he has created through the narrator a situation which appears as real to most of his readers as it does to the narrator and Roderick Usher, but this does not mean that Poe intended Madeline's reappearance to have any reality outside the deranged minds of the two protagonists in the tale. In a letter to James Russell Lowell, Poe said that he considered 'The Fall of the House of Usher' to be one of his finest productions, and this being so, it is unlikely he would have compromised the principles he outlined in his 'Preface' by using such a 'German' contrivance as a physical resurrection eight days after death. The purpose of the tale is to explore mental derangement rather than to present an elaborate Gothic horror story, and the terror it contains is psychological not 'German'. 'The Mad Trist' is an ironical title for the narrator to choose to read, for the trist obviously refers beyond Ethelred's fight with the dragon to the meeting of Roderick, the narrator, and Madeline, which is the fantastic product of deranged minds. Roderick is not killed by his sister, but is literally terrified to death by his environment and his distorted imagination, and succumbs 'a victim to the terrors he had anticipated'. The image of the house in the tarn which so alarmed the narrator when he first approached the House of Usher is a clear prefiguration of the catastrophe which completes the story, and the house-man who collapses into the tarn which ultimately caused his destruction, illustrates supremely well Poe's concept of a unified work of art.

Vampirism in "The Fall of the House of Usher"

Lyle H. Kendall Jr.

Lyle H. Kendall Jr. is a professor of English at Texas Christian University. Kendall explores the evidence of vampirism in "The Fall of the House of Usher." The House of Usher is seemingly cursed by the presence of the supernatural. Roderick Usher suffers from anemia, caused, as he explains, by a family evil, and his sister, Madeline, has the ability to enter a trancelike state of suspended animation. Upon prematurely entombing his sister, Usher knows that her return, short of staking her through the heart, is imminent. His terror arises not out of the guilt of entombing her but out of waiting for the vampire's revenge.

Roderick is the central figure of the narrative, Poe seeming at first glance to devote less than passing attention to Madeline as a character. Her personality seems unrealized, for she appears only three times: toward the middle of the story she passes "through a remote portion of the apartment"; some days after her supposed death she is seen in her coffin, with "the mockery of a faint blush upon the bosom and the face, and that suspiciously lingering smile upon the lip which is so terrible in death"; in the final paragraph but one she reappears to die again, falling "heavily inward upon the person of her brother." These brief appearances are nevertheless fraught with darkly suggestive significance, enough to inspire D.H. Lawrence's impressionistic diagnosis, although he takes a wrong turn: "The exquisitely sensitive Roger, vibrating without resistance with his sister Madeline, more and more exquisitely, and gradually devouring her, sucking her life like a vampire in his anguish of extreme love. And she was asking to be sucked."

Excerpted from "The Vampire Motif in 'The Fall of the House of Usher,'" by Lyle H. Kendall Jr., *College English*, October 1962.

EVIDENCE OF VAMPIRISM

Roderick, neither consumed by love nor acquiescent, faces a classic dilemma. He must put an end to Madeline—the lore dictates that he must drive a stake through her body in the grave—or suffer the eventuality of wasting away, dying, and becoming a vampire himself. As an intellectual he regards either course with growing horror and at length summons an old school friend, the narrator, whom Usher tentatively plans to confide in. From the outset the evidences of vampirism are calculated to overwhelm the narrator. Even before entering the house he feels the presence of supernatural evil. Reining in his horse to contemplate the "black and lurid tarn," he recalls Roderick's "wildly importunate" letter, speaking of *bodily* as well as mental disorder. He remembers that the Usher family has "been noted, time out of mind, for a peculiar sensibility of temperament, displaying itself, through long ages, in many works of exalted art, and manifested, of late, in repeated deeds of munificent yet unobtrusive charity" (a typically ironical Poe commentary upon charity as expiation). Before he rides over the causeway to the house, the visitor reflects further upon "the very remarkable fact, that the stem of the Usher race . . . had put forth, at no period, any enduring branch; in other words, that the entire family lay in the direct line of descent, and had always, with very trifling and very temporary variations [accounting for the twins], so lain."

Once within, the narrator wonders "to find how unfamiliar were the fancies which ordinary images were stirring up." On the staircase he meets the family physician, whose countenance wears a "mingled expression of low cunning [denoting knowledge of the Usher curse] and perplexity." He finds Roderick "terribly altered, in so brief a period," (an inconsistency: earlier the narrator says, "many years had elapsed since our last meeting") with lips "thin and very pallid," a skin of "ghastly pallor," oddly contrasting with the "miraculous lustre of the eye"; his manner is characterized by "incoherence—an inconsistency" and nervous agitation. He has, in fact, all the symptoms of pernicious anemia—extreme pallor, weakness, nervous and muscular affliction, alternating periods of activity and torpor—but it is an anemia, as Usher now makes perfectly clear, beyond the reach of mere medical treatment. He explains "what he conceived to be the nature of his malady . . . a constitutional and a family evil and one for which he despaired to find a remedy." He confesses that he is a "bounden slave" to an "anomalous species" of terror. Roderick discloses, further, that he is enchained by superstition in regard to the Usher house, and that "much of the peculiar gloom which thus afflicted him could be traced to a more natural and far more palpable origin—to the severe and long-continued illness—indeed to the evidently approaching dissolution—of a tenderly beloved sister." And the invalid reveals immediately that *tenderly beloved* is ironically intended by speaking with a "bitterness which I can never forget" of Madeline's impending death.

When Madeline herself now appears, at some little distance, the guest regards her with "an utter astonishment not unmingled with dread; . . . A sensation of stupor oppressed me [a characteristic reaction to the succubus] as my eyes fol-

---

THE BROTHER-SISTER DYAD

"The Fall of the House of Usher" prophesied the collapse of Victorian family structure.

"The Fall of the House of Usher," written mid-century, is prophetic in its anticipation of a vision of the collapse of a society built on the seemingly secure foundations of the family. One might say, in a certain sense, that Poe heralds—or, if you will, "ushers" in—a new era. Although innumerable studies have analyzed the symbolism of Poe's "House of Usher," and particularly that of the Usher twins, no one has yet discussed the twins as "simply" representing themselves: the apogee of the nineteenth century's figuration of the brother-sister dyad. Poe, unlike many of his contemporaries, makes not even a nominal attempt to include a parental presence; we have entered a world in which the nineteenth-century family has been reduced to its most basic unit: the sibling dyad. In this work, we witness, with Poe's narrator, "the hideous dropping off of the veil," wherein the fundamental building block of the Victorian family—the "ideal" brother-sister relation—once revealed for what it is and taken to its logical extreme, must necessarily (and horribly) self-destruct. As in texts as diverse as *Antigone, Frankenstein,* and *Wuthering Heights,* it is significantly the *sister* who must be sacrificed—here literally entombed, buried alive deep within the foundations of the familial edifice—and it is her breaking free from that entombment that provokes the collapse of the entire structure.

Leila S. May, "'Sympathies of a Scarcely Intelligible Nature': The Brother-Sister Bond in Poe's 'Fall of the House of Usher,'" *Studies in Short Fiction,* vol. 30, no. 3 (Summer 1993), pp. 387–96.

lowed her retreating steps." Roderick himself is quite evidently terror-stricken. Reluctant to grasp the import of the plain evidence with which he has so far been presented—not to mention the supernatural assault upon his own psyche—the narrator learns that Madeline's illness has been diagnosed as "of a partially cataleptical character," which is to say, to even the most casual student of necromancy, that she has the common ability of witches to enter at will upon a trance-like death-like state of suspended animation. Her "settled apathy" and "gradual wasting away of the person" are to be accounted for by the corresponding condition in her victim.

Following Madeline's presumed death the friends occupy themselves with poring over old books that have a curiously significant connection with Usher's dilemma. Among them are the "Chiromancy" of Robert Flud, Jean D'Indagine, and De la Chambre (dealing with palmistry). Even more significantly, "One favorite volume was a small octavo edition of the 'Directorium Inquisitorium,' by the Dominican Eymeric de Gironne" (on exorcising witches and ferreting out other sorts of heretics). But Usher's "chief delight, however, was found in the perusal of an exceedingly rare and curious book in quarto Gothic—the manual of a forgotten church—the *Vigiliae Mortuorum secundum Chorum Ecclesiae Maguntinae.*" The "wild ritual of this work"—the *Watches of the Dead according to the Choir of the Church of Mainz*—is, of course, the "Black Mass."

These books fail to provide a text for Roderick, who decides to imprison Madeline, as he says, by "preserving her corpse for a fortnight (previously to its final interment,) in one of the numerous vaults within the walls of the building." Here the plodding narrator at last scents the truth: "The brother had been led to his resolution . . . by consideration of the *unusual character of the malady of the deceased, of certain obtrusive and eager inquiries on the part of her medical men, and of the remote and exposed situation of the burial-ground of the family.* I will not deny that when I called to mind the sinister countenance of the person whom I met upon the staircase on the day of my arrival at the house, I had no desire to oppose what I regarded as at best but a harmless, and by no means an unnatural precaution" (italics mine).

THE VAMPIRE RETURNS

Alone the two friends encoffin the body and bear it to the vault. One last look at the *mocking* features of Madeline, and then the lid to the coffin is screwed down, the massive iron door secured. "Some days of bitter grief" ensue, but soon, sensing danger from a wonted quarter, Roderick Usher spends his restless hours consumed by the old horror, which he verges on confiding to the narrator: "There were times, indeed, when I thought his unceasingly agitated mind was laboring with some oppressive secret, to divulge which he struggled for the necessary courage." As he confesses later—"I *now* tell you that I heard her first feeble movement in the hollow coffin" (*hollow* in the sense that its vampiric occupant is scarcely physical in nature)—Usher is perfectly aware of Madeline's impending escape. And on the final night the guest himself suffers an experience which suggests that her evil spirit is already abroad. Endeavoring to sleep, he cannot "reason off the nervousness which had dominion over me." The room, he feels, is exerting a bewildering influence: "An irrepressible tremor gradually pervaded my frame; and, at length, there sat upon my very heart an *incubus* of utterly causeless alarm. *Shaking this off with a gasp and a struggle,* I uplifted myself upon the pillows" (italics mine), and now he hears "low and indefinite sounds." Shortly he is joined by Usher, radiating "mad hilarity" and restrained hysteria, who rushes to a casement window and throws it "freely open to the storm." It is not difficult to imagine that all the old fiendish Ushers in the distant cemetery are, disembodied, somehow present. A whirlwind (traditionally signalizing a spiritual presence) "had apparently collected its force in our vicinity; for there were frequent and violent alterations in the direction of the wind; and the exceeding density of the clouds . . . did not prevent our perceiving the life-like velocity with which they flew careening from all points against each other."

The last of the Ushers is persuaded to leave the window, which is closed against electrical phenomena of "ghastly origin," and the guest begins to read aloud from the "Mad Trist," whose descriptions of sound are horribly reproduced by Madeline as she leaves her prison and approaches the listeners. Roderick's final words are "a low, hurried, and gibbering murmur" punctuated by extraordinarily meaningful phrases: "'I *dared* not speak! . . . Oh! whither shall I fly? . . . Do I not distinguish that heavy and horrible beating of her heart?'" (Again, the slow and heavy pulse is traditionally characteristic of preternatural creatures.) Poe's accentuation of the miraculous aspects of the tale continues to the end. The sister reels upon the threshold, "then, with a low moaning cry, fell heavily inward upon the person of her brother, and in her violent and now final death-agonies, bore him to the floor a corpse, and a victim to the terrors he had anticipated." She is a vampire to the finish, and there is no escaping the shock of absolute recognition in "From that chamber, and from that mansion, I fled aghast."

In this view "The Fall of the House of Usher"—typical of Poe in its exploration of abysmal degradation—creates an experience that possesses, within itself, credibility and unity of technique once the basic situation is granted. And from the artist's treatment of the theme, the active existence of malignant evil in our world, emerges his partly optimistic and partly ironic commentary: Evil in the long run feeds incestuously upon itself, and it is self-defeating, self-consuming, self-annihilating; the short run is another matter.

Chronology

1809

Edgar Poe is born on January 19 in Boston.

1811

Poe's mother, Elizabeth Arnold Hopkins, dies on December 8; Poe is adopted by John and Frances Allan of Richmond, Virginia.

1815

Poe moves to Britain with the Allan family on July 28.

1818–1820

Poe is educated at Manor House School in Stoke-Newington, near London.

1820

On August 2 Poe returns to Richmond with the Allans and stays with Charles Ellis (John Allan's work partner).

1821

Poe moves with the Allans to Fifth Street; he attends Clarke School until December 1822.

1823

Poe enters William Burke's School on April 1.

1825

On June 28 the Allans purchase a house on Fifth and Main Streets in Richmond.

1826

Poe enters the University of Virginia at Charlottesville on February 14; on December 15, at the end of the first term, Poe is withdrawn from the university by John Allan.

1827

Poe and John Allan have a falling out; Poe leaves Richmond on March 24 and arrives in Boston on April 7; on May 26 Poe enlists in the U.S. Army under the name Edgar A. Perry; he is stationed at Fort Independence in Boston Harbor; *Tamerlane and Other Poems* is published anonymously "by a Bostonian" in Boston; between November 8 and 18, Poe's battery moves on to Fort Moultrie in Charleston, South Carolina.

1828

Between December 11 and 15, Poe's battery moves on to Fortress Monroe, Virginia.

1829

Poe is promoted to rank of sergeant major on January 1; Frances Allan dies in Richmond on February 29; on April 15 Poe retires from the army with an honorable discharge and heads to Washington to seek an appointment at West Point; that fall he stays in Baltimore with his aunt, Maria Clemm, and her daughter, Virginia; *Al Aaraaf, Tamerlane, and Minor Poems* is published in Baltimore in December.

1830

In June Poe receives appointment to the U.S. Military Academy at West Point in New York.

1831

Poe leaves West Point on February 19; in April the second edition of *Poems by Edgar A. Poe* is published in New York; that summer Poe again resides with the Clemms in Baltimore.

1832

Five of Poe's tales are published by the *Philadelphia Saturday Courier.*

1833

Poe's story "MS. Found in a Bottle" wins first prize in a competition in the *Baltimore Saturday Visitor* on October 12.

1834

John Allan dies on March 27, leaving nothing of his wealthy estate to Poe.

1835

Four of Poe's tales are published by the *Southern Literary Messenger* of Richmond; in August Poe becomes an assistant editor of the *Southern Literary Messenger* and leaves Baltimore for Richmond; the Clemms join Poe in Richmond on October 3.

1836

Poe marries his thirteen-year-old cousin Virginia on May 16.

1837

Poe leaves his post at the *Southern Literary Messenger* on January 3; in February Poe moves to New York, where he first lives at Sixth Avenue and Waverly Place, and later lives at 113½ Carmine Street.

1838

In July *The Narrative of Arthur Gordon Pym* is published in New York; Poe moves to Philadelphia that summer.

1839

The Conchologist's First Book is published in Philadelphia; in June Poe becomes assistant editor of Burton's *Gentleman's Magazine*.

1840

Tales from the Grotesque and Arabesque is published in Philadelphia; Poe leaves his editorial post at *Gentleman's Magazine*.

1841

Poe becomes editor of *Graham's Magazine* in April; in July he seeks, but does not receive, a clerk's position in the Treasury Department in Washington.

1842

Poe leaves *Graham's Magazine* in May.

1843

The Prose Romances of Edgar A. Poe is published in Philadelphia.

1844

Poe moves to New York on April 7, living near Eighty-Fourth Street and Broadway.

1845

On January 29 "The Raven" appears in the New York *Evening Mirror*, where Poe works as the assistant editor; on March 8 Poe becomes an editor at the *Broadway Journal;* in May he moves to 195 East Broadway, New York; Poe becomes the proprietor of the *Broadway Journal* on October 24; in November *The Raven and Other Poems* is published in New York; that winter Poe moves to 85 Amity Street, New York.

1846

Poe loses proprietorship of the *Broadway Journal* on January 3, and the journal ceases publication; in May Poe moves to a cottage in Fordham, New York.

1847

Virginia dies in Fordham on January 30.

1848

Poe reads *Eureka* at the New York Society Library on February 3; in June *Eureka* is published in New York; on June 10 Poe lectures at Lowell, Massachusetts, where he meets Nancy "Annie" Locke Heywood Richmond; Poe visits Richmond on July 17, and reports note that he is often drunk during this visit; on September 21 Poe travels to Providence, Rhode Island, where he meets and proposes marriage to Sarah Helen Whitman; in November Poe makes another journey to Providence to propose a second time to Whitman; he then proceeds to Boston, where he tries to commit suicide with an overdose of laudanum; Poe lectures in Providence on December 20; on December 22 a marriage agreement is drawn up between Poe and Whitman; the engagement, however, is broken off.

1849

Poe seeks the support of E.H.N. Patterson of Oquawka to start a new magazine that spring; on June 30 Poe goes to Richmond to share his ideas for the magazine; on July 2, in an apparent state of delirium, Poe arrives at the home of John Sartain in Philadelphia; on July 13 Poe travels to Richmond to meet Sarah Elmira Royster, whom he hopes to marry; on August 17, September 14, and September 24 Poe gives a lecture on *The Poetic Principle* in Richmond, Norfolk, and again in Richmond, respectively; on September 27 Poe travels to New York; on October 3 Poe is discovered unconscious in Baltimore and is taken to Washington College Hospital; he never fully regains consciousness; Poe dies at 5 A.M. on October 7.

FOR FURTHER RESEARCH

BIOGRAPHIES

William Bittner, *Poe: A Biography*. Boston: Little Brown, 1962.

Joanne Dodson, *The Raven and the Nightingale: A Modern Mystery of Edgar Allen Poe*. New York: Doubleday, 1999.

Benjamin Franklin Fisher IV, ed., *Poe and His Times: The Artist and His Milieu*. Baltimore: Edgar Allan Poe Society, 1990.

J.R. Hammond, *An Edgar Allan Poe Chronology*. New York: St. Martin's, 1998.

J. Gerald Kennedy, *Poe, Death, and the Life of Writing*. New Haven, CT: Yale University Press, 1987.

Wolf Mankowitz, *The Extraordinary Mr. Poe: A Biography of Edgar Allan Poe*. New York: Summit Books, 1978.

Jeffrey Meyers, *Edgar Allan Poe: His Life and Legacy*. New York: Charles Scribner's Sons, 1992.

Perry Miller, *The Raven and the Whale: Poe, Melville, and the New York Literary Scene*. Baltimore: Johns Hopkins University Press, 1997.

Kenneth Silverman, *Edgar A. Poe: Mournful and Never-Ending Remembrance*. New York: HarperCollins, 1991.

David Sinclair, *Edgar Allan Poe*. Totowa, NJ: Rowman and Littlefield, 1977.

Dwight Thomas, *The Poe Log: A Documentary Life of Edgar Allan Poe, 1809–1849*. Boston: G.K. Hall, 1987.

Lois Davis Vines, ed., *Poe Abroad: Influence, Reputation, Affinities*. Iowa City: University of Iowa Press, 1999.

John Evangelist Walsh, *Midnight Dreary: The Mysterious Death of Edgar Allan Poe.* New Brunswick, NJ: Rutgers University Press, 1998.

George E. Woodberry, *Edgar Allan Poe.* New York: AMS, 1968.

CRITICISM

Clive Bloom, *Nineteenth-Century Suspense: From Poe to Conan Doyle.* New York: St. Martin's, 1988.

Harold Bloom, ed., *Edgar Allan Poe.* New York: Chelsea House, 1985.

Michael L. Burduck, *Grim Phantasms: Fear in Poe's Short Fiction.* New York: Garland, 1992.

Killis Campbell, *The Mind of Poe and Other Studies.* New York: Russell & Russell, 1962.

Eric W. Carlson, ed., *A Companion to Poe Studies.* Westport, CT: Greenwood, 1996.

Graham Clarke, ed., *Edgar Allan Poe: Critical Assessments.* Mountfield, England: Helm Information, 1991.

Joan Dayan, *Fables of Mind: An Inquiry into Poe's Fiction.* New York: Oxford University Press, 1987.

Jeffrey DeShell, *The Peculiarity of Literature: An Allegorical Approach to Poe's Fiction.* Madison, NJ: Fairleigh Dickinson University Press, 1997.

Jonathan Elmer, *Reading at the Social Limit: Affect, Mass Culture, and Edgar Allan Poe.* Stanford, CA: Stanford University Press, 1995.

Thomas S. Hansen, *The German Face of Edgar Allan Poe: A Study of Literary References in His Works.* Columbia, SC: Camden House, 1995.

Kevin J. Hayes, *Poe and the Printed Word.* New York: Cambridge University Press, 2000.

Daniel Hoffman, *Poe Poe Poe Poe Poe Poe Poe.* New York: Paragon House, 1990.

William L. Howarth, ed., *Twentieth-Century Interpretations of Poe's Tales: A Collection of Critical Essays.* Englewood Cliffs, NJ: Prentice-Hall, 1971.

Tony Magistrale and Sidney Poger, *Poe's Children: Connections Between Tales of Terror and Detection.* New York: Peter Lang, 1999.

Shawn Rosenheim and Stephen Rachman, eds., *The American Face of Edgar Allan Poe.* Baltimore: Johns Hopkins University Press, 1995.

David R. Saliba, *A Psychology of Fear: The Nightmare Formula of Edgar Allan Poe.* Lanham, MD: University Press of America, 1980.

THE DETECTIVE STORIES

Ian Bell and Graham Daldry, eds., *Watching the Detectives: Essays on Crime Fiction.* New York: St. Martin's, 1990.

Bernard Benstock, ed., *Art in Crime Writing: Essays on Detective Fiction.* New York: St. Martin's, 1983.

Brian Docherty, *American Crime Fiction: Studies in the Genre.* New York: St. Martin's, 1988.

David Geherin, *The American Private Eye: The Image in Fiction.* New York: F. Ungar, 1985.

Howard Haycraft, ed., *The Art of the Mystery Story: A Collection of Critical Essays.* New York: Simon and Schuster, 1946.

Gary Hoppenstand, *The Defective Detective in the Pulps.* Bowling Green, OH: Bowling Green State University Popular Press, 1983.

John T. Irwin, *The Mystery to a Solution: Poe, Borges, and the Analytic Detective Story.* Baltimore: Johns Hopkins University Press, 1994.

Peter Thoms, *Detection and Its Designs: Narrative and Power in Nineteenth-Century Detective Fiction.* Athens: Ohio University Press, 1998.

GOTHIC LITERATURE

Linda Bayer-Berenbaum, *The Gothic Imagination: Expansion in Gothic Literature and Art.* London: Associated University Press, 1982.

Matthew Brennan, *The Gothic Psyche: Disintegration and Growth in Nineteenth-Century English Literature.* Columbia, SC: Camden House, 1997.

INDEX

ium